CW00660493

RECEIVING GIFTS OF THE SPIRIT

OTHER BOOKS AND AUDIO BOOKS
BY MATTHEW B. BROWN:

Symbols in Stone:
Symbolism on the Early Temples of the Restoration
(WITH PAUL THOMAS SMITH)

The Gate of Heaven:
Insights on the Doctrines and Symbols of the Temple

The Plan of Salvation:
Doctrinal Notes and Commentary

Plates of Gold:
The Book of Mormon Comes Forth

Joseph Smith:
The Man, the Mission, the Message
(WITH PHOTOGRAPHS BY VAL W. BRINKERHOFF)

RECEIVING GIFTS OF THE SPIRIT

MATTHEW B. BROWN

Covenant Communications, Inc.

Cover design © 2005 by Covenant Communications, Inc.
Cover art: reference dove photo by Alan & Sandy Carey © 2005 Photodisc Green/Getty Images, Inc.; painting by Jonathan Brown.

Published by Covenant Communications, Inc.
American Fork, Utah

Printed in Canada
First Printing: October 2005

11 10 09 08 07 06 05 10 9 8 7 6 5 4 3 2 1

ISBN 1-59811-028-4

May God increase the gifts among
[the Saints] for His Son's sake.

—Joseph Smith, Journal, 29 October 1833

CONTENTS

INTRODUCTION

A gentleman once asked the Prophet Joseph Smith if he could join himself to the cause and kingdom of God by baptism but choose not to pay any attention to the gifts of the Spirit. The Prophet replied that taking this particular course of action would be like asking the host of a house for food and having it placed upon the table, but then leaving the building without ever taking a bite. This person's hunger, explained the Prophet, would *not* be satisfied.[1] This scenario applies to all of us in the restored Church of Jesus Christ. The Lord has invited each of His servants to an ongoing spiritual banquet, but some live in a state of hunger, even malnourishment, because of infrequent visits to the dining hall, or hesitation to try some of the unfamiliar items on the menu.

Latter-day Saints have not only the opportunity, but also the divinely mandated obligation to discover and develop their spiritual gifts. Only in doing so can they reach their full religious potential. George Q. Cannon said that "if men or women become members of the Church and receive the Holy Ghost their work does not end there; it has hardly begun." He further stated that if the Saints "do not cultivate the Holy Spirit, it will not increase in them; neither will the gifts and blessings of the gospel increase within them."[2] On another occasion he explained that "we cannot be the people that God designs we should be, unless we seek after and obtain these spiritual gifts. . . . [I]t should be the constant prayer of all the Latter-day Saints for the Lord to give us those gifts that are suited to our condition, and that will make us perfect, because the bestowal of these gifts is for the express purpose of making those who are entitled to them perfect before the Lord."[3]

The gifts of the Spirit have other purposes as well. Elder James E. Talmage taught that visions, miracles, healings, and the gift of tongues all serve as ways whereby the Lord can manifest His heavenly powers within our temporal sphere.[4] In this way He certifies His existence to those who may wonder or doubt. The manifestation of these powers in modern times also demonstrates that God is the same in dealing with the followers of truth in every age of the world; He is just as willing to bestow spiritual gifts upon Latter-day Saints as upon their former-day counterparts.[5] Charles W. Penrose provided an additional perspective on this subject. He believed that spiritual gifts serve as two different types of witnesses. First, their existence in the restored Church of Jesus Christ signals to baptized observers that they do indeed belong to God's true fold. And second, the bestowal of spiritual gifts upon an individual is an indication to them that they have done something acceptable in their life that has merited the blessings of their Heavenly Father.[6]

Even if we have experienced some of these marvelous tokens of heavenly approbation and power, we may still limit the gifts that we could receive if we do not continue to seek after them. Elder Orson Pratt testified that during his lifetime he had experienced some remarkable spiritual gifts such as revelations, prophecies, and dreams. Yet, he admitted that he had not attained all of the blessings that were available to him. He taught that even though some mortals—such as the leading prophets of dispensations—are blessed with an abundance of gifts, the typical Latter-day Saint is not hindered from enjoying blessings of a similar nature. And he also made this important observation: "I have thought the reason why we have not enjoyed these gifts more fully is, because we have not sought for them as diligently as we ought. I speak for one, I have not sought as diligently as I might have done. . . . [W]e do not receive [the gifts of the Spirit] in their fullness, because we do not seek for them as diligently and faithfully as we should."[7]

There are several different sets of spiritual gifts that have been identified either in or by authoritative sources and this book will categorize and examine each of them. Perhaps the best known set of gifts can be found in virtually identical lists in the New Testament, Book of Mormon, and Doctrine and Covenants (1 Cor. 12; Moro. 10; D&C 46). They are twelve in number (testimony of Jesus

Christ, administration, operations, wisdom, knowledge, faith, healing, miracles, prophecy, angels and spirits, speaking in tongues, and interpretation of tongues). Another group of four gifts has been identified in the sayings of Jesus Christ and the writings of the Prophet Joseph Smith (revelation, dreams, visions, and casting out evil spirits).[8] They will be combined, in categories, with the previous twelve. And finally there are multiple gifts that have been acknowledged by more modern apostles and prophets. These are discussed in appendix 1 of this volume. Appendix 2 addresses several questions that are commonly asked about the Spirit's extraordinary blessings, and appendix 3 constitutes a directory and harmony of the longest scriptural gift records.

The purpose of this book is threefold. The first goal is to teach about spiritual gifts. This will be achieved through the presentation of various scriptural teachings and also commentary that has been offered by recognized Church authorities. The second aim is to illuminate the gifts of the Spirit. This will be accomplished through discussion and analysis, as well as through numerous examples from leaders and common members of the latter-day Church. The third purpose of this volume is by far the most important. It is to encourage members of the Church to take Elder Pratt's previously mentioned words to heart and step forward to claim their rich spiritual inheritance. Spiritual gifts present an opportunity for personal experience with the power of God. And experience with this holy power serves to impart the quality of godliness to the recipient, thus changing them for the better and making them more effective servants of the Lord.

It is the sincere hope of the author that those who peruse the pages of this book will come away from it with a desire to accept the Lord's invitation to the abundant spiritual feast that He has prepared for them.

NOTES TO INTRODUCTION

1. See Brigham H. Roberts, ed., *History of The Church of Jesus Christ of Latter-day Saints* (Salt Lake City: Deseret Book, 1948–1950), 5:218–19; hereafter cited as HC. Elder Orson F. Whitney said, "The gospel is more than a code of laws and ordinances, an embodiment of eternal principles, obedience to which must precede entrance into the Church and Kingdom of God. The machinery is one thing; the power that moves the machinery is another. God is the author and giver of both. Divine authority, the authority of the Priesthood, comes with the gospel, to make operative for man its laws and ordinances and the eternal principles of which it is composed. The gifts of the Holy Spirit are also necessary—imperatively so, in order to render effective the great plan of salvation" (Conference Report, April 1927, 97).
2. *Millennial Star,* vol. 23, no. 34, 24 August 1861, 538.
3. Ibid., vol. 62, no. 23, 7 June 1900, 354.
4. See *Improvement Era,* vol. 36, no. 2, December 1932, 69.
5. See *HC,* 1:322.
6. See Brian H. Stuy, ed., *Collected Discourses* (Burbank, CA, and Woodland Hills, UT: B.H.S. Publishing, 1987–1992), 3:55; see also George D. Watt, ed., *Journal of Discourses* (Liverpool, England: Samuel W. Richards and Sons, 1852–1886), 23:352.
7. Ibid., 25:145–46.
8. Joseph Smith included "revelation" and "visions" among the gifts of the Spirit in Article of Faith 7. In a letter dated March 22, 1839, the Prophet told Isaac Galland the following: "We believe that we have a right to revelations, visions, and dreams from God, our Heavenly Father" (Dean C. Jessee, ed., *The Personal Writings of Joseph Smith* [Salt Lake City: Deseret Book, 1984], 421). President Smith listed "casting out devils" along with other "spiritual gifts" when he spoke to a gathering of Relief Society sisters in Nauvoo, Illinois (HC, 4:602–603). Jesus Christ included casting out evil spirits among the gifts and signs of the gospel in both ancient and modern scripture (see Matt. 10:8; Mark 3:15; 16:17–18; Morm. 9:24; D&C 24:13; 35:9).

UNDERSTANDING SPIRITUAL GIFTS

CHAPTER ONE
The Nature of Spiritual Gifts

A gift can be defined as anything that is voluntarily transferred from one individual to another without the expectation of compensation to the giver.[1] The Greek word that underlies the word "gifts" in the Apostle Paul's discourse on those of a spiritual nature is *charisma,* which can be translated as "deliverance," "gratuity," "endowment," "qualification," or "faculty." The word *charisma,* in turn, is derived from the Greek word *charis,* which is "the divine influence upon the heart, and its reflection in the life" of a person.[2] Thus, a gift of the Spirit can be understood as a freely given endowment, delivered through the agency of the third member of the Godhead, which enhances the life of the recipient and influences their heart.

When individuals desire to enhance their religious life through experience with the gifts of the Spirit, there are questions that will naturally arise in their minds. They will ask themselves things such as: What is the nature of spiritual gifts? How do they function? What will happen if I am successful in receiving them? A concerted effort will be made on the following pages to assist in broadening understanding in these areas. This will be accomplished through a discussion of such topics as the origin of spiritual gifts, the means whereby they are made accessible to mortals, the method used to transfer them from the heavenly world to the mortal sphere, and what realistic expectations people should have in connection with the reception of these sublime blessings.

The Origin of Spiritual Gifts

As taught in the scriptures, spiritual gifts originate with Deity. A close examination of canonical texts reveals the interesting fact that all three members of the Godhead play a role in connection with these otherworldly powers.

First, there is mention of God the Father. In the book of Moroni we find that spiritual gifts are referred to as "the gifts of God" (10:8), and in the Joseph Smith Translation of the book of Luke we read that our "[H]eavenly Father [shall] give good gifts . . . to them who ask Him" (11:14). Elder Bruce R. McConkie of the Quorum of the Twelve has written that "spiritual gifts come from God. They are the gifts of God; they originate with Him and are special blessings that He bestows upon those who love Him and keep His commandments."[3] This latter-day Apostle also stated that "it is at [God's] direction . . . that the gifts of the Spirit are poured out upon the faithful."[4] With this perspective in mind, it becomes apparent that in the ultimate sense, "the gifts of the Holy Spirit . . . are of the same kind, in a small degree, as those powers possessed by our Heavenly Father in the celestial realms, in infinite perfection."[5] Spiritual gifts are, therefore, the means whereby mortals become partakers of the powers of godliness.

The scriptures make a connection between the second member of the Godhead and spiritual gifts when they teach in the book of Moroni that "every good gift cometh of Christ" (10:18). Also, in Ephesians the Apostle Paul speaks of the Savior giving "gifts unto men" (4:8). It appears that Paul, in the book of 1 Corinthians, "identifies Heavenly Father as the origin from which all gifts derive their existence," but he also "refers [there] to Christ's universal role in administering the gifts."[6] It does not appear that the manner by which the Redeemer administers spiritual gifts is described anywhere in holy writ, but it seems probable that even in the case of these particular heavenly blessings He acts in the role of a divine Mediator between God and man (see 1 Tim. 2:5; 2 Ne. 2:27; D&C 107:19).

Finally, we come to the third member of the Godhead. In the book of Hebrews, Paul refers to the plural "*gifts* of the Holy Ghost" (2:4, emphasis added). And in the book of Moroni we find mention that spiritual gifts "are given by the manifestations of the Spirit of God unto men" (10:8). This is similar to the information found in the Joseph Smith Translation of Luke's gospel, where we read that our Father in heaven "give[s] good gifts, through the Holy Spirit" (11:14).

The gift of the Holy Ghost, which is received during the confirmation of every baptized Saint, is an indispensable component that enables a person to access the gifts of God on a continuing basis. The Prophet Joseph Smith taught this concept when he said that blessings such as prophecy, tongues, visions, revelations, and healings "cannot be enjoyed without the gift of the Holy Ghost" because they are "obtained through that medium."[7] Various scriptures corroborate this connection. When Stephen was full of the Holy Ghost, the heavens opened and he saw heavenly beings (see Acts 7:55–56); when the Holy Ghost fell upon the Saints of Christ's day, they spoke in tongues (see Acts 2:4); when Adam was full of the Holy Ghost he was able to prophesy (see D&C 107:56) and also receive revelation (see Moses 5:9); Paul worked a miracle when he was filled with the Holy Ghost (see Acts 13:6–12); Peter was able to testify of Christ when filled with the Spirit (see Acts 4:8–10; 10:34–44) and was also able to teach knowledge by the same power (see Acts 11:15); when Moses was filled with the Holy Ghost it was possible for him to behold visions (see Moses 1:24–28).

Elder Orson Pratt provided some insightful commentary on the connection between the initial gift that every Saint receives and the subsequent gifts that are associated with it. He stated that

> God has . . . ordained that when He bestows upon the children of men spiritual gifts that they must be received in order; they must be given according to the laws and institutions of the Church, through the administration of that authority and power that He has established here on the earth. Hence, Paul, in writing to the Saints in his day, said to them on a certain occasion that he greatly desired to visit certain branches of the Church in order that he might impart to them some spiritual gifts. Why not receive these spiritual gifts in some other way? Why not receive these great and choice heavenly blessings according to our own will? Because God is a God of order and His house is not a house of confusion. If He desires to bestow any great, choice heavenly gift upon His servants and handmaidens He has ordained an authority and set that authority in His Church, and through the administration of the ordinances that pertain to that heavenly gift they may be made partakers thereof.[8]

The question of how spiritual gifts are delivered from Deity to mortals is an interesting one. It appears that in order for the Holy Ghost (who is a spirit personage) to bridge the gap between the celestial world where He resides and the telestial world in which we dwell, He utilizes the omnipresent spiritual power known as the Light of Christ. Elder Bruce R. McConkie wrote that "the light of Christ (also called the Spirit of Christ and the Spirit of the Lord) is a light, a power, and an influence that proceeds forth from the presence of God to fill the immensity of space." This light, said Elder McConkie, "is the agency of God's power and the law by which all things are governed. It is also the agency used by the Holy Ghost to manifest truth and dispense spiritual gifts to many people at one and the same time."[9]

Availability of Spiritual Gifts

Some Latter-day Saints may be under the impression that the gifts of the Spirit are only available to or experienced by people who hold positions of high authority in the Church's hierarchy. But this is simply not the case. George Q. Cannon discounted this notion when he said, "I hope the idea will never prevail among our people that God confines His gifts and graces to the First Presidency or to the Twelve Apostles or to the Seven Presidents of Seventies. I know that God is the God of this people, and every young man or middle-aged man or aged man who will seek for the power of God can obtain it."[10] Elder Bruce R. McConkie expanded the scope of availability by pointing out that "where spiritual things are concerned, as pertaining to all of the gifts of the Spirit, with reference to the receipt of revelation, the gaining of testimonies, and the seeing of visions, in all matters that pertain to godliness and holiness and which are brought to pass as a result of personal righteousness—in all these things men and women stand in a position of absolute equality before the Lord." He then emphasized the fact that God "is no respecter of persons nor of sexes, and He blesses those men and those women who seek Him and serve Him and keep His commandments."[11]

The main prerequisite, then, for reception of a spiritual gift is not our status in the Church but rather our standing before the Lord. President Heber C. Kimball once asked a gathering of Saints, "Are you faithful to your vows?" And he explained that "if you are, you will have dreams, and visions, and revelations from the world of light, and you will be comforted by night and by day. But if you do not fulfill your covenants you cannot enjoy these blessings."[12] This same nineteenth-century counselor in the First Presidency also taught that "there is no person in this Church who can increase in the knowledge of God, in the spirit of revelation, in the gift of prophecy, in visions or in dreams, unless they cleave unto God with full purpose of heart, but by being faithful these gifts will be multiplied unto the Saints."[13] Another counselor who served in this quorum, President George Q. Cannon, offered a similar assessment. He affirmed it as being "certainly true" that "the men who obey the laws of God most perfectly, and the women who do so, have the greatest faith, and God will bless them in proportion to their faith." Specifically, "the gifts of the Spirit will be manifested more in their behalf than upon those who deliberately violate or are careless concerning the word of God."[14]

Manifestation of Spiritual Gifts

In order to better understand the nature of spiritual gifts it is helpful to know something about how and when they might be manifested. Elder Dallin H. Oaks draws attention to the fact that "spiritual gifts do not come visibly, automatically, and immediately to all who have received the gift of the Holy Ghost."[15] Indeed, the Prophet Joseph Smith taught that even if spiritual gifts were bestowed upon an individual at the time of the laying on of hands for the gift of the Holy Ghost, an observer that was standing nearby would be completely unaware if they had received the gifts of knowledge, wisdom, or faith. Neither would an observer know if the newly baptized Saint had received such gifts as the discerning of spirits, the interpretation of tongues, the ability to heal the sick or the power to work miracles. As the Prophet pointed out, "it would require time and circumstances to call these gifts into operation."[16]

The same principle applies when gifts that have been bestowed upon individuals are identified through patriarchal blessings. One example of this can be seen in the life of Lorenzo Snow. In his patriarchal blessing he was promised the gift of "healing the sick by the power of faith." Yet he could not actually exercise this gift until an occasion arose wherein he could go forward to bless the sick and afflicted.[17] Another example comes from Zina D. Huntington. She was informed in her patriarchal blessing that she would be a witness to the ministering of angels. But it was not until some time later, when she visited the consecrated ground of the Kirtland Temple, that the promised gift was enjoyed.[18]

Elder Charles W. Penrose recalled that when he had the gift of the Holy Ghost bestowed upon him after baptism he "felt no physical manifestation" or "exhibition of power"—though he was expecting one—and was therefore a little disappointed. But the spiritual gift bestowed upon him through this agency was one that was internally discerned, and it took time and circumstance to activate it. He said of his edifying and useful gift,

> When I prayed for knowledge and understanding concerning the things of God, they were manifested to me. It brought to me that which is called in the scriptures, "the peace of God [which] passeth all understanding" [Philip. 4:7]. The joy, the peace, the satisfaction that it brought to me could not be described in words. I knew that my Redeemer lived; I knew that I was born again; I knew the Holy Spirit was working in my heart. Truths were manifested to me that I had never heard of or read of, but which I afterwards heard preached by the servants of the Lord.[19]

Misapplication of Spiritual Gifts

Once we are blessed with the gifts of the Spirit, it is vitally important that we are careful not to treat them inappropriately or misapply them. The Prophet Joseph Smith offered a word of caution to the Saints in this regard when he said, "The gifts of God are all useful in their place, but when they are applied to that which God does not intend, they prove an injury, a snare and a curse instead of a blessing."[20] Joseph F. Smith (the Prophet's nephew) provided a useful illustration that is connected with this idea. He said,

> We have found occasionally that men blessed with some peculiar gift of the Spirit have exercised it in an unwise—shall we say, improper—manner. For instance, brethren strongly gifted with the power of healing have visited far and near amongst the Saints (to the neglect sometimes of other duties), until it has almost become a business with them. And their visits to the homes of

> the Saints have assumed somewhat the character of those of a physician, and the people have come to regard the power so manifested *as though coming from man.* And [the brother] himself has sometimes grown to so feel, and not that he was simply an instrument in the hands of God of bringing blessings to their house. This view is exceedingly unfortunate when indulged in and is apt to result in the displeasure of the Lord. It has sometimes ended in the brother possessing this gift (if he encouraged such a feeling) losing his power to bless and heal.[21]

Thus there is a definite possibility that a person who has been blessed with great spiritual power can lose their gift through improper conduct or an unfitting attitude. This is the desire of the adversary, said Elder Dallin H. Oaks. "Satan will . . . attempt to cause our spiritual downfall through tempting us to misapply our spiritual gifts." It is therefore of the utmost importance to remember that "a spiritual gift is given to benefit the children of God, not to magnify the prominence or to gratify the ego of the person who receives it."[22]

It must also be kept in mind that individuals will be deprived of the gifts that they have been granted if they turn themselves to unrighteousness. The Book of Mormon clearly indicates that when people manifest wickedness in their lives (including the spirit of rebelliousness) the Lord will take His power out of their midst. Under such conditions there will be no ability to work miracles or to perform healings. If any of the Saints choose to cultivate unbelief, or otherwise engage in iniquitous behavior, then the Holy Ghost will be withdrawn from them and there will be "no gifts from the Lord" (Morm. 1:13–14, 16).

Another way that spiritual gifts can be misapplied or misused is when a person attempts to seal one of these gifts upon another individual. Elder Wilford Woodruff made note of the fact that "we lay hands upon the heads of those who embrace the gospel and we say unto them, 'In the name of the Lord Jesus Christ receive ye the Holy Ghost.'" Properly authorized priesthood holders have the right to "seal this blessing upon the heads of the children of men." But Elder Woodruff made it clear that "we have no right, power nor authority to seal the *gifts* of the Holy Ghost upon anybody. . . . [T]he *gifts* of the Holy Ghost are His property to bestow as He sees fit."[23] This type of misapplication should not be confused with the ability of a patriarch to properly identify, by revelation from the Holy Ghost, those gifts that have been granted to a Latter-day Saint.

Misconceptions about Spiritual Gifts

There are a few misconceptions about spiritual gifts that call for brief enumeration and explanation. First, there is the misguided idea that once a person receives the gifts of the Spirit, they have reached a stage of spirituality where earthly weaknesses have been vanquished. The fact of the matter is that after the Lord bestows a gift upon someone He may, in His wisdom, choose to counterbalance it. First Presidency counselor George Q. Cannon taught,

> The Lord shows His servants their weaknesses. They are made to feel how impotent they are without Him. He will keep them constantly reminded of their dependence upon Him, conscious that they are poor, fallible creatures, and that their only strength is in the Lord. If a man is blessed of the Spirit of the Lord, with great gifts and power, with visions and revelations, [the Lord] will accompany these gifts and graces perhaps with weaknesses, in order that the man may be kept humble, and not be lifted up in the pride of his heart, and forget the source of his blessings. We who look upon him may see him in his weaknesses, and say, "What a weak, poor man he is!" And yet the Lord may have given him these weaknesses in order to keep him from being lifted up to his overthrow.[24]

Another misconception about spiritual gifts is that recipients of these heavenly endowments have risen above their human nature and are therefore not susceptible to the loss of spirituality. Once again we learn from Elder Cannon that "it would appear, looking at matters naturally, that if men and women had tasted the word of God, had received revelation from God, had knowledge poured into their souls concerning this being the work of God, they would always be faithful to the truth; but it is not so." The reality is that "men may behold the heavens opened and see Jesus, they may see visions, and have revelations given to them, and yet if they do not live as they should do, and cherish the Spirit of God in their hearts, all this knowledge, and these revelations and wonderful manifestations fail to keep them in the Church, to preserve them from the power of the adversary, and to deliver them from the snares that he spreads for the feet of all the children of God."[25] Since agency is never taken away from those who are in a state of earthly probation, it is possible for even those who have partaken of a portion of the power of God to fall by the wayside. Elder Orson Pratt illustrated this point. He referred to what happened during the Kirtland era of Church history when he said,

> We were commanded to seek to behold the face of the Lord; to seek after revelation; to seek after the spirit of prophecy, and the gifts of the Spirit; and many testify to what they saw. But yet [some of the Saints] were inexperienced; they had not proven themselves in their religion long enough. They obtained blessings greater than some of them were prepared to receive. They perhaps might have been faithful if they had exercised the agency which God gave them. But how easily are mankind toppled first this way, then that way, and are led astray, even after the heavens were opened and chariots and horses of fire, as well as angels were seen: still many of those brethren apostatized.[26]

The third misconception in regard to spiritual gifts that we will address in this chapter is the idea that experiencing or handling the power of God somehow precludes one from having to deal with the power of the devil. President Brigham Young taught that just the opposite is true. He asked, "[I]s there a reason for men and women [to be] exposed more constantly and more powerfully to the power of the enemy by having visions than by not having them?" He answered affirmatively, "There is, and it is simply this—God never bestows upon His people, or upon an individual, superior blessings without a severe trial to prove them, to prove that individual, or that people, to see whether they will keep their covenants with Him, and keep in remembrance what He has shown them." The general rule then, as explained by President Young, is this: "[T]he greater the vision, the greater the display of the power of the enemy. . . . So when individuals are blessed with visions, revelations, and great manifestations, look out, then the devil is nigh you, and you will be tempted in proportion to the vision, revelation or manifestation you have received."[27]

Conclusion

Each Latter-day Saint, regardless of their position in the Church, is blessed with the potential to receive spiritual gifts from the Father, in the name of the Son, and through the power of the Holy Ghost. These gifts present recipients with the remarkable opportunity to have personal experience with the power and characteristics of God. The gifts of the Spirit may be given to individuals but remain unnoticed until they are activated under the right circumstances or identified through proper sources. As long as the nature of these gifts is not misunderstood and the power and abilities that come with them are not misapplied, they will prove to be a great benefit to recipients and to those around them. Indeed, the Saints should diligently seek after these gifts because they will enhance their lives and influence their hearts in good and holy ways.

NOTES TO CHAPTER 1

1. Noah Webster, *An American Dictionary of the English Language* (New York: S. Converse, 1828), s.v., "gift."
2. James Strong, *The New Strong's Exhaustive Concordance of the Bible* (Nashville, TN: Thomas Nelson Publishers, 1995), Concise Dictionary of the Words in the Greek Testament, 98.
3. Bruce R. McConkie, *A New Witness for the Articles of Faith* (Salt Lake City: Deseret Book, 1985), 270; hereafter cited as *NWAF.*
4. Conference Report, October 1969, 80; hereafter cited as CR.
5. Hyrum M. Smith and Janne M. Sjodahl, *Doctrine and Covenants Commentary,* rev. ed. (Salt Lake City: Deseret Book, 1960), 542.
6. Robert C. Freeman, "Paul's Earnest Pursuit of Spiritual Gifts," in *The Apostle Paul, His Life and His Testimony: The Twenty-third Annual Sidney B. Sperry Symposium* (Salt Lake City: Deseret Book, 1994), 36.
7. Brigham H. Roberts, ed., *History of The Church of Jesus Christ of Latter-day Saints* (Salt Lake City: Deseret Book, 1948–1950), 5:27–28; hereafter cited as *HC.* Confirmation of this teaching can be found in the *Evening and Morning Star,* vol. 2, no. 17, February 1834, 130; *Messenger and Advocate,* vol. 1, no. 6, March 1835, 84; ibid., vol. 1, no. 12, September 1835, 184; *Times and Seasons,* vol. 1, no. 8, June 1840, 126; Orson Spencer, *Letters Exhibiting the Most Prominent Doctrines of The Church of Jesus Christ of Latter-day Saints* (Salt Lake City: George Q. Cannon and Sons, 1891), 68; CR, April 1956, 72; Daniel H. Ludlow, ed., *Encyclopedia of Mormonism* (New York: Macmillan,

1992), 2:543. By way of clarification, Elder Bruce R. McConkie has said that "Gentiles, which includes all nonmembers of the Church, do not have the gifts of the Spirit; these spiritual outpourings of divine grace are reserved for those who have the gift of the Holy Ghost, who is the very Spirit whose gifts are bestowed upon men" (*Doctrinal New Testament Commentary* [Salt Lake City: Bookcraft, 1971], 2:366; hereafter cited as *DNTC).*

8. George D. Watt, ed., *Journal of Discourses* (Liverpool, England: Samuel W. Richards and Sons, 1852–1886), 14:272–73; hereafter cited as *JD.*
9. *NWAF,* 70; see also Bruce R. McConkie, *Mormon Doctrine,* 2nd ed. (Salt Lake City: Bookcraft, 1966), 314; *DNTC,* 2:371.
10. Jerreld L. Newquist, comp., *Gospel Truth: Discourses and Writings of George Q. Cannon* (Salt Lake City: Deseret Book, 1987), 158.
11. *Ensign,* January 1979, 61.
12. *JD,* 3:112.
13. Ibid., 10:245.
14. Ibid., 24:147.
15. *Ensign,* September 1986, 69.
16. *HC,* 5:29–30.
17. Eliza R. Snow, *Biography and Family Record of Lorenzo Snow* (Salt Lake City: Deseret News, 1884), 263.
18. See Janet Peterson and LaRene Gaunt, *Elect Ladies* (Salt Lake City: Deseret Book, 1990), 47.
19. *JD,* 23:350–51.
20. *HC,* 5:31–32.
21. *Juvenile Instructor,* vol. 37, no. 2, 15 January 1902, 51 (emphasis added).
22. *Ensign,* October 1994, 12–13.
23. *JD,* 13:157 (emphasis added).
24. Brian H. Stuy, ed., *Collected Discourses* (Burbank, CA, and Woodland Hills, UT: B.H.S. Publishing, 1987–1992), 5:305.
25. *JD,* 18:83–84.
26. Ibid., 19:16.
27. Ibid., 3:205–206; Orson Pratt: "If you were, within one week from this time, to be let into all the visions that the brother of Jared had, what a weight of responsibility you would have upon you; how weak you would be, and how unprepared for the responsibility; and after the vision had closed up in your minds, and you [were] left to yourselves, you would be tempted in proportion to the light that had been presented before you. Then would come the trial, such as you never have had. This is the principle upon which the devil is allowed to try us. We have a circumstance in relation to Moses' being tempted; when the vision withdrew, and the heavens closed, the devil presented himself and said, 'Moses, son of man, worship me.' Moses replied, 'Who are you?' 'I am the son of God,' was the answer. Then said Moses, 'You call me son of man and say that you are the son of God, but where is your glory?' Could Moses

have withstood that terrible manifestation if he had not practiced for many years the principles of righteousness? A mere vision would not have strengthened him, and even to show him the glory of God in part would not have enabled him to combat with the powers of darkness that then came to him. It was by his knowledge of God, by his perseverance, his diligence and obedience in former years, that he was enabled to rebuke the devil, in the name of Jesus Christ, and drive him from him.

"So it will be with you, whether you have the necessary preparation or not, for the Lord will say to the powers of darkness, 'You are now at liberty to tempt my servants in proportion to the light that I have given. Go and see if they will be steadfast to that light; use every plan so far as I permit you, and if they will yield they are not worthy of me nor of my kingdom, and I will deliver them up and they shall be buffeted. You, Satan, shall buffet and torment them, until they shall learn obedience by the things that they suffer.'

"Hence the propriety of preparing for these things, that when they come you will know how to conquer Satan, and not want for experience to overcome, but be like Michael, the archangel, who, with all the knowledge and glory that he had gained through thousands of years of experience, durst not bring a railing accusation, because he knew better. And when Moses withstood Satan face to face, he knew who he was and what he had come for. He had obtained his knowledge by past trials, by a long series of preparation; hence he triumphed.

"So it must be with Latter-day Saints, and if we prepare ourselves we shall conquer. We must come in contact with every foe, and those who give way will be overcome.

"If we are to conquer the enemy of truth his power must be made manifest, and the power which will be given of the Lord through faithfulness must be in our possession. Do you wish to prevail—to conquer the powers of darkness when they present themselves? If you do, prepare yourselves against the day when these powers shall be made manifest with more energy than is now exhibited. Then you can say, the evil powers that have been made manifest, the agents that came and tempted me, came with all their force, I met them face to face and conquered by the word of my testimony, by patience, by the keys which have been bestowed upon me, and which I held sacred before God, and I have triumphed over the Adversary and over all his associates" (ibid., 3:353).

CHAPTER TWO
The Lord's Instructions

The most authoritative source of information on the gifts of the Spirit is the forty-sixth section of the Doctrine and Covenants. This revelation from the Lord Jesus Christ was given to the Prophet Joseph Smith on March 8, 1831, in Kirtland, Ohio. It was published for the first time in Independence, Missouri, in 1832 by William W. Phelps—who was acting in the capacity of official printer for the Church.[1] In this insightful section of canonized scripture the Lord provides valuable instructions for the "profit and learning" of His Saints (v. 1) in regard to the gifts that have been "given unto the Church" in the latter days (v. 10).

The discussion that follows will focus attention on key statements that were made by the Lord in section 46 and then expound upon these sayings by drawing upon statements made by the recognized leaders of His restored Church.

Every Saint Receives a Gift

In section 46 of the Doctrine and Covenants the Savior reveals that one of the gifts of the Spirit is bestowed upon each of His earthly disciples (see v. 11). This is a blessing for which we should all be truly grateful. One might well ask, "How does the transference or delivery of these gifts take place between the heavenly and temporal worlds?" We learn from the Prophet Joseph Smith and others that it is by securing the gift of the Holy Ghost that an individual is enabled to regularly receive spiritual gifts such as prophecy, visions, and dreams.[2] Elder Orson Pratt of the Quorum of the Twelve Apostles commented upon both of the previously mentioned ideas when he stated that "whenever the Holy Ghost takes up its residence in a person, it not only cleanses, sanctifies, and purifies him, in proportion as he yields himself to its influence, but also imparts to him some gift, intended for the benefit of himself and others. No one who has been born of the Spirit, and who remains sufficiently faithful, is left destitute of a spiritual gift."[3] President George Q. Cannon of the First Presidency suggested that "there is one general gift which we all receive: the gift of revelation. It becomes a source of knowledge of the mind and will of God." He further expounded this notion by saying, "no man or woman can receive the gift of the Holy Ghost without the spirit of revelation also." And he pointed out that "it may be that those who have received this talent do not feel the full force of what they have received. They may not be aware of the full extent of the power of the gift that has been bestowed upon them [cf. 3 Ne. 19:8–9]."[4]

Distribution of Spiritual Gifts

Next, we learn from the Lord in Doctrine and Covenants section 46 that the gifts of the Spirit are widely dispersed among His followers. "To some is given one, and to some is given another," He says, "that all may be profited thereby" (vv. 11–12). In the twelfth chapter of the book of 1 Corinthians, the Apostle Paul referred to this concept when he compared the Church of Jesus Christ to the human body. He pointed to the fact that the body has many "members" or parts (vv. 12, 14), which give the whole organism a variety of abilities. If the entire body consisted of an eye, he says, it would have no ability to hear; and if the entire body consisted of an ear, there would be no way for it to smell (see v. 17). Paul explained that just as all of the parts of the human body are necessary for it to function properly (see v. 22), so each of the gifts of the Spirit "need" to be in the Church (v. 21) in order for it to function as a unified entity and for the individuals within it to be sufficiently cared for (see v. 25).

The Lord, with His infinite knowledge and wisdom, decides where spiritual gifts will do the most good for His people, and He distributes them accordingly (see vv. 11, 18). This idea is repeated in Doctrine and Covenants section 46, where we are told that the gifts of the Spirit are dispensed "as it will be pleasing unto the . . . Lord, according as the Lord will, suiting his mercies according to the conditions of the children of men" (v. 15). In reference to this last-mentioned element, we have the words of Elder Orson Pratt. He taught that "spiritual gifts are distributed among the members of the Church, according to their faithfulness, circumstances, natural abilities, duties, and callings; that the whole may be properly instructed, confirmed, perfected, and saved."[5]

Purposes of Spiritual Gifts

Elder Pratt's statement leads us into the next section of this chapter, covering the various purposes behind spiritual gifts. An examination of section 46 of the Doctrine and Covenants reveals that "all these gifts come from God, for the benefit of the children of God" (v. 26). There are at least five distinct ways whereby these heavenly blessings can benefit mankind.

Benefit 1: Strength

In addressing the Latter-day Saints directly, President Wilford Woodruff said, "Brethren and sisters, let us try to live our religion and sanctify ourselves before the Lord. Seek for the Holy Spirit; pray for it; and labor for visions, for dreams, for revelations and for the gifts of the gospel of Christ, that they may strengthen us in the good work."[6] On January 10, 1877, Elder Franklin D. Richards wrote a letter that brought up the same theme. He said in this written communication that during some earlier joint meetings of the young men's and young women's associations the gifts of the Spirit had been made manifest. He reported that by means of these gifts "strength was infused into the meetings" and this strength was both "abiding and sincere."[7] We have a third proponent of this notion in the Prophet Joseph Smith, who noted that witnesses of "the gifts and blessings of the Holy Ghost" tended to be inspired with "fresh zeal and energy in the cause of truth."[8]

Benefit 2: Guidance

The connection of spiritual gifts with the concept of guidance was put forward by President Harold B. Lee. He taught the Saints with the following words: "If we live worthy, then the Lord will guide us—by a personal appearance, or by His actual voice, or by His voice coming into our mind, or by impressions upon our heart and our soul. And oh, how grateful we ought to be if the Lord sends us a dream in which are revealed to us the beauties of eternity or a warning and direction for our special comfort. Yes, if we so live, the Lord will guide us for our salvation and for our benefit."[9]

Benefit 3: Protection

Once again in section 46 of the Doctrine and Covenants, verse 7 specifically states that the spiritual gifts of God are bestowed upon the Latter-day Saints so that they will not be deceived by the "doctrines of devils, or the commandments of men." That is the protection that the power of God affords us. Elder Bruce R. McConkie issued the ominous warning that "if we do not receive gifts and guidance and doctrine and commandments from on high, we shall of necessity receive them from some other source. Others," he said, "have guidance to offer, doctrine to teach, and commandments to give."[10] It is imperative that we shield ourselves from influences or ideologies that are opposed to the building up and maintenance of God's kingdom. This concept will be treated in greater detail in the final chapter of this book.

Benefit 4: Improvement

Improvement in all aspects of life should be a goal for each of God's children. And George Q. Cannon explained how spiritual gifts fit into such an agenda. He stated that "if any of us are imperfect, it is our duty to pray for the gift that will make us perfect. . . . No man ought to say, 'Oh, I cannot help this; it is my nature.' He is not justified in it, for the reason that God has promised to give strength to correct these things, and to give gifts that will eradicate them." And in an appeal to the first chapter and fifth verse of the book of James he said, "If a man lack[s] wisdom, it is his duty to ask God for wisdom. The same with everything else. That is the design of God concerning His Church. He wants His Saints to be perfected in the truth. For this purpose He gives these gifts, and bestows them upon those who seek after them."[11]

Benefit 5: Preparation

Since we all must eventually pass from the mortal sphere to that which lies beyond the veil, it is advisable to prepare for this inevitable transition. In discoursing upon the Saints who lived in previous dispensations of the gospel, early nineteenth-century Church leader Oliver Cowdery mentioned that "visions, dreams, revelations and prophesyings enlarged their minds, and prepared them for the society of the blessed."[12] It is interesting to note that according to George Q. Cannon, God does not expect or desire the Latter-day Saints to put off acquiring the gifts that rightly belong to the heavenly world until they get there. They have the ability, here and now, to receive their Father's choice blessings. The Saints, said Brother Cannon, "believe in doing everything here that will help to prepare them for life eternal in [God's] presence. They look upon this world as a place where they should attend to these things. By baptism? Yes. By having hands laid upon them? Yes. [By acquiring] the *gifts* of the Holy Ghost? Certainly, have them here as well as hereafter; have them here to a partial extent to prepare them for the life that is to come."[13]

Seek Ye Earnestly

As stated above, we are all given a spiritual gift by a gracious and loving Heavenly Father at the time that we are confirmed and commanded to receive the gift of the Holy Ghost. But it is apparent that there is no expectation on the Lord's part that His sons and daughters be limited to a single heavenly endowment. In fact, we find a directive (one might even say, an invitation) from the Lord in the forty-sixth section of the Doctrine and Covenants to earnestly seek after spiritual gifts beyond those with which each Saint has initially been blessed (see v. 8). Joseph Fielding Smith, who wrote under the direction of the Quorum of the Twelve Apostles, assured us that "more than one gift may be received by any person who diligently seeks for these things."[14] Charles W. Penrose verified in an official LDS publication that "one person may receive several of them."[15] President Harold B. Lee, however, added the stipulation that "we shall never be given more of the gifts of the Spirit until we demonstrate our ability to use those He has already given us."[16]

Yet the directive to seek additional blessings at the hand of our Creator and King is exceptionally clear. Counselor George Q. Cannon posed some pertinent questions and made some provocative remarks in regard to this issue. He said,

> How many of you are seeking for these gifts that God has promised to bestow? How many of you, when you bow before your Heavenly Father in your family circle or in your secret places, contend for these gifts to be bestowed upon you? How many of you ask the Father in the name of Jesus to manifest Himself to you through these powers and these gifts? Or do you go along day by day like a door turning on its hinges, without having any feeling upon the subject, without exercising any faith whatever, content to be baptized and be members of the Church and to rest there, thinking that your salvation is secure because you have done this?
>
> I say to you, in the name of the Lord, as one of His servants, that you have need to repent of this. You have need to repent of your hardness of heart, of your indifference and of your carelessness. There is not that diligence, there is not that faith, there is not that seeking for the power of God that there should be among a people who have received the precious promises we have.[17]

How do baptized believers go about petitioning the Almighty for gifts that originate in the world of holiness and light? Fortunately, our Redeemer has provided a set of instructions on this very topic. We will now continue to recite and expound upon His words as recorded in section 46 of the Doctrine and Covenants.

Ask in the Spirit

In Doctrine and Covenants 46:28 and 30, we read that "he that asketh in Spirit shall receive in Spirit." We are then educated on why this action will produce this particular result. We are told that "he that asketh in the Spirit asketh according to the will of God; wherefore it is done even as he asketh." The phrase "in the Spirit," then, is interpreted to mean "as the Spirit dictates."[18]

Elder Bruce R. McConkie has written that "in the pure and perfect and proper sense, no one can speak or pray in the name of Christ unless he speaks or prays by the power of the Holy Ghost. It is within our capability, as the Lord's people, to do this because 'we have the mind of Christ' (1 Cor. 2:16). That is, we have the gift of the Holy Ghost, which is the right to the constant companionship of that member of the Godhead, based on faithfulness." This Apostle also explains that God the Father grants a petition spoken in the Spirit "because, having been offered in the name of the Son, it is, in fact, the petition of the Son. . . . Perfect prayers are always answered; proper petitions are always granted. The Lord never rejects a prayer uttered by the power of the Spirit, or denies a petition sought in the name of Christ, that accords with the divine will." And then he makes this significant observation: "[P]erfect prayers are spoken by the power of revelation."[19]

Ask in the Name of Jesus Christ

Elder McConkie's comments lead us directly into the next requirement for seeking spiritual gifts, since verse 31 of section 46 stipulates that "all things must be done in the name of Christ, whatsoever you do in the Spirit. " This is the very same instruction that an angel gave to Adam once he had been expelled from the Garden of Eden (see Moses 5:8). In the book of 3 Nephi the Savior explains to His disciples that, "whatsoever ye shall ask the Father in my name, which is right, believing that ye shall receive, behold it shall be given unto you" (18:20).

The words of Elder James E. Talmage help us to understand why this is so. He pointed to the fact that God the Father "has one Son who has done more than all the rest; one Son who has been more dutiful than all the others; one Son who never broke a commandment of His; one Son who thinks and feels as He thinks and feels; who is so like unto Him that if you see the one you have seen the other." Therefore, said Elder Talmage, "if a petition comes up to Him in the name of that well-beloved Son, depend upon it [that] it will receive consideration at His hands; depend upon it that He will be moved and His heart will be softened because of that." And then Elder Talmage made a significant connection. He said, "It is for that reason that we have been told to offer all our supplications, and to perform all our ceremonies and ordinances of the Church, in the name of Jesus Christ. It is for that reason that we partake of the sacramental bread and water in the name of Jesus Christ. It is for that reason that we administer to the sick in His name. For it is a name of power."[20]

Ask in a State of Worthiness

If we are to be so bold as to approach the throne of the Father and ask for blessings in the name of His Beloved Son, it is required that we also imitate the Master in the way that we live. The Prophet Joseph Smith's teaching was that even though Latter-day Saints have a "right" to the gifts of the Spirit, they must render themselves worthy in the sight of God before they can lay hold upon those blessings.[21] This requirement is laid out in section 46 of the Doctrine and Covenants. There we are taught that those who desire to receive spiritual gifts must walk "uprightly" before the Lord; they must "practice virtue and holiness before [Him] continually" (vv. 7, 33). Deity makes a concession for the fact that no mortal is perfect. And so in verse 9 of this same section of scripture we are told that these gifts "are given for the benefit of those who love [God] and keep all [His] commandments, and *him that seeketh so to do*" (emphasis added). This is a merciful allowance for which we should all be most grateful.

Gratitude for Gifts Received

Finally, we are instructed in Doctrine and Covenants section 46 that "[we] must give thanks unto God in the Spirit for whatsoever blessing [we] are blessed with" (v. 32). Notice that once again the command is for us to act "in the Spirit." It would appear from this directive that after God has blessed us with spiritual power He desires that we respond on a spiritual level, perhaps to demonstrate that we have become active participants (or even partners with Him) in rising above our telestial or fallen condition.

When Elder George Q. Cannon was serving as a member of the Quorum of the Twelve Apostles in the mid-nineteenth century, he addressed the issue of offering thanks for blessings received when he said,

> It is right that we, as a people and as individuals, should be continually grateful to God for what He has done for us. Unless we appreciate these blessings, it is not likely they will be increased upon us—it is not reasonable that greater blessings than those already received will be bestowed upon us; but if we are humble, meek, and filled with thanksgiving and gratitude to our Father and God under all circumstances, appreciating and putting a high value on the mercies He extends unto us, it is

> more than probable that those blessings and mercies will be increased upon us according to our wants and necessities, and we shall still have increased cause for gratitude and thanksgiving before Him.[22]

Seeking for Signs

There is one cautionary note in section 46 of the Doctrine and Covenants that calls for attention here. In verse 9 the Lord stresses that those who seek after spiritual gifts are not to do so for the purpose of seeking a sign from Him. As Charles W. Penrose once wrote, the desires of those who seek after spiritual gifts "must be pure in order to obtain the blessings for which they ask. These are not given as signs to be consumed on anyone's lust. Neither are they bestowed as wonders to create astonishment or feed the love of the marvelous."[23]

It is an evil and adulterous generation that seeks after signs, said the Savior in the meridian dispensation of the gospel (see Matt. 12:39). In modern scripture He expounds upon this theme. In Doctrine and Covenants section 63 He states that sign-seekers have existed from the beginning, and they exist even now among the Latter-day Saints. With such people the Lord is not well pleased. And He informs us that signs and wonders do not produce faith in those that witness them, but rather signs are meant to follow after the exercise of faith. Signs are never produced by the will of mortals but only by the will of God, and they are granted unto the faithful not for their own aggrandizement but "for the good of men" unto God's glory (see vv. 7–12).

It is important that we recognize the difference between heavenly inducement and earthly impulse. "To seek the gifts of the Spirit through faith, humility, and devotion to righteousness," said Elder Bruce R. McConkie, "is not to be confused with sign-seeking."[24]

Conclusion

The forty-sixth section of the Doctrine and Covenants is a guide for latter-day disciples of Christ who desire to bridge the gap between heaven and earth and repair the breach between their native spiritual nature and their current fallen state. It is a handbook for placing interested individuals in a situation where they can better themselves now with divine support and prepare themselves for the world to come. Perhaps most importantly, section 46 teaches us that we have the potential to become a benefit to our fellow sojourners on the earth. In all of these things the kingdom of God is built up and the glory of God is increased. And because of all these things, the gifts of the Spirit can be viewed as seeds of godliness.

NOTES TO CHAPTER 2

1. *Evening and Morning Star,* vol. 1, no. 3, August 1832, 17; hereafter cited as *EMS.*
2. The Prophet Joseph Smith taught that the gifts of the Spirit "cannot be enjoyed without the gift of the Holy Ghost" because they are "obtained through that medium" (Brigham H. Roberts, ed., *History of The Church of Jesus Christ of Latter-day Saints* [Salt Lake City: Deseret Book, 1948–1950], 5:27–28; hereafter cited as *HC).* This concept is confirmed in *EMS,* vol. 2, no. 17, February 1834, 130; *Messenger and Advocate,* vol. 1, no. 6, March 1835, 84; hereafter cited as *M&A;* ibid., vol. 1, no. 12, September 1835, 184; *Times and Seasons,* vol. 1, no. 8, June 1840, 126; Orson Spencer, *Letters Exhibiting the Most Prominent Doctrines of The Church of Jesus Christ of Latter-day Saints* (Salt Lake City: George Q. Cannon and Sons, 1891), 68; Conference Report, April 1956, 72; Daniel H. Ludlow, ed., *Encyclopedia of Mormonism* (New York: Macmillan, 1992), 2:543.
3. Nels B. Lundwall, comp., *Masterful Discourses and Writings of Orson Pratt* (Salt Lake City: N. B. Lundwall, 1946), 539.
4. Brian H. Stuy, ed., *Collected Discourses* (Burbank, CA, and Woodland Hills, UT: B.H.S. Publishing, 1987–1992), 2:256; hereafter cited as *CD.*
5. Lundwall, comp., *Masterful Discourses and Writings of Orson Pratt,* 541.
6. *CD,* 1:265.
7. *The Contributor,* vol. 3, no. 4, January 1882, 116.
8. *HC,* 1:85–86.
9. Harold B. Lee, *Stand Ye in Holy Places* (Salt Lake City: Deseret Book, 1975), 144.
10. Bruce R. McConkie, *A New Witness for the Articles of Faith* (Salt Lake City: Deseret Book, 1985), 370; hereafter cited as *NWAF.*
11. *Millennial Star,* vol. 56, no. 17, 23 April 1894, 260.
12. *M&A,* vol. 2, no. 20, May 1836, 308.
13. George D. Watt, ed., *Journal of Discourses* (Liverpool, England: Samuel W. Richards and Sons, 1852–1886), 17:231 (emphasis added); hereafter cited as *JD.*

14. Joseph Fielding Smith, *Church History and Modern Revelation* (Salt Lake City: The Council of the Twelve Apostles of The Church of Jesus Christ of Latter-day Saints, 1953), 1:201.
15. *The Contributor,* vol. 2, no. 3, December 1880, 71.
16. Clyde J. Williams, ed., *The Teachings of Harold B. Lee* (Salt Lake City: Bookcraft, 1996), 130.
17. Jerreld L. Newquist, comp., *Gospel Truth: Discourses and Writings of George Q. Cannon* (Salt Lake City: Deseret Book, 1987), 154–55.
18. Hyrum M. Smith and Janne M. Sjodahl, *Doctrine and Covenants Commentary,* rev. ed. (Salt Lake City: Deseret Book, 1960), 276.
19. *NWAF,* 383–84.
20. *CD,* 3:12–13.
21. Dean C. Jessee, ed., *The Personal Writings of Joseph Smith* (Salt Lake City: Deseret Book, 1984), 421.
22. *JD,* 11:67–68.
23. *The Contributor,* vol. 2, no. 3, December 1880, 71.
24. Bruce R. McConkie, *Mormon Doctrine,* 2nd ed. (Salt Lake City: Bookcraft, 1966), 715.

GIFTS OF THE INWARD SENSES

CHAPTER THREE
Testimony of Jesus Christ

To some it is given by the Holy Ghost to know that Jesus Christ is the Son of God.

—*Doctrine and Covenants 46:13*

President J. Reuben Clark Jr. taught that there are two different kinds of testimony. One of them comes through the physical senses, and the other comes through the Spirit of God. Both of these kinds of testimony may be involved in the process of gaining a knowledge of the Savior's divinity. The Apostle Thomas obtained a sure knowledge that Jesus was the Christ when he saw the resurrected Lord face to face and physically felt the wounds of the crucifixion. But President Clark pointed to the fact that Jesus subsequently said to this particular disciple, "Thomas, because thou hast seen me, thou hast believed: blessed are they that have not seen, and yet have believed" (John 20:25–29). "And that is the testimony of the Christ which must come to most of us," said President Clark, "the testimony of believing without seeing, a testimony which the Lord blessed. And this testimony is the testimony of the Spirit. . . . We should all seek for it. If the Lord wishes to add the testimony of the senses, we should be grateful; but the testimony of the Spirit is within the call of all of us. All we need to do to get it, is to live for it and seek it."[1]

One of the official functions of the Holy Ghost is to bear record of the Son of God (see Moses 1:24; John 15:26; D&C 42:17). Elder Bruce R. McConkie provided an insightful perspective on the connection between these two members of the Godhead. He said,

> The Holy Ghost is Christ's revelator to bear witness of His divine Sonship and of the saving truths of His gospel. . . . As a spirit personage, the Holy Spirit, by laws which are ordained, has power to speak to the spirit within man and to convey truth with absolute certainty. This revealed knowledge becomes a personal testimony to the recipient. By definition a testimony of the gospel is to know by personal revelation from the Holy Ghost that Jesus is the Christ through whom salvation comes.[2]

President Joseph Fielding Smith taught that "each member of the [LDS] Church is *entitled* to have that revelation given to him by which he may know that Jesus Christ is the Son of God."[3] President Gordon B. Hinckley took this idea one step further. He proclaimed that "every Latter-day Saint has the *responsibility* to know for himself or herself with a certainty beyond doubt that Jesus is the resurrected, living Son of the living God."[4]

There is a definite distinction between having secondhand belief in something and having firsthand knowledge of it. In both of the lists of spiritual gifts found in the Book of Mormon and Doctrine and Covenants, it is plainly stated that a person can "know" that Jesus is the Christ by the power of the Holy Ghost (Moro. 10:7; D&C 46:13). In the King James Bible's list of spiritual gifts, it is said that "no man can *say* that Jesus is the Lord, but by the Holy Ghost" (1 Cor. 12:3; emphasis added), but in a public sermon the Prophet Joseph Smith modified this statement to read, "No man can *know*"[5]—thus bringing all three of the scriptural lists into line with each other. Charles W. Penrose provided some concise but thought-provoking commentary on the biblical verse just quoted when he said,

> Now, there may be a great many people [who] say that Jesus is the Christ. How do you *know?* "Well, I believe it." Why? "Because I have been brought up [as] a Christian, and therefore I believe it." But do you *know* that Jesus is the Christ? No, you cannot *know* unless you get a revelation from God to that effect. You may believe that Jesus is the Christ, you may have been trained up in that belief, but you cannot know it unless God shall reveal it to you. It is only by the power of the Holy Ghost that this knowledge can come to the children of men.[6]

An article published in the *Encyclopedia of Mormonism* points out why revealed knowledge in this area is so desirable and vital. It says that true Christian discipleship is achieved "in the fullest spiritual sense only when a personal testimony of Jesus is received."[7] It is one thing to hold an idea close to one's heart and quite another to step beyond the boundary of belief and into the realm of revealed certainty.

Testimony through Revelation

There are several scriptural examples of people gaining a testimony of Jesus' divinity through the power of the Holy Ghost. We begin with a man named Simeon, whose story is told on the pages of the New Testament. The Holy Ghost revealed to him that he would see the Christ before his eyes closed in death. This promise was fulfilled when the baby Jesus was taken by His parents to the temple at Jerusalem and the Spirit directed Simeon to go up to that holy house and see Him (see Luke 2:25–32).

Next is John the Baptist. This priest after the order of Aaron reportedly witnessed "the Spirit descending from heaven like a dove" and abiding upon the Messiah after His baptism had taken place. This was a foreordained sign. The man upon whom the dove sign rested was thereby identified as "the Lamb of God, which taketh away the sin of the world," even "the Son of God"—and John was enabled by his experience to so testify (John 1:29–34). The scripture that is quoted at the beginning of this chapter from Doctrine and Covenants section 46 holds out the possibility that each of us can gain the same testimony of the Redeemer in a similar, and directly connected, fashion. It reads: "To some it is given *by the Holy Ghost* to know that Jesus Christ is the Son of God, and that He was crucified for the sins of the world" (v. 13, emphasis added).

In the Book of Mormon, Alma the Younger testifies that after a season of fasting and prayer, he was taught about the redeeming power of the blood of Christ. He reports that this information was transmitted to him through "the Holy Spirit of God," and he therefore knew for himself of its surety (Alma 5:21, 38, 45–46).

The last example of scriptural accounts comes from a story about the first man Adam, which account is found in the book of Moses. In that source is written: "And in that day the Holy Ghost fell upon Adam, which beareth record of the Father and the Son, saying: 'I am the Only Begotten of the Father from the beginning, henceforth and forever, that as thou hast fallen thou mayest be redeemed, and all mankind, even as many as will'" (5:9). Thus we learn that Adam gained a revealed testimony of Jesus Christ through the power of the Holy Ghost.

Leaders of the Lord's restored Church have borne public witness that they have received assurances from the Spirit of God that Jesus Christ is indeed the Redeemer of mankind. Joseph F. Smith, for instance, has said, "I say to this congregation that the Holy Spirit of God has spoken to me—not through the ear, not through the eye, but to my spirit, to my living and eternal part—and has revealed unto me that Jesus is the Christ, the Son of the living God. I testify to you that I know that my Redeemer lives."[8]

Marion G. Romney bore a similar witness as an Apostle of the Lord. From the general conference pulpit he boldly declared, "I know that my Redeemer lives. I shall not know it better when I stand before the bar of God to be judged. I know that Jesus is the Redeemer. I bear that witness to you, not from what people have told me; I bear it out of a knowledge revealed to me by the Holy Spirit." And he indicated that he was willing to bear that eternal truth to men and women everywhere—saint and sinner alike.[9]

Another modern Apostle, Elder Melvin J. Ballard, made a frank admission while speaking before a worldwide gathering of the faithful. He said simply, "I haven't seen Him." Nevertheless, this ordained special witness could say without hesitation, "I know, within my heart and in my soul, as I live and stand before you today, that Jesus Christ is the Son of God, the Savior of the world. When I shall stand before Him, in His presence, and see Him face to face as He is, I shall not know any better the truth that He is the Christ, and that He lives, than I do today." This steadfast knowledge was given, said Elder Ballard, "by the witness and testimony of the Spirit of God in [his] heart and soul."[10]

President Lorenzo Snow left behind a remarkable account of how he received a heavenly witness of the Master. Brother Snow was born into a home of Baptists, and so he was raised from childhood to believe in the divinity of Christ. When he became a member of the restored Church of Christ on April 5, 1835, he reaffirmed his belief in the Lord Jesus. Here is his report.

> Some two or three weeks after I was baptized, one day while engaged in my studies, I began to reflect upon the fact that I had not obtained a *knowledge* of the truth of the work—that I had not realized the fulfillment of the promise [that] "he that doeth my will shall know of the doctrine" [see John 7:16–17], and I began to feel very uneasy. I laid aside my books, left the house, and wandered around through the fields under the oppressive influence of a gloomy, disconsolate spirit, while an indescribable cloud of darkness seemed to envelop me. I had been accustomed, at the close of the day, to retire for secret prayer, to a grove a short distance from my lodgings, but at this time I felt no inclination to do so. The spirit of prayer had departed and the heavens seemed like brass over my head. At length, realizing that the time had come for secret prayer, I concluded I would not forego my evening service and, as a matter of formality, knelt as I was in the habit of doing, and in my accustomed retired place, but not feeling as I was [accustomed] to feel.
>
> I had no sooner opened my lips in an effort to pray, than I heard a sound, just above my head, like the rustling of silken robes, and immediately the Spirit of God descended upon me, completely enveloping my whole person, filling me from the crown of my head to the soles of my feet, and oh, the joy and happiness I felt! No language can describe the almost instantaneous transition from a dense cloud of mental and spiritual darkness into a refulgence of light and knowledge, as it was at that time imparted to my understanding. I then received a perfect knowledge that God lives, that Jesus Christ is the Son of God, and of the restoration of the holy priesthood, and the fullness of the gospel. It was a complete baptism—a tangible immersion in the heavenly principle or element, the Holy Ghost; and even more real and physical in its effects upon every part of my system than the immersion by water; dispelling forever, so long as reason and memory last, all possibility of doubt or fear in relation to the fact handed down to us historically, that the "Babe of Bethlehem" is truly the Son of God.[11]

Conclusion

It is probably significant that in each of the three detailed scriptural discourses on spiritual gifts, the testimony of Christ is the first to be named. This is undoubtedly so because it has primacy of importance. There is no gift of the Spirit that has greater relevance and none that can instigate such dramatic, positive changes in the lives of its recipients. A revealed witness of the divine nature of the Son of God is tremendously meaningful because it touches each individual in such a personal way, being inseparably interwoven with their eternal salvation. This gift awaits delivery to all those who desire it, for it is the intent of God that this particular present be widely dispersed. We are not only entitled to this blessing as Latter-day Saints, but it is our responsibility to request it from the Father of us all.

NOTES TO CHAPTER 3

1. *Improvement Era,* August 1949, 495, 539–40. When President Clark mentions "the testimony of the senses" he is referring to the doctrine of receiving the Second Comforter. This privilege, as Joseph Fielding Smith points out, can only be obtained "by the most faithful adherence to every principle of righteousness. . . . This great gift has been received by many of the prophets. Nephi and Jacob testify of this visitation. Abraham, Moses, Daniel, Elijah and many others anciently were so blessed. There have been some in our own dispensation besides the Prophet Joseph Smith who have realized the blessing of [the] promise" found in John 14:16–23 (Joseph Fielding Smith, *Church History and Modern Revelation* [Salt Lake City: The Church of Jesus Christ of Latter-day Saints, 1949], 4:35).

 A desire for the reception of this priceless gift was once voiced by a stake president named William McLachlan, who was invited to speak during a session of general conference. He said on this occasion: "There is a revelation in the Book of Doctrine and Covenants from which I shall read the first verse, contained in the ninety-third section:

 "'Verily, thus saith the Lord, it shall come to pass that every soul who forsaketh [his] sins and cometh unto me and calleth on my name, and obeyeth my voice and keepeth my commandments, shall see my face and know that I am.'

 "This is a passage that has interested me very much of late. I have had a constant and increasing desire grow up in my heart to obtain the testimony that is promised unto those who keep the commandments of God, to behold the face of Him who came into the world in the meridian of time, and who did so much for you and for me. I desire to live in harmony with the Lord, so that

I can receive, in His own due time, this testimony, that shall enable me to bear record of Him in truth. While I know by the revelation of the Spirit of God that this is His work, I also know that it has been promised in His word through the Prophet Joseph Smith, that the Second Comforter will come unto the Latter-day Saints who have kept the commandments of God, who have been steadfast in their faith in His work" (Conference Report, April 1906, 70; hereafter cited as CR).

2. Bruce R. McConkie, *Doctrinal New Testament Commentary* (Salt Lake City: Bookcraft, 1965), 1:756.
3. Joseph Fielding Smith, *Take Heed to Yourselves* (Salt Lake City: Deseret Book, 1966), 228 (emphasis added).
4. Gordon B. Hinckley, *Teachings of Gordon B. Hinckley* (Salt Lake City: Deseret Book, 1997), 285 (emphasis added).
5. Andrew F. Ehat and Lyndon W. Cook, eds., *The Words of Joseph Smith: The Contemporary Accounts of the Nauvoo Discourses of the Prophet Joseph* (Orem, UT: Grandin Books, 1991), 115 (emphasis added); see also Brigham H. Roberts, ed., *History of The Church of Jesus Christ of Latter-day Saints* (Salt Lake City: Deseret Book, 1948–1950), 4:602–603; 5:27.
6. George D. Watt, ed., *Journal of Discourses* (Liverpool, England: Samuel W. Richards and Sons, 1852–1886), 22:88–89 (emphasis in original).
7. Daniel H. Ludlow, ed., *Encyclopedia of Mormonism* (New York: Macmillan, 1992), 4:1472.
8. Brian H. Stuy, ed., *Collected Discourses* (Burbank, CA, and Woodland Hills, UT: B.H.S. Publishing, 1987–1992), 5:230.
9. CR, April 1953, 124.
10. Ibid., April 1910, 45.
11. Eliza R. Snow, *Biography and Family Record of Lorenzo Snow* (Salt Lake City: Deseret News, 1884), 7–8 (emphasis in original).

CHAPTER FOUR
Administration

To some it is given by the Holy Ghost to know the differences of administration.

—DOCTRINE AND COVENANTS 46:15

The gift of knowing the differences of administration has been identified by Elder Bruce R. McConkie as having "administrative ability,"[1] which is "used in administering and regulating the Church."[2] The text of Doctrine and Covenants section 46 plainly states that this is much more than just an inherent knack for conducting ecclesiastical business or carrying out the diverse dealings of the Lord's earthly kingdom—it is to have the assistance of the third member of the Godhead in doing so (v. 15).

The affairs of the Church should be administrated by the power of the Holy Ghost. When John Taylor was serving as the President of the Church, he stressed that "there is no man living in and of himself, [who] can guide the ship of Zion or regulate the affairs of the Church and kingdom of God unaided by the Spirit of God."[3] Elder John A. Widtsoe of the Quorum of the Twelve asserted that as a privilege "all officers of the Church, in the Priesthood, or the auxiliary organizations in their official labors, have the *right* to enjoy that spirit of guidance which we call the spirit of inspiration."[4] And, indeed, the Lord confirms this concept in the Doctrine and Covenants where He states that "it always has been given to the elders of my Church from the beginning, and ever shall be, to conduct all meetings as they are directed and guided by the Holy Spirit" (D&C 46:2; cf. 20:45; 107:68, 71). Elder Matthias F. Cowley told the Saints in relation to the scripture just cited that "this is the law of God to every bishop, to every stake president, and to the president of every quorum or association in the Church. They are to be guided by the Holy Spirit."[5] And it would seem that no administrative task is too mundane to be included under the umbrella of this spiritual gift. Wilford Woodruff recorded in his journal that the Lord gave a revelation through the Prophet Joseph Smith wherein He said that the Twelve Apostles who held office in 1842 were to govern the printing of all Church publications as they were directed by the Holy Spirit.[6]

In a very interesting letter written on August 31, 1835, and signed by the presidencies of Kirtland, Ohio, and Independence, Missouri (i.e., Joseph Smith, Oliver Cowdery, and Sidney Rigdon; and Frederick G. Williams, William W. Phelps, and John Whitmer), it was related that the Lord, through His Spirit, had issued a specific revelation for the government of the Church. He had manifested that the priesthood officers in these two locations were more or less in a state of transgression because they had "not enjoyed the Spirit of God sufficiently to be able to comprehend their duties respecting themselves and the welfare of Zion." This was detrimental to everyone's interests. They were urged to rectify this undesirable situation by letting God "open the eyes of their understanding" and manifest His designs and purposes to them. This letter also encouraged the Saints to always stay within appointed boundaries when regulating the affairs of the Church.[7]

An example of divinely enriched Church administration can be seen in the Old Testament story of Moses and the seventy elders of Israel. In Numbers 11, the Lord commanded Moses to gather the elders to the Tabernacle, where He would take the Spirit that was upon Moses and disperse it among the elders also. This was done specifically so that these other men could share the burden of Church government (see vv. 16–17, 24–25).

In the New Testament we read of an instance where the Holy Ghost became directly involved with the Church's governmental affairs when the Lord revealed who should be called to certain missionary labors (see Acts 13:1–5). The Spirit also reportedly governed the meridian Saints in matters of a ritual nature (see Acts 15:23–29).

For latter-day examples of the gift under discussion we turn first to Heber C. Kimball. He was seated at the Melchizedek Priesthood pulpits inside the Kirtland Temple on June 4, 1837, when the Prophet Joseph Smith approached him and said, "Brother Heber, the Spirit of the Lord has whispered to me, saying: 'Let my servant, Heber, go to England and proclaim my gospel, and open the door of salvation to that nation.'"[8] This was to be the first overseas mission since the Church had been formally organized in 1830. The Prophet indicated that this administrative revelation was not only given to him for the salvation of Great Britain, but it was also connected with "the salvation of [God's] Church."[9]

As a member of the First Presidency, George Q. Cannon mentioned another incident where the Spirit of God played a crucial role in the government and administration of the entire LDS Church. This was in connection with the standing of each Apostle in the Quorum of the Twelve. When Joseph and Hyrum Smith were murdered in Carthage, Illinois, in 1844, John Taylor was severely wounded by gunfire but survived through the providence of God. There were several men ahead of him in seniority in the quorum who should not have been. This circumstance was corrected by President Brigham Young, but Orson Hyde and Orson Pratt were still senior to Elder Taylor. President Young was "prompted by the Spirit of God" to rearrange the seniority standings within the quorum since Elders Taylor, Woodruff, and Smith each held the apostleship during a time when Elders Hyde and Pratt did not hold that power. It was because of this administrative move that Elder Taylor eventually became the presiding President of the Church—being the senior Apostle when President Young passed away. Brother Cannon maintained that it was by this manner that God brought to the forefront the man whom He desired to lead His Church.[10]

Ezra Taft Benson related an experience about guidance of the Spirit in important administrative matters. Once he was assigned to go with S. Dilworth Young to attend a stake conference in Sandy, Utah, and so he, as usual, carefully went over the stake's records beforehand. While searching these documents, he received a strong impression that an alternate high councilman was to be the next stake president. The next day he reviewed the records again and had the same impression. When he met with Brother Young he told him what he thought but, not wanting to influence someone else's decisions, he said they should go forward with the usual interviews and see what happened. He said of their meetings, "We interviewed the bishops, the high council, the stake presidency, and a few other officers. As I remember, every man but one recommended the junior member of the alternate high councilmen as the stake president. I know the Spirit operates. It is a great assurance that we can reorganize a stake presidency or divide a stake and have the witness of the Spirit."[11]

Elder Dallin H. Oaks recalled a situation where the Spirit of the Lord directly intervened to prevent some interference in the administration of an important Church matter. He said of this incident,

> One of my first experiences in being restrained by the Spirit came soon after I was called as a counselor in a stake presidency in Chicago. In one of our first stake presidency meetings our stake president made a proposal that our new stake center be built in a particular location. I immediately saw four or five good reasons why that was the wrong location. When asked for my counsel, I opposed the proposal, giving each of those reasons. The stake president wisely proposed that each of us consider the matter prayerfully for a week and discuss it further in our next meeting.
>
> Almost perfunctorily I prayed about the subject and immediately received a strong impression that I was wrong, that I was standing in the way of the Lord's will, and that I should remove myself from opposition to it. Needless to say, I was restrained and promptly gave my approval to the proposed construction. Incidentally, the wisdom of constructing the stake center at that location was soon evident, even to me. My reasons to the contrary turned out to be short-sighted, and I was soon grateful to have been restrained from relying on them.[12]

Elder M. Russell Ballard provides a concluding example of the gift of administration. He tells of a conversation he once had with a bishop who was new to his calling and trying to decide who should be the next Young Women's president in his ward. He had a clear impression in his mind who this person should be, but his counselors presented him with another name. He decided to rely on his respect for them instead of on his own spiritual sensitivity and accepted their recommendation. The call was issued but the woman who was presented with it felt that the call didn't feel right, and so she asked for some time to reconcile her feelings. She also asked the counselor who issued the invitation for service to ask the bishop if he was sure that this was what the Lord really wanted to happen.

> "Of course she feels uncomfortable," the bishop said when his counselor explained the situation. "This isn't what the Lord wants. He let me know who the new Young Women president is supposed to be, and I've been ignoring Him."
>
> The bishop instructed his counselor to let the sister know that there was nothing wrong with her spiritual sensitivity. Then he was to go ahead and extend the calling to the sister the bishop had been originally impressed to call.
>
> Her response was validating: "I've had the impression for two weeks that this calling was coming."
>
> "The experience didn't teach me to ignore my counselors," the bishop said. "Their input was important—the woman they suggested was called to serve as a Young Women adviser, and she did a wonderful job there. But I did learn that of all the voices I was to listen to as bishop, the most important one was the voice of the Spirit as it guided my thoughts, my words, and my actions."[13]

Conclusion

Being called to function in an administrative role in the Lord's latter-day Church is a great responsibility, which requires the guidance of the Holy Ghost. The regulation and maintenance of God's kingdom is sure to be handled more efficiently and effectively when the Holy Ghost's direction is put before our own understanding. In the due time of the Lord, recipients of the spiritual gift of administration are sure to have their burdens lightened if they will heed the inspirational thoughts and impulses that are granted to them.

NOTES TO CHAPTER 4

1. Bruce R. McConkie, *A New Witness For the Articles of Faith* (Salt Lake City: Deseret Book, 1985), 271.
2. Ibid., 278.
3. George D. Watt, ed., *Journal of Discourses* (Liverpool, England: Samuel W. Richards and Sons, 1852–1886), 26:32; hereafter cited as *JD.*
4. Conference Report, October 1934, 10 (emphasis added).
5. Ibid., October 1902, 60.
6. Scott G. Kenney, ed., *Wilford Woodruff's Journal: 1833–1898* (Midvale, UT: Signature Books, 1983), 2:153.
7. Dean C. Jessee, ed., *The Personal Writings of Joseph Smith* (Salt Lake City: Deseret Book, 1984), 345–46.
8. Jeni Broberg Holzapfel and Richard Neitzel Holzapfel, eds., *A Woman's View: Helen Mar Whitney's Reminiscences of Early Church History* (Provo, UT: BYU Religious Studies Center, 1997), 90–91.
9. Brigham H. Roberts, ed., *History of The Church of Jesus Christ of Latter-day Saints* (Salt Lake City: Deseret Book, 1948–1950), 2:489–90.
10. *JD,* 24:275–76.
11. Ezra T. Benson, *The Teachings of Ezra Taft Benson* (Salt Lake City: Bookcraft, 1988), 146.
12. *New Era,* September 1982, 42.
13. M. Russell Ballard, *Counseling with Our Councils: Learning to Minister Together in the Church and in the Family* (Salt Lake City: Deseret Book, 1997), 69–70.

CHAPTER FIVE
Operations

It is given by the Holy Ghost to some to know the diversities of operations, whether they be of God.

—DOCTRINE AND COVENANTS 46:16

The gift of operations is at first a bit difficult to define when we read through the three parallel scriptural texts that mention it. In the Apostle Paul's discourse, he tells us that "there are diversities of operations . . . [by] God . . . [through] the manifestation of the Spirit" (1 Cor. 12:6–7). In the prophet Moroni's discussion on this topic he only relates that "the gifts of God . . . are given by the manifestations of the Spirit" and does not mention the term "operations"at all—though his thoughts clearly follow along the same track as Paul's (Moro. 10:8). It is not until we examine the Lord's explanation of spiritual gifts in latter-day scripture that we get some clarification on this issue. He states that "it is given by the Holy Ghost to some to know the diversities of operations, *whether they be of God*" (D&C 46:16, emphasis added). Thus we learn that this particular gift consists of a divinely assisted ability to tell the difference between an operation initiated by Deity and one that is not. As Elder Bruce R. McConkie has stated, "It is to the gift of discernment that reference is here made."[1]

Elder McConkie provided a concise overview of the opposing spiritual forces that mankind is obliged to discern between and in the process illustrated why the gift of operations is so desirable. He taught that two general spirits are abroad in our earthly realm:

> *One is of God, the other of the devil.* The spirit which is of God is one that leads to light, truth, freedom, progress, and every good thing; on the other hand, the spirit which is of Lucifer leads to darkness, error, bondage, retrogression, and every evil thing. One spirit is from above, the other from beneath; and that which is from beneath never allows more light or truth or freedom to exist than it can help. All religion, philosophy, education, science, governmental control—indeed, all things—are influenced and governed by one or the other (in some cases, part by one and part by the other) of these spirits (Moro. 7).
>
> It should be understood that these two influences in the world are manifest through the ministrations of actual spirit personages from the unseen world. The power and influence wielded by Satan is exercised through the host of evil spirits who do his bidding and who have power, according to laws that exist, to impress their wills upon the minds of receptive mortals. On the other hand, much of the power and influence of Deity is exercised by and manifest through spirit beings who appear and give revelation and guidance as the Lord's purposes may require. In general, the more righteous and saintly a person is, the easier it will be for him to receive communications from heavenly sources; and the more evil and corrupt he is, the easier will it be for evil spirits to implant their nefarious schemes in his mind and heart.[2]

This modern-day Apostle has made one other important point that bears repeating. He said that the "appointed leaders [of the Church] must be able . . . to discern between true spirits and false ones."[3] This is precisely the same precept that is presented in Doctrine and Covenants section 46 where the Lord relates that "unto the bishop of the Church, and unto such as God shall appoint and ordain to watch over the Church and to be elders unto the Church, are to have it given unto them to *discern* all those gifts lest there be any among you professing and yet be not of God" (v. 27, emphasis added, cf. v. 16). The Prophet Joseph Smith reiterated this fact when he told the Saints of his day that "the gift of discerning spirits will be given to the presiding Elder" of a congregation, and he admonished members of the restored Church with these words: "pray for him that he may have this gift."[4]

Elder Stephen L. Richards reached beyond the aforementioned ecclesiastical boundary and included all of the Latter-day Saints among those who are in need of this spiritual blessing. He said, "The gift and power of discernment in this world of contention between the forces of good and the power of evil is essential equipment for *every* son and daughter of God."[5] We all need the power of discernment, said Elder James E. Talmage, "that we may know the spirits with whom we have to deal, and recognize those who are speaking and acting under the influence of heaven, and those who are the emissaries of hell." This is "a gift of the Spirit, to which we are entitled and we will have it as we live for it," he explained. "With that gift we shall be free, to a great extent, from the deception that otherwise might lead us astray."[6]

George Q. Cannon made note of the fact that the gift of operations or discernment is not only useful in an outward, public setting but may also be applied on a personal level—that which is inward and private. He pointed out that this gift

> not only gives men and women who have it the power to discern the spirit with which others may be possessed or influenced, but it gives them the power to discern the spirit which influences themselves. They are able to detect a false spirit, and also to know when the Spirit of God reigns within them. . . . [I]n private life this gift is of great importance to the Latter-day Saints. Possessing and exercising this gift, they will not allow any evil influence to enter into their hearts or to prompt them in their thoughts, their words or their acts. They will repel it; and if perchance such a spirit should get possession of them, as soon as they witness its effects they will expel it or, in other words, refuse to be led or prompted by it.[7]

According to President Brigham Young the gift of discernment can become so well developed within a gifted Saint that they "can discern the [essential] spirit of a person, whether it is good or evil. They have such power, that when a person enters [their presence] they can tell the spirit of such [a] person."[8]

Ancient and Latter-Day Examples

A survey of the Bible reveals several stories where the gift of discernment was either sorely needed or was enjoyed by the Lord's faithful followers.

First, there is the story of Moses and the magicians of Egypt. Moses was commanded to display the power of the Lord by casting Aaron's rod before the Pharaoh, whereupon it would be changed into a serpent. This directive was carried out and the miracle performed. But then the Pharaoh had his sorcerers perform the exact same feat. Without the gift of operations or discernment it would have been impossible for a typical bystander to tell the difference between the two powers displayed. And Pharaoh did, in fact, fail to discern properly—even after the power of Jehovah overcame the power of his wonder-workers (see Ex. 7:8–13).

Another failure to obtain and exercise the gift of divinely aided discernment can be seen in the story of Jesus Christ healing a blind and mute man. Even with the Savior of mankind standing before them, the Pharisees, who belonged to the chosen house of Israel, were unable to determine the source of the power that wrought these mighty miracles (see Matt. 12:22–24).

An instance where the power of discernment was properly exercised is found in Acts chapter 16. In verses 16 through 18 there is an account of a girl who publicly proclaimed that a group of meridian Saints were "servants of the most high God" who could show others "the way of salvation." But the Apostle Paul was not fooled by this pretended exhibition of honor and approbation. He was able to discern that this young woman was actually possessed by an evil spirit, and he proceeded to cast it out of her.

A tale told in the New Testament provides an excellent example of the power of discernment being granted through the assistance of the Spirit. In the fifth chapter of the book of Acts we read:

> [A] certain man named Ananias, with Sapphira his wife, sold a possession,
>
> And kept back part of the price, his wife also being privy to it, and brought a certain part, and laid it at the apostles' feet.
>
> But Peter said, Ananias, why hath Satan filled thine heart to lie to the Holy Ghost, and to keep back part of the price of the land?

> Whiles it remained was it not thine own? and after it was sold, was it not in thine own power? why hast thou conceived this thing in thine heart? Thou hast not lied unto men, but unto God.
>
> And Ananias hearing these words fell down, and gave up the ghost: and great fear came on all them that heard these things.
>
> And the young men arose, wound him up, and carried him out, and buried him.
>
> And it was about the space of three hours after, when his wife, not knowing what was done, came in.
>
> And Peter answered unto her, Tell me whether ye sold the land for so much? And she said, Yea, for so much.
>
> Then Peter said unto her, How is it that ye have agreed together to tempt the Spirit of the Lord? behold, the feet of them which have buried thy husband are at the door, and shall carry thee out.
>
> Then fell she down straightway at his feet, and yielded up the ghost: and the young men came in, and found her dead, and, carrying her forth, buried her by her husband (vv. 1–10).

During the latter-day dispensation of the gospel, the gift of operations or discernment has also been bestowed upon the Lord's servants. Brigham Young referred to the time when he first met the Prophet Joseph Smith. A meeting was held by a few of the brethren, and they conversed together upon the things of God's kingdom. The Prophet called upon Brother Young to pray, and the future Apostle and prophet mentioned what happened next. He said, "In my prayer I spoke in tongues. As soon as we arose from our knees the brethren flocked around [the Prophet], and asked his opinion concerning the gift of tongues that was upon me. He told them that it was the pure Adamic language. Some said to him they expected he would condemn the gift brother Brigham had, but he said, 'No, it is of God.'"[9]

First Presidency counselor Heber C. Kimball acknowledged that he had enjoyed this very same gift and declared that he could utilize it under the same set of circumstances. Said he, "When any of you get up to speak in tongues, whether you do so by the power of God or of the devil, I can tell you which source that tongue came from."[10]

Another mention of the gift of discernment comes out of the Merthyr Tydfil branch of Christ's restored Church in the country of Wales. Near the end of 1848, a conference was planned for this branch, but there were two young women who found themselves uninvited because they were constantly annoying those who were present in the meetings that they attended. Dan Jones, who was the presiding elder in the branch, directed them not to attend the conference but they ignored his judgment against them and went anyway. Soon they started raving and shrieking so loudly that they drowned out the voice of the speaker. A commentator on this incident wrote that, "When a presiding Elder has the spirit of his office upon him it is his privilege to know the proper course to take in any emergency. It is his privilege to enjoy communion with the Holy Spirit and have the Lord dictate through him that which will be for the best good of the members over whom he is set to preside. It is also his privilege to discern by what spirit the people with whom he is brought in contact are actuated." Brother Jones discerned that these young women were under the influence of evil spirits, and he sent some brethren to cast the intruders out. But this action failed to expel the foul entities. So Brother Jones proposed, according to his best judgment, that the girls be excommunicated on the spot. As soon as this course was approved by the congregation, the spirits abandoned their ill-gotten tenements, since they could no longer use members of the Church to annoy other members. The girls eventually confessed the wrongdoing that brought them into a state of bondage to the powers of darkness and were rebaptized.[11]

Lastly, we will take a look at an incident that took place in the Hulet branch of the LDS Church in Independence, Missouri, in the year 1834. Some of the members of this branch started imbibing certain principles in connection with spiritual gifts that were out of step with the Church at large. They believed that they had been blessed with communication from the Lord through an authentic gift of tongues. But they professed that they would not receive the teachings of ordained members of the Church—not even of the Prophet Joseph Smith himself—unless they accorded with the teachings that they had received through the manifestation of tongues. These people also began to brag that they had come up to their privileges more than the rest of the Church. Ironically, one of the individuals who was a participant in this incident claimed that she had received the power of discernment as a spiritual gift. A tell-tale sign of the true origin of the 'gifts' that were found in the Hulet branch surfaced when a prophecy was given through tongues but proved to be false. The president of the high council in Missouri at the time (David Whitmer) said of these occurrences, "As for the gift of tongues in the manner it was used in the Hulet Branch, the devil deceived them, and they obtained not the word of the Lord, as they supposed, but were deceived; and as for the gift of 'seeing,' as held by the Hulet Branch, it is of the devil, saith the Lord God."[12] It is interesting to note that members of this congregation eventually admitted that they had been duped by "false spirits."[13]

Conclusion

The gift of being divinely assisted to discern between operations initiated by God and those instigated at the behest of earthly or even infernal powers is one of sterling worth in our world. It is an especially strong antidote for the poison of deception that is so prevalent in our day. Who would not consider themselves doubly blessed if they were able to know what spirit actuated themselves and others on countless issues? What Church leader would not be greatly benefited from being able to accurately understand the underlying forces that motivate the people they must oversee or counsel or call to various positions? Certainly this is a spiritual gift of great utility, which should be sought after, cultivated, and cherished.

NOTES TO CHAPTER 5

1. Bruce R. McConkie, *A New Witness For the Articles of Faith* (Salt Lake City: Deseret Book, 1985), 278; hereafter cited as *NWAF.* Elder McConkie noted that discernment has several different stages, the first of which is granted to all men and women and is not in the category of spiritual gifts per se. He said, "To all men in some degree and to the faithful Saints in particular is given the spirit, gift, and power of discernment. This ability is conferred upon people generally by the operations of the light of Christ (Moro. 7:12–18), but in addition the

faithful saints receive discerning power through revelation from the Holy Ghost (D&C 63:41). In its most important aspect, discernment is used to distinguish between good and evil (Moro. 7:12–18), between the righteous and the wicked (D&C 101:95; Mal. 3:18; 3 Ne. 24:18), between the false or evil spirits and those spirits who truly manifest the things of God (D&C 46:23; 1 Cor. 12:10). In its fullest manifestation the gift of the discerning of spirits is poured out upon presiding officials in God's kingdom; they have it given to them to discern all gifts and all spirits, lest any come among the Saints and practice deception (D&C 46:27)" (Bruce R. McConkie, *Mormon Doctrine,* 2nd ed. [Salt Lake City: Bookcraft, 1966], 197).

2. Ibid., 270–71 (emphasis in original).
3. *NWAF,* 278.
4. Andrew F. Ehat and Lyndon W. Cook, eds., *The Words of Joseph Smith: The Contemporary Accounts of the Nauvoo Discourses of the Prophet Joseph* (Orem, UT: Grandin Books, 1991), 12.
5. Stephen L. Richards, *Where Is Wisdom?* (Salt Lake City: Deseret Book, 1955), 199 (emphasis added).
6. Conference Report, April 1931, 28.
7. *Juvenile Instructor,* vol. 31, no. 19, 1 October 1896, 573.
8. George D. Watt, ed., *Journal of Discourses* (Liverpool, England: Samuel W. Richards and Sons, 1852–1886), 16:164; hereafter cited as *JD.*
9. *Millennial Star,* vol. 25, no. 28, 11 July 1863, 439.
10. *JD,* 4:170.
11. George Q. Cannon, ed., *Early Scenes in Church History* (Salt Lake City: Juvenile Instructor Office, 1881), 55–57.
12. Brigham H. Roberts, ed., *History of The Church of Jesus Christ of Latter-day Saints* (Salt Lake City: Deseret Book, 1948–1950), 2:139–41.
13. Ibid., 2:147.

CHAPTER SIX
Wisdom

To one is given by the Spirit of God, that he may teach the word of wisdom.

—*Moroni 10:9*

Wisdom can be defined in a number of different ways. In one person's manner of thinking it is the sum of learning accumulated over extended ages of time. In the words of a separate individual it might be described as the trait of common sense or good judgment. Still another person could consider wisdom to be the application of understanding or insight. Elder Stephen L. Richards of the Quorum of the Twelve Apostles pointed to the fact that "wisdom cannot be disassociated from discernment, but," said he, "it involves some other factors, and its applications are rather more specific. Wisdom is sometimes defined as sound judgment and a high degree of knowledge." However, Elder Richards was inclined to define wisdom as being "the beneficent application of knowledge in decision." He thought of wisdom "not in the abstract but as functional. Life is largely made up of choices and determinations," he said. And he could "think of no wisdom that does not contemplate the good of man and society." In his view, "wisdom is true understanding."[1] Derek A. Cuthbert of the Quorum of the Seventy concurred with these sentiments. He averred that "we need to acquire wisdom . . . so that [we can] make righteous judgments." He also acknowledged that "many of us are not wise, for we are blinded by the material world around us. Wisdom comes from a realization of true values and priorities. It is a spiritual quality, for it is founded on discernment and an understanding heart."[2]

It is evident that there are two different types of wisdom available to mortal beings: heavenly and earthly. We are informed in the book of Mosiah that "God . . . has all wisdom" (4:9), and an invitation to tap into this heavenly repository is extended in the book of James. A passage that is eminently familiar to Latter-day Saints reads: "If any of you lack wisdom, let him ask of God, that giveth to all men liberally, and upbraideth not; and it shall be given him" (1:5). In modern times the Lord has issued a commandment that His disciples "seek . . . for wisdom" (D&C 6:7), and He has also provided these additional instructions:

> Let him that is ignorant learn wisdom by humbling himself and calling upon the Lord his God, that his eyes may be opened that he may see, and his ears opened that he may hear; for my Spirit is sent forth into the world to enlighten the humble and contrite (D&C 136:32–33).

There are certain hallmarks by which heavenly wisdom can be distinguished from that of another type. "The wisdom that is from above," says another passage in the book of James, "is first pure, then peaceable, gentle, and easy to be intreated, full of mercy and good fruits, without partiality, and without hypocrisy" (3:17). This is the kind of wisdom that is to be prized above all. In the eighty-eighth section of the Doctrine and Covenants the Lord commands the Latter-day Saints to search for words of wisdom "out of the best books" (v. 118). This directive encompasses wisdom that is available both from earth-centered and heaven-centered books (i.e., the scriptures). The Lord further states that once these words of wisdom have been obtained by an individual, they are not to be selfishly hidden in the recesses of their mind but are to be put to good use by being passed on; the Saints, specifically, are to "teach one another words of wisdom" (ibid.).

It should be noted that in the Book of Mormon's discourse on spiritual gifts, the person who enjoys the gift of wisdom is specifically designated as a conveyor of it (see Moro. 10:9). This is not all that should be noticed, however. It is also made known in this canonized passage that the recipient of this gift is enabled to relay wisdom in conjunction with the Spirit of God. Several leading Latter-day Saints have expounded upon these themes. Elder Wilford Woodruff, for instance, acknowledged that "wisdom is one of the greatest gifts of God." He earnestly exhorted those members of the Church who stand in the capacity of teachers or messengers to tap into this divine power and pursue a wise course as they present the principles of the gospel to their respective audiences.[3] "The gift to teach the word of wisdom . . . by the Spirit is much to be desired," said Elder Boyd K. Packer. And he asked, "Why should such a gift not come to us if we desire it? If we desire to succeed as a teacher and we're willing to earn that ability, why should it not come to us? If we're willing to ask for it and pray for it, and we believe with sufficient faith that we can possess it, why should it be withheld from us?"[4] Elder Bernard P. Brockbank, who served as an Assistant to the Quorum of the Twelve Apostles, offered this advice to those who spread the word of the Lord: "When you teach, follow the Savior's counsel and 'let your light shine.' Pray always before you teach for . . . wisdom, and the inspiration of the Holy Ghost."[5]

Heaven-Sent Wisdom

Perhaps the best-known biblical recipient of the gift of wisdom is King Solomon. The Old Testament book of 1 Kings describes the moment when this earthly ruler of Israel asked God for this gift and had his petition granted.

> In Gibeon the Lord appeared to Solomon in a dream by night: and God said, Ask what I shall give thee.
>
> And Solomon said, Thou hast sh[o]wed unto thy servant David my father great mercy, according as he walked before thee in truth, and in righteousness, and in uprightness of heart with thee; and thou hast kept for him this great kindness, that thou hast given him a son to sit on his throne, as it is this day.
>
> And now, O Lord my God, thou hast made thy servant king instead of David my father: and I am but a little child: I know not how to go out or come in.

> And thy servant is in the midst of thy people which thou hast chosen, a great people, that cannot be numbered nor counted for multitude.
>
> Give therefore thy servant an understanding heart to judge thy people, that I may discern between good and bad: for who is able to judge this thy so great a people?
>
> And the speech pleased the Lord, that Solomon had asked this thing.
>
> And God said unto him, Because thou hast asked this thing, and hast not asked for thyself long life; neither hast asked riches for thyself, nor hast asked the life of thine enemies; but hast asked for thyself understanding to discern judgment;
>
> Behold, I have done according to thy words: lo, I have given thee a *wise* and an understanding heart; so that there was none like thee before thee, neither after thee shall any arise like unto thee. (1 Kgs. 3:5–12; emphasis added)

The king's subsequent infusion of wisdom from above seems to have far exceeded the amount or possibly the quality acquired by the typical wise men of his day, for it is recorded in the book of 1 Kings that "all the earth sought to Solomon, to hear his wisdom, which God had put in his heart" (10:24).

As remarkable as King Solomon's wisdom was, he was surpassed by an even greater King. It is reported in the book of Luke that as Jesus Christ grew from childhood, "the grace of God was upon Him," and He "waxed strong in spirit," and was "filled with wisdom" (2:40). And He "increased in wisdom and stature, and in favor with God" (v. 52). His wisdom was once displayed in a synagogue where He was given an opportunity to teach the congregation. It is reported that His wisdom was of such an astonishing character that the attendees wondered where He had gotten it from (see Matt. 13:54).

The Savior promised His disciples in the meridian of time that He would give them wisdom that even their adversaries would be unable to gainsay or resist (see Luke 21:12–15). The fulfillment of this promise can be seen in an incident involving a disciple named Stephen. He was chosen to perform certain acts of service in the

Church of his time because he was "full of the Holy Ghost and wisdom." At one time when members of a synagogue got into a dispute with him they found that "they were not able to resist the wisdom and the [S]pirit by which he spake" (Acts 6:3, 5, 9–10).

The Apostle Paul was another follower of the Messiah who received the gift of heaven-sent "wisdom" (1 Cor. 2:6). In addressing the Corinthians, he said of himself: "When I came to you, [I] came not with excellency of speech or of wisdom, declaring unto you the testimony of God. . . . And my speech and my preaching was not with enticing words of man's wisdom, but in demonstration of the Spirit and of power." His message was delivered "not in the words which man's wisdom teacheth, but which the Holy Ghost teacheth." And he explained why this method of delivery was necessary and desirable. It was so that the faith of those to whom he was speaking would "not stand in the wisdom of men, but in the power of God" (vv. 1, 4–5, 13).

We turn now to examples of the gift of wisdom that have been manifest since the Restoration took place in the early nineteenth century. President George Q. Cannon referred to one of the great overarching miracles wrought among the Lord's latter-day disciples when he noted that "there have been Elders of this Church who could not read, who have gone forth to preach; but they had in them the power of God, they had the inspiration of the Almighty." These men, even though they were "ignorant and unlearned, and not capable of teaching by their own wisdom, have been the means of bringing salvation to hundreds and thousands of souls, and of bringing them into the Church of Christ."[6]

Elder Parley P. Pratt was one of the early ministers of the LDS Church and had been able to acquire for himself a decent amount of education. Nevertheless, he recalled that his abilities were appreciably augmented when he was blessed in receiving the gift of teaching wisdom by the Spirit. He wrote,

> In the latter part of summer and in the autumn [1833], I devoted almost my entire time in ministering among the churches; holding meetings; visiting the sick; comforting the afflicted, and giving counsel. A school of Elders was also organized, over which

> I was called to preside. This class, to the number of about sixty, met for instruction once a week. The place of meeting was in the open air, under some tall trees, in a retired place in the wilderness, where we prayed, preached and prophesied, and exercised ourselves in the gifts of the Holy Spirit. Here great blessings were poured out, and many great and marvelous things were manifested and taught. The Lord gave me great wisdom, and enabled me to teach and edify the Elders, and comfort and encourage them in their preparations for the great work which lay before us.[7]

Elder Pratt was able to recognize when the gift of teaching wisdom by the Spirit was being manifested through other Saints as well. When he attended a Sabbath day meeting in St. Louis, Missouri, on March 1, 1857, he saw that Erastus Snow was blessed with this ability. A notation in his journal reads: "I preached in the forenoon, and Erastus Snow and others in the afternoon. We had [the] sacrament, and the gift of the Holy Ghost was upon us. Brother Snow spake by it in great wisdom."[8]

The Prophet Joseph Smith was another person upon whom this gift was bestowed. Newel Knight recounted the Hiram Page seerstone crisis in Fayette, New York, and the effect that it had upon the young Prophet. Some Church members were believing in the false revelations that were coming through Hiram's stone and it created feelings of dissension. Brother Knight said, "Joseph was perplexed and scarcely knew how to meet this new exigency." But the solution to the problem was sought in the proper way. President Smith spent the greater part of a night in prayer and supplication to God. A Church conference was then convened, and the situation was considered. Newel related how the Lord intervened. He said,

> During this time we had much of the power of God manifested among us and it was wonderful to witness the wisdom that Joseph displayed on this occasion, for truly God gave unto him great wisdom and power, and it seems to me, even now, that none who saw him administer righteousness under such trying circumstances, could doubt that the Lord was with him, as he acted—not with the wisdom of man, but with the wisdom of God. The Holy Ghost came upon us and filled our hearts with unspeakable joy.

The consequence of these proceedings was that the revelations through Hiram's stone were renounced, and unity among Church members was preserved.[9]

Conclusion

Wisdom is one of the fundamental attributes of Deity, one which God commands His children to seek after. In this way we can imitate our Creator. But His instructions go further. We are to take the wisdom that we gain and pass it on to others; we are to become teachers of wisdom. If we desire to imitate our God even more closely, we may apply to Him for the gift of teaching wisdom with the assistance of the third member of the Godhead. When we allow the Lord to put such wisdom in our hearts we become more effective instruments in His hands.

NOTES TO CHAPTER 6

1. Stephen L Richards, *Where Is Wisdom?* (Salt Lake City: Deseret Book, 1955), 200.
2. *Ensign,* November 1982, 55.
3. *Millennial Star,* vol. 5, no. 8, January 1845, 141–42.
4. Boyd K. Packer, *Teach Ye Diligently* (Salt Lake City: Deseret Book, 1975), 16.
5. Conference Report, October 1963, 67.
6. George D. Watt, ed., *Journal of Discourses* (Liverpool, England: Samuel W. Richards and Sons, 1852–1886), 22:121.
7. Parley P. Pratt, *Autobiography of Parley P. Pratt* (Salt Lake City: Deseret Book, 1985), 75–76.
8. Ibid., 406.
9. George Q. Cannon, ed., *Scraps of Biography* (Salt Lake City: Juvenile Instructor Office, 1883), 64–65.

CHAPTER SEVEN
Knowledge

To another [is given], that he may teach the word of knowledge by the . . . Spirit.

—*Moroni 10:10*

The gift of knowledge, as represented in the book of Moroni, has a very precise definition. To have this gift is to be able to teach knowledge by the power of the Holy Ghost (10:10). And the type of knowledge that is associated with the enjoyment of this gift is evidently very specific. Elder Bruce R. McConkie of the Quorum of the Twelve Apostles explained that this gift pertains "not [to] random knowledge, not knowledge in general or as an abstract principle, but gospel knowledge, [meaning] a knowledge of God and His laws."[1] This viewpoint is sustained by the following passages from the Doctrine and Covenants, where the Lord Jesus Christ speaks. He says,

> – "expound scriptures . . . according as it shall be given thee by my Spirit" (D&C 25:7).
>
> – "thou shalt teach [the Saints] by the Comforter, concerning the revelations and commandments which I have given" (D&C 28:1).
>
> – "Wherefore, I the Lord ask you this question—unto what were ye ordained? To preach my gospel by the Spirit, even the Comforter which was sent forth to teach the truth" (D&C 50:13–14).

> – "proclaim the everlasting gospel, by the Spirit of the living God" (D&C 68:1).
>
> – "thou art called . . . to proclaim mine everlasting gospel . . . and you shall have power to declare my word in the demonstration of my Holy Spirit" (D&C 99:1–2).
>
> – "you should open your mouths in proclaiming my gospel, the things of the kingdom, expounding the mysteries thereof out of the scriptures, according to that portion of Spirit and power which shall be given unto you, even as I will" (D&C 71:1).

One theme that stands out prominently in some of the scriptures just cited is that those who teach knowledge of the gospel can be blessed with the accompanying power of the Holy Ghost, which will bear a general witness to the truth of the words spoken. A scripture from the Book of Mormon reinforces this idea: "When a man speaketh by the power of the Holy Ghost the power of the Holy Ghost carrieth it unto the hearts of the children of men" (2 Ne. 33:1). According to George Q. Cannon, "It is the Spirit of God that reaches the hearts of the honest. A few words accompanied by that Spirit, though they may be awkwardly expressed, will have more effect upon the people than the most eloquent discourses which are not sealed upon the hearts of the listeners by the Holy Spirit."[2]

Another theme that emerges in the previous passages is that words can be given to a teacher by the Holy Ghost while teaching (see D&C 25:7). The following scriptures should be considered in connection with this concept. In Doctrine and Covenants section 42, Jesus Christ refers to instances where the words or thoughts being delivered by the Spirit to the speaker are actually His own. Thus we read: "the Spirit shall be given unto you by the prayer of faith. . . . And as ye shall lift up your voices by the Comforter, ye shall speak . . . as seemeth *me* good" (vv. 14, 16, emphasis added). It is upon this same principle that a passage in the book of 2 Nephi applies. It says, "Angels speak by the power of the Holy Ghost; wherefore, they speak the words of *Christ*" (32:3, emphasis added). This means that a Saint who speaks with the power of the Holy Ghost upon them could potentially relay words that literally represent the mind and will of the Lord.

The Prophet Joseph Smith had an appropriate word of caution for those persons who find that they have been blessed with this spiritual gift. He said,

> When the Twelve [Apostles] or any other witness of Jesus Christ stands before the congregations of the earth and they preach in the power and demonstration of the Holy Ghost and the people are astonished and confounded at the doctrine and say that that man has preached a powerful discourse, a great sermon, then let that man or those men take care that they do not ascribe the glory unto themselves, but be careful that they are humble and ascribe the praise and glory to God and the Lamb, for it is by the power of the . . . Holy Ghost that they have power thus to speak.[3]

Ancient and Latter-Day Examples

Instances of the gospel being preached by the power of the Spirit can be found throughout holy writ. In the beginning of mankind's sojourn on the earth there were no mortals to teach Adam, and so, as we learn in the book of Moses, the gospel was taught to him directly through the agency of the "the gift of the Holy Ghost" (5:58–59). Thereafter the Spirit strengthened the preaching of the gospel through human intermediaries.

The Apostle Peter mentions that in his day preachers were blessed with the gift of teaching the gospel "with the Holy Ghost" (1 Pet. 1:12). Men such as Paul, Silvanus, and Timotheus are identified in a New Testament text as belonging to that group. They wrote to the Thessalonians saying, "Our gospel came not unto you in word only, but also in power, and in the Holy Ghost, and in much assurance. . . . And ye . . . received the word . . . with joy of the Holy Ghost" (1 Thes. 1:5–6).

This gift is also spoken of on the pages of the Book of Mormon. In the book of Helaman, for instance, it is recorded that Nephi and Lehi were able to "speak forth marvelous words" because "the Holy Spirit of God did come down from heaven, and did enter into their hearts" (5:44–45). The reception of this blessing brought them unspeakable joy, which is precisely what the Thessalonians experienced when they heard the gospel preached by the same power (as noted above). Alma and Amulek are two other servants of the Lord who went forth to "declare the words of God" that were allotted to them when they were "filled with the Holy Ghost." They preached "unto the people, according to the [S]pirit and power which the Lord had given them" (Alma 8:27, 30, 32). Similarly, Ammon makes it known that a portion of the Holy Spirit dwelt within him and supplied him with "knowledge" that he was supposed to "teach" to other people (Alma 18:34–35).

Many examples of the gift of knowledge are recorded in latter-day Church history. On January 17, 1896, David W. Jeffs, a carpenter and brick mason, was ordained as a Seventy and then set apart by Elder John Henry Smith to serve a mission in the southern portion of the United States. In a sketch of his missionary labors he writes that he had very little knowledge of the content of the Bible and no experience in public preaching. He was, therefore, greatly dependent upon the Holy Spirit for guidance. Despite this state of affairs, Brother Jeffs resolved in his heart not to shirk any type of missionary labor. When he and his companion were in North Carolina they set up an appointment to hold a meeting inside of a house. When some of the enemies of the Church heard that the Mormons were going to gather, they dispatched a well-known preacher from the state of Georgia to "defeat" them. When this person arrived at the place of meeting, Brother Jeffs's heart seemed to stop beating, his mind went perfectly blank, and he started to tremble like a leaf. But once the opening hymn began, all fear left him. He related, "[A]s I arose to my feet to speak I was as cool and collected as if I had been in the work for years. The Spirit of God rested upon me in mighty power and by the help of my Father in heaven, I spoke for one hour and twenty-five minutes, and quoted scripture that I could not remember ever having read and my mind was filled with knowledge."[4]

Early Church convert Philo Dibble gives another account. A group of non-Mormons composed of people from a variety of Christian denominations wished to learn about the Saints' religious organization, and John P. Greene was appointed to preach to them. The attendees were so well pleased with what they heard that they called for another meeting. But before the next appointment, Brother Greene was taken ill and was therefore unable to attend. After some consultation, Philo, A. J. Stewart, and Levi Stewart (his brother) decided that they would fill in for the ailing elder. Philo told the others that he could not preach, and so A. J. Stewart said he would fulfill that particular duty—with the provision that if he ran into any difficulty the others would help him out. Brother Stewart ran into trouble almost immediately, and Philo recalled what happened next.

> He then called on me. I arose to speak. The Holy Ghost came down and enveloped me, and I spoke for over two hours. When I found the Spirit leaving me I thought it time to close, and told my hearers it was the first time I had spoken to a public congregation.
>
> A Brother Mills, who was present, felt so well that he went home with me and declared that I had delivered the greatest discourse he had ever heard. Said I: "Brother Mills, I don't know what I have said. It was not me; it was the Lord!"[5]

Finally, there is this recollection which comes from the memory of President Brigham Young. He was baptized in a little mill stream on a Sunday morning in 1832, and before his clothes were dry he had been ordained to the office of an elder. One week from that day he met with a large congregation, and since there were four experienced elders present, he expected to hear them address the Saints who were assembled. "They," however, "said that the Spirit of the Lord was not upon them to speak to the people. . . . I was but a child so far as public speaking and a knowledge of the world was concerned," said Brother Brigham. "But the Spirit of the Lord was upon me, and I felt as though my bones would consume within me unless I spoke to the people and told them what I had seen, heard and learned—what I had experienced and rejoiced in; and the first discourse I ever delivered I occupied over an hour. I opened my mouth and the Lord filled it."[6]

Conclusion

While the acquisition of knowledge is a common occurrence, it is far less common to be able to relay what one knows in conjunction with a divine agency. The advantage of being able to combine teaching with this particular gift of the Spirit is that the words spoken are accompanied by a divine power, and they therefore have a deeper and more lasting effect on the listener. This gift is also useful when the one who is blessed with it does not have appropriate or necessary knowledge to convey. The Lord has all knowledge (see 2 Ne. 9:20), and He is able to supply that which we lack. We must remember, however, as with all spiritual gifts, that the Lord only grants this blessing when it is according to His will and when His purposes will be advanced through such a manifestation.

NOTES TO CHAPTER 7

1. Bruce R. McConkie, *Doctrinal New Testament Commentary* (Salt Lake City: Bookcraft, 1971), 2:370.
2. *Juvenile Instructor,* vol. 25, no. 7, 1 April 1890, 210.
3. Andrew F. Ehat and Lyndon W. Cook, eds., *The Words of Joseph Smith: The Contemporary Accounts of the Nauvoo Discourses of the Prophet Joseph* (Orem, UT: Grandin Book, 1991), 7.
4. Andrew Jenson, *Latter-day Saint Biographical Encyclopedia* (Salt Lake City: Deseret News Press, 1914), 2:51–52.
5. George Q. Cannon, ed., *Early Scenes in Church History* (Salt Lake City: Juvenile Instructor Office, 1882), 91–92.
6. George D. Watt, ed., *Journal of Discourses* (Liverpool, England: Samuel W. Richards and Sons, 1852–1886), 13:211.

CHAPTER EIGHT
Faith

To another [is given] . . . faith.

—*Moroni 10:11*

Faith has several different dimensions. It can be viewed in a general sense and also in spiritual terms. In order to understand how faith is tied to the gifts of the Spirit, it is helpful to first understand its general aspects. In the days of the Prophet Joseph Smith, faith was delineated in a popular dictionary as simply "belief; the assent of the mind to the truth of what is declared by another, resting on his authority and veracity, without other evidence; the judgment that what another states or testifies is the truth."[1] This definition accords well with scriptural texts. In the Joseph Smith Translation of the book of Hebrews we find the statement that "faith is the assurance of things hoped for, the evidence of things not seen" (11:1). And in the book of Alma we read that "faith is not to have a perfect knowledge of things; therefore if ye have faith ye hope for things which are not seen, which are true" (32:21; cf. Ether 12:5–9). Faith of this nature can be applied in the spiritual realm as well as in everyday circumstances. Elder Bruce R. McConkie offered some thoughts on how faith can be thus applied. He said, "Individuals who have not yet advanced in spiritual things to the point of gaining for themselves personal and direct revelation from the Holy Ghost may yet have power to believe what others, speaking by the power of the Spirit, both teach and testify. They have power within themselves," he affirmed, "to recognize the truth of the words of others who do speak by the power of the Spirit, even though they cannot attune themselves to the Infinite so as to receive the divine word direct from heaven."[2]

The type of faith just mentioned is the same as that spoken of in the Doctrine and Covenants list of spiritual gifts. In section 46 we are told that to some people "it is given to believe on [the] words [of another individual], that they also might have eternal life if they continue faithful" (v. 14). Examples of this type of faith can be found scattered throughout the scriptures. Adam taught his children the truths of the everlasting gospel, and many of them had sufficient faith in his words to press forward and "become the sons of God" (Moses 7:1). Nephi did "believe all the words" of his father, Lehi, concerning that which the Lord had commanded him; and Sam, in turn, believed the words of his brother Nephi in regard to "the things which the Lord had manifested unto [him] by his Holy Spirit" (1 Ne. 2:16–17). It is recorded in the New Testament that when the Redeemer spoke to a gathering of Israelites in the temple courts at Jerusalem about His identity, the source of His doctrine, and His forthcoming atonement, faith was kindled within them and "many believed on him" (see John 8:1–2, 12–30).

Next, we turn to an examination of faith that is appreciably enhanced by a divine source; faith which is of an extraordinary character. Faith can be "*a gift of God bestowed as a reward for personal righteousness,*" said Elder McConkie. But Elder McConkie also called attention to the fact that "the greater the measure of obedience to God's laws the greater will be the endowment of faith."[3] There seems to be, then, a progressive scale of gifted faith. It is interesting to note that in the Book of Mormon list of spiritual gifts, faith is spoken of in terms of the far end of the scale—that which is "exceedingly great" (Moro. 10:11). This is the type of faith with which miraculous events become possible, even the moving of mountains by vocal command (see Matt. 17:20; 21:18–21; Ether 12:30).

It appears that there is a key to exercising this kind of uncommon faith, which key is attached to an undeviating law. The law is laid out in 2 Nephi 27:23 wherein the Lord says, "I am God . . . and I work not among the children of men save it be according to their faith." The key, which is found in the Doctrine and Covenants, is also identified by the Lord. He declares:

> "[H]e that hath *faith in me* to be healed, and is not appointed unto death, shall be healed.
>
> He who hath faith [in me] to see shall see.
>
> He who hath faith [in me] to hear shall hear.
>
> The lame who hath faith [in me] to leap shall leap" (D&C 42:48–51; emphasis added; cf. 46:19).

The key, then, is to believe unreservedly in the divine power of Almighty God. As the Book of Mormon so clearly states, "The Lord is able to do all things according to His will, for the children of men, if it so be that they exercise *faith in Him*" (1 Ne. 7:12; emphasis added).

Scriptural instances of the higher gift of faith are not too difficult to find. Melchizedek is identified as "a man of faith, who . . . stopped the mouths of lions, and quenched the violence of fire" (JST, Gen. 14:26). The brother of Jared had such "exceeding faith" that he was enabled to see past the veil that separates the temporal and spiritual spheres and behold the premortal spirit of Jesus Christ (see Ether 3:6–14). The Apostle Peter exercised tremendous faith as he stepped out of a boat that was floating at sea and walked across the top of the water (see Matt. 14:24–31).

There are many accounts found in LDS-related records that tell of the exercise of great faith in God. For the purposes of this book, three instances will be cited that exemplify this gift. The first is told by President Thomas S. Monson. He reports the following incident that took place while he was serving as a member of the Quorum of the Twelve Apostles.

> On my first visit to the fabled village of Sauniatu, so loved by President [David O.] McKay, my wife and I met with a large gathering of small children. At the conclusion of our messages to these shy, yet beautiful, youngsters, I suggested to the native Samoan teacher that we go forward with the closing exercises. As he announced the final hymn, I suddenly felt compelled to personally greet each of these 247 children. My watch revealed that the time was too short for such a privilege, so I discounted the impression. Before the benediction was to be spoken, I again

> felt this strong impression to shake the hand of each child. This time I made the desire known to the instructor, who displayed a broad and beautiful Samoan smile. He spoke in Samoan to the children, and they beamed their approval of his comments.
>
> The instructor then revealed to me the reason for his and their joy. He said, "When we learned that President McKay had assigned a member of the Council of the Twelve to visit us in faraway Samoa, I told the children if they would each one earnestly and sincerely pray and exert faith like the Bible accounts of old, that the Apostle would visit our tiny village at Sauniatu, and through their faith, he would be impressed to greet each child with a personal handclasp." Tears could not be restrained as each of those precious boys and girls walked shyly by and whispered softly to us a sweet "talofa lava." The gift of faith had been evidenced.[4]

The next account comes from Lucy Mack Smith, mother of the Prophet Joseph Smith. In the spring of 1831 a group of eighty Latter-day Saints tried to engage passage on a ship in Buffalo, New York. This was to be one leg of a journey that would eventually take them to Kirtland, Ohio. This group was detained in their travel because deep ice had formed in the harbor. Mother Smith relates in her autobiography,

> Once the depth of the ice was discovered and it was said that the ship might have to wait in the harbor for two weeks William whispered in my ear, "Mother, do see the confusion yonder; won't you go and put a stop to it!"
>
> I went to that part of the boat where the principal portion of our company were. There I found several of the brethren and sisters engaged in a warm debate, others murmuring and grumbling. . . .
>
> I stepped into their midst, "Brethren and sisters," said I, "we call ourselves Saints and profess to have come out from the world for the purpose of serving God at the expense of all earthly things; and will you, at the very onset, subject the cause of Christ to ridicule by your own unwise and improper conduct? You profess to put your trust in God, then how can you feel to murmur and complain as you do? You are even more unreasonable than the

children of Israel were; for here are my sisters pining for their rocking chairs, and brethren from whom I expected firmness and energy declare that they positively believe they shall starve to death before they get to the end of their journey. And why is it so? Have any of you lacked? Have I not set food before you every day, and made you who had not provided for yourselves as welcome as my own children? And even if this were not the case, where is your faith? Where is your confidence in God? Do you not know that all things are in His hands, that He made all things and overrules them? If every Saint here would just lift their desires to Him in prayer, that the way might be opened before us, how easy it would be for God to cause the ice to break away, and in a moment's time we could be off on our journey. But how can you expect the Lord to prosper you when you are continually murmuring against Him? . . .

Now, brethren and sisters, if you will all of you raise your desires to heaven that the ice may be broken before us, and we be set at liberty to go on our way, as sure as the Lord lives, it shall be done." At that moment a noise was heard like bursting thunder. The captain cried out, "Every man to his post," and the ice parted, leaving barely a pathway for the boat that was so narrow that, as the boat passed through, the buckets were torn with a crash from the waterwheel. This, with the noise of the ice, the confusion of the spectators, the word of command from the captain, and the hoarse answering of the sailors, was truly dreadful. . . .

Our boat and one other had just time enough to get through, and the ice closed again and remained three weeks longer.[5]

Finally, we have stories about John Taylor as told by assistant Church historian Andrew Jenson. Elder Taylor was "a man of great faith in God" and continually petitioned Heavenly Father for assistance in carrying out his labors in the restored kingdom. Here are a few of the many examples of his "inexhaustible store of faith."

When they were about to sail from New York to Liverpool, he and two other brethren were almost destitute of means, not having sufficient to pay one passage, much less three. Notwithstanding their predicament, a very short time before the

> vessel was to sail Elder Taylor told one of his companions to go and engage passage for all three to Liverpool. His fellow-laborers were nonplussed and asked where on earth could they get means in so short a time. Elder Taylor answered that there was plenty of means in the world and the Lord would send them enough before the vessel sailed to pay their way. His words were most remarkably fulfilled. He asked no person for money, and yet immediately after he made the prediction one after another came to them and proffered assistance, until enough was provided to meet their expenses to Liverpool. . . .
>
> While laboring on the Isle of Man he had secured the printing of some tracts, which he wrote in reply to the falsehoods circulated by ministers and others regarding the character and doctrines taught by the Prophet Joseph Smith. When the tracts were ready the printer would not deliver them until every penny was paid which was due him. Elder Taylor did not have sufficient to meet the demand, and being very anxious to obtain the tracts went immediately into a private room, and, kneeling down, told the Lord in plain simplicity exactly how much he needed to pay for the matter he had published in defense of His cause. In a few minutes after his prayer was offered a young man came to the door, and upon being invited to enter handed Elder Taylor an envelope and walked out. The young man was unknown to him. The envelope contained some money and a little note which read: "The laborer is worthy of his hire," and no signature was placed thereon. In a few minutes later a poor woman engaged as a fish vender came to the house and offered a little money to assist him in his ministerial labors. He told her there was plenty of money in the world and he did not wish to take her money. She insisted that the Lord would bless her the more and she would be happier if he would accept it, whereupon he received the offering, and to his surprise the poor woman's mite, added to what the young man had given him, made exactly the amount sufficient to pay the printer the balance due him.[6]

Conclusion

Each Latter-day Saint can benefit from the gift of faith, whether it is the simple type that enables us to believe in the existence of a loving, unseen Heavenly Father or the more robust type that enables us to raise a person from the dead in the Savior's holy name. If we believe unreservedly in the Lord's almighty power, then there are unlimited possibilities that lie before us.

NOTES TO CHAPTER 8

1. Noah Webster, *An American Dictionary of the English Language* (New York: S. Converse, 1828), s.v., "faith."
2. Bruce R. McConkie, *A New Witness For the Articles of Faith* (Salt Lake City: Deseret Book, 1985), 372.
3. Bruce R. McConkie, *Mormon Doctrine,* 2nd ed. (Salt Lake City: Bookcraft, 1966), 264 (emphasis in original).
4. Conference Report, October 1966, 9–10.
5. Lavina F. Anderson, ed., *Lucy's Book: A Critical Edition of Lucy Mack Smith's Family Memoir* (Salt Lake City: Signature Books, 2001), 530–33.
6. Andrew Jenson, *Latter-day Saint Biographical Encyclopedia* (Salt Lake City: Deseret News Press, 1901), 1:15–16.

CHAPTER NINE

Revelation

The revelations of God . . . come . . . by the gift and power of the Holy Ghost.

—*Doctrine and Covenants 20:35*

When the Prophet Joseph Smith published a list of the basic tenants of Latter-day Saint belief in 1842, he included "the gift of . . . revelation" among them (Article of Faith 7). Several other nineteenth-century LDS publications also categorized personal revelation as one of the spiritual gifts of the restored gospel.[1] An article printed in the *Encyclopedia of Mormonism* emphasizes the fundamental importance of this gift. It states that "receiving personal revelation is a vital and distinctive part of the LDS religious experience. Response to personal revelation is seen as the basis for true faith in Christ, and the strength of the Church consists of that faithful response by members to their own personal revelations."[2]

The ancient American prophet Mormon experienced the gift of revelation firsthand, and he identified the force that empowers this extraordinary spiritual phenomenon. He said that "the word of the Lord came to [him] by the power of the Holy Ghost." Even though the words that were spoken to Mormon were "the words of Christ," yet it was "the Holy Ghost" who manifested these words unto him (Moro. 8:7–9). The same principle is referred to in the book of Acts where it is mentioned that some of the leaders of the Lord's meridian Church received a revelation of His will through "the Holy Ghost" (13:2). And in the book of Moses we read that the prophet Moses heard the voice of the Almighty speak to him after he had been "filled with the Holy Ghost" (1:24–25).

Elder Bruce R. McConkie explained that when legal administrators of the Church place their hands upon the heads of newly baptized Saints and command them to receive the Holy Ghost, "this gives [them] the right to the constant companionship of that member of the Godhead, based on faithfulness, in consequence of which [they] are entitled and qualified . . . to receive personal revelation."[3] Elder M. Russell Ballard clarified that personal revelation is not reserved for an elite few. "God doesn't speak only to those who have been called to be prophets and revelators," he said. "You and I can receive personal revelation for our own lives and for our families and personal responsibilities if we will live in such a way that we can be open and receptive to the whisperings of the Holy Spirit when they come."[4] Joseph Fielding Smith likewise affirmed that "revelation may be given to every member of the Church." But he went further than this by teaching that "it is not only the privilege but the *duty* of each member of the Church to know the truth which will make him free. This he cannot know unless it is revealed to him. . . . The gift of the Holy Ghost is given to the members of the Church so that they may have the spirit of . . . revelation."[5]

There are no bounds to the scope of the revelatory gift. As Elder McConkie stressed, it is not limited to the common revelations that bring one a testimony of the Lord's divinity or to guidance in personal and family affairs. "In truth and in verity," said he, "there is no limit to the revelations each member of the Church may receive."[6] This concept is embodied in a profound passage of scripture found in the seventy-sixth section of the Doctrine and Covenants. Here the Savior says to members of His fold,

> I, the Lord, am merciful and gracious unto those who fear me, and delight to honor those who serve me in righteousness and in truth unto the end.
>
> Great shall be their reward and eternal shall be their glory.
>
> And to them will I reveal all mysteries, yea, all the hidden mysteries of my kingdom from days of old, and for ages to come, will I make known unto them the good pleasure of my will concerning all things pertaining to my kingdom.

> Yea, even the wonders of eternity shall they know, and things to come will I show them, even the things of many generations.
>
> And their wisdom shall be great, and their understanding reach to heaven; and before them the wisdom of the wise shall perish, and the understanding of the prudent shall come to naught.
>
> For by my Spirit will I enlighten them, and by my power will I make known unto them the secrets of my will—yea, even those things which eye has not seen, nor ear heard, nor yet entered into the heart of man (vv. 5–10).

God can bestow a revelation upon an individual at any given moment, even when such a blessing has not been actively sought after. But there are times when Latter-day Saints deliberately approach the Lord and seek after a heaven-sent message. The Prophet Joseph Smith had some advice for those who contemplate engaging in seeking a revelation from God. He said that when an individual seeks knowledge through humble and sincere prayer, they should "never inquire at the hand of God for special revelation only in case of there being no previous revelation to suit the case." A careful perusal of the Lord's revealed word is, therefore, recommended as a preliminary step to petitioning Him directly for knowledge. The Prophet also cautioned that "it is a great thing to inquire at the hands of God, or to come into His presence" and, for his part, he felt "fearful to approach Him on subjects that are of little or no consequence."[7]

The Voice of God's Spirit

In verses 34 and 35 of Doctrine and Covenants section 18 the Lord reveals that He speaks to mortal men and women by the voice of His Spirit. This voice is described in the scriptures as being "still" and "small" (see 1 Kgs. 19:9–12; 1 Ne. 17:45; D&C 85:6). It is "not a voice of thunder," neither is it "a voice of a great tumultuous noise." Rather it is "a still voice of perfect mildness," like a whisper, that has the ability to pierce the fabric of a person's soul as it is manifested inside their mind (see Hel. 5:30; Enos 1:10).

This heavenly voice is separate and distinct from other types of spiritual phenomena such as inspiration. Elder James E. Talmage emphasized this distinction when he wrote,

> The word *inspiration* is sometimes invested with a signification almost identical with that of *revelation,* though by origin and early usage it possessed a distinctive meaning. To inspire is literally to animate with the spirit; a man is inspired when under the influence of a power other than his own. Divine inspiration may be regarded as a lower or less comprehensive manifestation of the heavenly influence upon man than is shown in revelation. The difference therefore is rather one of degree than of kind. . . . [I]n the giving of revelation, a more direct influence is exercised upon the human recipient of the God-given message than is the case under the weaker, though no less truly Divine, effect of inspiration.
>
> The directness and plainness with which God may communicate with man is dependent upon the purity and general fitness of the person. One may be susceptible to inspiration in its lower and simpler phases only; another may be so thoroughly responsive to this power as to be capable of receiving direct revelation; and this higher influence again may manifest itself in varying degrees, and with a greater or lesser shrouding of the Divine personality.[8]

It is vitally important that we as Latter-day Saints learn to distinguish between the revelatory voice of the Lord and our own inner thoughts and feelings. George Q. Cannon taught that this is one thing that all Church members need to be very careful about. He said that in his experience he had seen individuals who had their spirit appreciably moved by some significant event, and then "they imagined that it was the Spirit of God, and it was difficult in some instances to tell the difference between the suggestions of their own spirit and the voice of the Spirit of God. This is a gift of itself to be able to distinguish that which suggests itself to our own hearts and that which comes from God. And we are misled sometimes by our own feeling, because of our inability to distinguish between the voice of the Spirit of God and the suggestions of our own spirit."[9]

Keys for discerning the difference between heaven-sent revelations and those of a purely earthly origin have been provided by modern prophets. Joseph Smith, for one, said that we can tell we have experienced the "spirit of revelation . . . when [we] feel pure intelligence flowing unto [us]." The effect will be that we are given "sudden strokes of ideas."[10] Another key is offered by Elder S. Dilworth Young who suggested that when a person has a revelatory experience, the word of God will come into their mind through their thoughts, "accompanied by a feeling in the region of [their] bosom. It is a feeling which cannot be described, but the nearest word we have is 'burn' or 'burning.' Accompanying this always is a feeling of peace, a further witness that what one heard is right."[11]

There are numerous stories about the reception of personal revelation scattered throughout the pages of LDS literature. It is evident from available examples that these manifestations can vary from short, simple thoughts to extensive, complex paragraphs.

On December 4, 1831, Newel K. Whitney was called by revelation through the Prophet Joseph Smith to serve as the bishop of Kirtland, Ohio. The Lord said, "And now, verily I say unto you, my servant Newel K. Whitney is the man who shall be appointed and ordained unto this power. This is the will of the Lord your God, your Redeemer. Even so. Amen" (D&C 72:8). But the thought of assuming this type of responsibility was almost more than this inexperienced man could bear. He laid his concerns before the Prophet but said that if this was the Lord's will then he would certainly try to perform this task. Brother Joseph assured Newel that he could go straight to his Heavenly Father and learn of the divine origin of this calling for himself. And so Brother Whitney took the advice of the Lord's anointed and approached God in humble prayer. There, in the solitude of his chamber, he heard a voice from heaven say in minimal but meaningful words, "Thy strength is in me." With his doubts now dispelled, Newel sought out the Prophet and accepted the opportunity to serve.[12]

President Wilford Woodruff disclosed the fact that he had heard the voice of the Spirit whisper brief words of instruction to him on one occasion. He reported this event in the following words.

> After I came to these valleys and returned to Winter Quarters, I was sent to Boston by President Young. He wanted me to take my family there and gather all the Saints of God in New

> England, in Canada, and in the surrounding regions, and stay there until I gathered them all. I was there about two years. While on the road there, I drove my carriage one evening into the yard of Brother Williams. Brother Orson Hyde drove a wagon by the side of mine. I had my wife and children in the carriage.
>
> After I turned out my team and had my supper, I went to bed in the carriage. I had not been there but a few minutes when the Spirit said to me, "Get up and move that carriage." I told my wife I had to get up and move the carriage. She said, "What for?" I said, "I don't know." That is all she asked me on such occasions; when I told her I did not know, that was enough.
>
> I got up and moved my carriage four or five rods and put the off fore wheel against the corner of the house. I then looked around me and went to bed. The same Spirit said, "Go and move your animals from that oak tree." They were two hundred yards from where my carriage was. I went and moved my horses and put them in a little hickory grove. I again went to bed. In thirty minutes a whirlwind came up and broke that oak tree off within two feet from the ground. It swept over three or four fences and fell square in that dooryard, near Brother Orson Hyde's wagon, and right where mine had stood.
>
> What would have been the consequences if I had not listened to that Spirit? Why, myself and wife and children doubtless would have been killed. That was the still, small voice to me—no earthquake, no thunder, no lightning; but the still, small voice of the Spirit of God. It saved my life. It was the spirit of revelation to me.[13]

Elder Moses Thatcher related a story where an individual received a short but very important revelation that concerned their spiritual welfare. Elder Thatcher admonished the Saints not to say harsh things about other people in the presence of their children because it might prove an injury to their way of thinking. A young man once said to him, "For a long, long time I had feelings of jealousy and envy against an Apostle in this Church caused by the careless words of my father uttered in my hearing. He was tried in business relations. When he visited his family, I used to hear him speak harsh words of this man of

God." The father's words planted a feeling of bitterness in the heart of this young man, and for ten years he felt badly toward the unjustly vilified servant of the Lord. He told Elder Thatcher that he never would have overcome his bitter feelings had it not been for a "direct revelation" from God by means of an "audible voice," which said to him, "As God lives, unless you forgive the trespasses of your brother against you, I will not forgive your trespasses against me!" Immediately after this happened the young man went to the Apostle whom his father had verbally degraded, and when he got near to him he knew internally that the things said against him were founded upon nothing more than bias and prejudice. He declared to Elder Thatcher that "it was the power of God by direct revelation" that saved him, both here and hereafter.[14]

An example of a more detailed personal revelation comes from the writings of Elder Orson F. Whitney. He reminisced that in November of 1882 he was endeavoring to write an editorial for the *Millennial Star,* a periodical that was published in England. But he was feeling overworked and run-down, resulting in "a decided lack of physical and mental vigor." Try as he might, Elder Whitney could not seem to produce anything worth reading and continued in this condition throughout the entire day. At last he threw down his pen and burst into tears from the vexation and discouragement that he felt. At that moment the Spirit whispered to him, "Why don't you pray?" He protested that he prayed five times a day and almost petulantly asked, "Why can't I get some help?" The reply of the Spirit was, "Pray now and ask for what you want." Elder Whitney recounted, "I saw the point. It was a special not a general prayer that was needed. I knelt and sobbed out a few simple words. I did not pray for the return of the Ten Tribes nor for the building of the New Jerusalem. I asked the Lord in the name of Jesus Christ to help me write that article. I then arose, seated myself, and began to write. My mind was now perfectly clear, and my pen fairly flew over the paper. All I needed came as fast as I could set it down—every thought, every word in place. In a short time the article was completed to my entire satisfaction."[15]

For a final example we turn to a document produced by Elder Heber C. Kimball. He received a revelation of considerable length at Far West, Missouri, on April 6, 1839. He said that the Spirit instructed him to write the following words down as they flowed into his mind.

> A word from the Spirit of the Lord to my servant Heber C. Kimball: Verily, I say unto my servant Heber, thou art my son in whom I am well pleased; for thou art careful to hearken to my words, and not transgress my law nor rebel against my servant Joseph Smith; for thou hast a respect to the words of mine anointed, even from the least to the greatest of them; therefore, thy name is written in heaven, no more to be blotted out forever, because of these things; and this spirit and blessing shall rest down upon thy posterity forever and ever; for they shall be called after thy name, for thou shalt have many more sons and daughters, for thy seed shall be as numerous as the sands upon the sea shore.
>
> Therefore, my servant Heber, be faithful; go forth in my name and I will go with you, and be on your right hand and on your left, and my angels shall go before you and raise you up when you are cast down and afflicted. Remember that I am always with you, even to the end; therefore, be of good cheer, my son, and my Spirit shall be in your heart, to teach you the peaceable things of the kingdom.
>
> Trouble not thyself about thy family, for they are in my hands; I will feed them and clothe them and make unto them friends. They never shall want for food nor raiment, houses nor lands, fathers nor mothers, brothers nor sisters; and peace shall rest upon them forever, if thou wilt be faithful and go forth and preach my gospel to the nations of the earth; for thou shalt be blessed in this thing.
>
> Thy tongue shall be loosed to such a degree that has not entered into thy heart as yet, and the children of men shall believe thy words, and flock to the water, even as they did to my servant John; for thou shalt be great in winning souls to me, for this is thy gift and calling. And there shall be no gift withheld from thee, if thou art faithful; therefore, be faithful, and I will give thee favor in the eyes of the people. Be humble and kind, and thou shalt obtain kindness; be merciful, and thou shalt obtain mercy; and I will be with thee even unto the end. Amen.[16]

Conclusion

The God of heaven is willing to speak personally to His mortal children (regardless of their ecclesiastical position) through the voice of the Spirit if they are willing to comply with the prerequisites for the enjoyment of this gift and then seek after such an experience in the prescribed way. The clarity of the voice that recipients of this gift will hear will depend largely upon how directly the Lord chooses to communicate His mind and will and how well we train ourselves to listen for the messages that may be sent to us. Whether these messages are short or long, whispered or trumpeted, simple or profound, they are marvelous gifts to receive.

NOTES TO CHAPTER 9

1. See *Millennial Star,* vol. 2, no. 12, April 1842, 188; see also *Times and Seasons,* vol. 3, no. 1, 15 November 1841, 579; hereafter cited as *T&S.*
2. Daniel H. Ludlow, ed., *Encyclopedia of Mormonism* (New York: Macmillan, 1992), 3:1225.
3. Bruce R. McConkie, "Seek the Spirit," in *BYU Speeches of the Year* (Provo, UT: Extension Publications, 1964), 3–4. As the Prophet Joseph Smith said, "no man can receive the Holy Ghost without receiving revelations. The Holy Ghost is a revelator" (Andrew F. Ehat and Lyndon W. Cook, eds., *The Words of Joseph Smith: The Contemporary Accounts of the Nauvoo Discourses of the Prophet Joseph* [Orem, UT: Grandin Books, 1991], 256; hereafter cited as *WJS).*
4. M. Russell Ballard, *Our Search for Happiness: An Invitation to Understand The Church of Jesus Christ of the Latter-day Saints* (Salt Lake City: Deseret Book, 1993), 96–97. Brigham Young taught the same principle: "Every member has the right of receiving revelations for themselves, both male and female. It is the very life of the Church of the living God. . . . It is the right of an individual to get revelations to guide himself. It is the right of the head of a family to get revelations to guide and govern his family. . . . [Y]ou have the right to obtain revelations for your own salvation" (*T&S,* vol. 5, no. 19, 15 October 1844, 683; see also Joseph F. Smith, *Gospel Doctrine* [Salt Lake City: Deseret Book, 1949], 34).
5. Joseph Fielding Smith, *Church History and Modern Revelation* (Salt Lake City: The Council of the Twelve Apostles of The Church of Jesus Christ of Latter-day Saints, 1949), 4:36 (emphasis added).
6. Bruce R. McConkie, *A New Witness for the Articles of Faith* (Salt Lake City: Deseret Book, 1985), 489–90.

7. Brigham H. Roberts, ed., *History of The Church of Jesus Christ of Latter-day Saints* (Salt Lake City: Deseret Book, 1948–1950), 1:339.
8. James E. Talmage, *The Articles of Faith* (Salt Lake City: Deseret News Press, 1901), 308–309 (emphasis in original).
9. George D. Watt, ed., *Journal of Discourses* (Liverpool, England: Samuel W. Richards and Sons, 1852–1886), 22:104. Brother Cannon stated on another occasion: "It requires the utmost care upon the part of the people who have received the Spirit of the Lord by the laying on of hands, to distinguish between the voice of that Spirit and the voice of their own hearts, or other spirits which may take possession of them. Experience and watchfulness will enable the Saint to recognize the voice of the Holy Spirit.

   "It is a still, small voice in the hearts of the children of men. It is not boisterous, loud or aggressive, and if those who receive it carefully watch its suggestions, it will develop more and more within them, and it will become an unfailing source of revelation. But the necessity always remains of exercising care in distinguishing its voice from the voice of other influences in the heart" (*Juvenile Instructor,* vol. 21, no. 23, 1 December 1886, 364).
10. *WJS,* 5.
11. Conference Report, April 1976, 34.
12. *The Contributor,* vol. 6, no. 4, January 1885, 126.
13. Brian H. Stuy, ed., *Collected Discourses* (Burbank, CA, and Woodland Hills, UT: B.H.S. Publishing, 1987–1992), 2:266–67.
14. Ibid., 2:320–21.
15. Orson F. Whitney, *Through Memory's Halls: The Life Story of Orson F. Whitney* (Independence, MO: Zion's Printing and Publishing, 1930), 151–52.
16. Helen Mar Whitney, comp., *Journal of Heber C. Kimball* (Salt Lake City: Juvenile Instructor Office, 1882), 70–71.

CHAPTER TEN
Dreams

I will pour out my Spirit . . . [and you] shall dream dreams.
—*Joel 2:28*

Dreaming is a universal experience among mortals. But, as President Spencer W. Kimball pointed out, "most of our dreams are flighty and have no meaning."[1] President Charles W. Penrose admitted that in his own personal experience he had "dreamed a great deal that was nothing but vanity . . . followed by a vexation of spirit."[2] And it was the astute observation of Elder George A. Smith that "a great many dreams are the result, perhaps, of fatigue, of over-exercise, of over-eating before retiring to rest, or some other cause."[3]

Nevertheless, some dreams originate outside of our finite minds and have a distinctly divine purpose. In a letter dated March 22, 1839, the Prophet Joseph Smith wrote to a person who was not a member of the restored Church and informed him that the Latter-day Saints "believe that [they] have a right to . . . dreams from God, our heavenly Father."[4] In a Church periodical from the same time period, dreams were classified among the "spiritual gifts" of the gospel.[5]

Examples of God-given dreams can be found in scriptural texts such as Genesis chapter 37, where Joseph, the son of Jacob, is taught in two symbolic dreams concerning the preeminent station he would occupy within his father's family (see vv. 5–11). And in the book of 1 Kings we read that the Lord made an appearance to King Solomon while he slept and granted him blessings according to the desire of his heart (see 3:5–12).

Elder Bruce R. McConkie provided us with a few words of insightful commentary on the nature of heaven-sent dreams. He stated that "an inspired dream is a vision given to a person while he sleeps. . . . *All inspired dreams are visions* . . . [and] it is only when the vision occurs during sleep that it is termed a dream."[6] It can be concluded from reading the thirty-third chapter of Job that the Lord employs dreams as a means of communication between heaven and earth because mortals are so preoccupied with earthly events that they often have difficulty perceiving His voice during waking hours (see vv. 14–16). Elder Parley P. Pratt expounded upon this concept. He noted that during sleep the physical organs of thought and perception are released from activity, and then their spiritual counterparts experience a certain degree of liberty. "In this situation," said Elder Pratt, "the spiritual organs are susceptible of converse with Deity, or of communion with angels, and the spirits of just men made perfect." These beneficent beings sometimes "seek to communicate with our spirits, to warn us of dangers or temptation, to comfort and soothe our sorrow, or to ward off the ills which might befall us."[7] An article printed in the *Millennial Star* in 1864 similarly states that inspired dreams are not furnished arbitrarily but "are given for a definite purpose, either as warnings of judgments to come, or telling of duties to perform in the present or the future." Those dreams that are "beneficial to us and productive of happiness and joy are from a good and holy source, and are given for the purpose of strengthening our determinations and confirming our faith, or of warning us of difficulties which will be presented before us by the adversary, to daunt our courage and lure us on to destruction."[8] In light of this, we should pay particular attention to the advice of Wilford Woodruff. He proposed that "whenever you have a dream that you feel is from the Lord, [you should] pay attention to it."[9]

There are certain hallmarks that differentiate a God-given dream from a regular or diabolic dream. Elder George A. Smith said that "when a man's mind is illuminated by a dream [which is guided by the Spirit of God], it leaves a vivid and pleasant impression: . . . it leaves the mind happy and comfortable, and the understanding clear."[10] President Heber C. Kimball likewise stated that dreams initiated by the Holy Ghost will "edify and comfort" those who receive them.[11] Again, from the pages of the *Millennial Star* we read that "one mark of a dream from God is that it is distinguished for the clearness and simplicity of the impress[ion] that it makes upon the mind of him that dreams. A dream from the Lord, being always true in all its legitimate bearings, will be so disembarrassed from error and uncertainty to him that has the spirit of truth in lively exercise, that he will know it perfectly in distinction from all false hallucinations or deceptions of the mind."[12]

The Purposes of God-Given Dreams

The Lord can decide to bestow purposeful dreams upon His children for an infinite number of reasons. Examples of divine dreams can help us to understand what some of these reasons might be.

For example, President John Taylor told of an incident that occurred around the year 1839, where the Lord taught an English convert one of the principles of His gospel through the gift of dreams. The leaders of the Church who were sent to England were instructed by the Prophet Joseph Smith not to preach the doctrine of gathering, since at the time there was no suitable place for the Saints to assemble. These men obeyed the directive that they had been given, but on one occasion a sister in the Church approached Elder Taylor and asked him to interpret a dream that she had received. Elder Taylor inquired as to the nature of the dream and was told by this woman, "I thought . . . there were a number of Saints standing on the pier head (the place where the vessels start from), and they seemed as if they were bound for somewhere. They said they were going to Zion, and they sang the songs of Zion; and you were with them. Now, can you interpret the dream for me?" Elder Taylor said that he supposed he could but advised her to leave it alone for the present time. He commented on this experience by saying, "We could not prevent people from being impressed in this way. We could not help the Lord giving them dreams, neither could Joseph Smith. It was the privilege of the Saints to have revelation for themselves."[13]

Another purpose of God-given dreams is to spread the restored gospel of Jesus Christ. James H. Moyle served as a missionary in the Southern States Mission beginning in July 1879. He was, by his own admission, not much of a dreamer. But one night he was shown a vivid view of houses and barns on the Tar River, specifically in the extreme eastern part of North Carolina. He was not familiar with this locality and did not think that any missionaries had ever been sent there before. But because of the strong nature of his dream, he recommended to the mission president that two elders be sent to this place. About six months later James met the missionaries that had been dispatched at his urging and described for them the buildings that he had seen in his dream. The missionaries told Elder Moyle that the structures from his night vision matched those belonging to some recent converts.[14]

It is possible for some people to be given knowledge of imminent Church callings through the gift of dreams. Such was the case with Franklin D. Richards. He wrote of a prophetic dream that would find fulfillment within two years. He said,

> I awoke from a dream in which I seemed to have been with President Brigham Young in the temple at Nauvoo. We sat opposite each other, with our feet in a clear, lively pool of water, and we conversed together. He asked, "Brother Franklin, would you accept it if I should appoint you one of the quorum [of the Twelve]?" I replied, "Brother Brigham, I always have accepted, and as far as I could, have obeyed every appointment that has been given to me, and I always intend to." He then showed me several books containing peculiar drawings and diagrams, many of which were lightly colored and in the Prophet Joseph Smith's own handwriting. While I was examining the books I awoke, and felt as happy as if I had really been in the company of President Young and the holy influence seemed to rest upon my whole person.[15]

Dreams can be sent from above to forewarn people of dangerous circumstances. During a time when several Church leaders in Kirtland, Ohio, apostatized from the truth, Heber C. Kimball found himself mourning in his heart. The only consolation he could find in these troubled times was to kneel before God and ask for His sustaining influence. Heber did not want to fall into the same snares that the apostates had, and he knew that they felt no shame in recruiting others to join them in their wickedness. The following is a rehearsal of one of the spiritual gifts that Heber received during this trying period of Church history.

> I dreamed that I entered into the house of John Boynton, in which there was a panther; he was jet black and very beautiful to look upon, but he inspired me with fear. When I rose to leave the house he stood at the door, with the intention to seize on me, and seeing my fear he displayed his beauty to me, telling me how sleek his coat was, and what beautiful ears he had; and also his claws, which appeared to be of silver; and then he showed me his teeth, which also appeared to be silver. John F. Boynton told me that if I made myself familiar with him he would not hurt me; but if I did not he would. I did not feel disposed to do so, and while the panther was displaying to me his beauty, I slipped through the door and escaped, although he tried to keep me back by laying hold of my coat; but I rent myself from him.
>
> The interpretation of this dream was literally fulfilled. The panther represented an apostate who I had been very familiar with, and is well known by thousands, though I will not mention his name. I felt to thank the Lord for this dream and other intimations that I had which, by His assistance, kept me from falling into snares.[16]

It is evident from other examples that the Lord may employ the gift of dreams in an effort to encourage a person to take some course of action. One year after the mother of a man known only as Brother Miller died, she appeared to him in a dream. Her hair was unkempt, her eyes were red, and her face was drawn out in an expression of sorrow. She wrung her hands and wept, yet she said no words, and the dream ended. This nocturnal vision was subsequently repeated, night after night. This worried Brother Miller, but he did not know what his mother wanted him to do. He knew that before she had died she was not satisfied with her religious standing, but in the dream she never expressed the cause of her distress. She had taught him to pray as a little child, and so he turned to God and petitioned Him for knowledge about what to do. A few days later he found that Mormon missionaries had left several tracts at his place of residence, and among them was one on salvation for the dead. He eagerly read through this publication and decided that he must go to the temple and offer saving ordinances to his deceased parents. That night his mother did not appear to him. But after he had spent his time and earnings hunting up his genealogy she made one more appearance.

This time she was dressed in white, her hair was braided, and she had a smile of peace on her face. Brother Miller cried out, "Oh mother, am I doing right?" She then clasped her hands together joyfully and vanished from his sight.[17] This manifestation encouraged Brother Miller to move forward and complete the work of salvation that he had previously begun.

The Interpretation of Dreams

Divinely inspired dreams can sometimes be difficult to understand because they contain symbolic elements. It is possible that some dreams are infused with symbols as a way of signaling to the recipient that they are not originating from their own subconscious image library—something like a special postmark indicating that a letter is coming from an important place. When this kind of manifestation occurs, the dream is not meant to be a stumbling block but rather an opportunity for mental exercise and spiritual training.

The Lord communicates by dreams in order "to teach us a principle," said Wilford Woodruff. "We may never see anything take place exactly as we see it in a dream . . . yet it is intended to teach us a principle."[18] The recipient of a God-given dream must, therefore, look beyond the symbolic elements that are being presented to their mind's eye and interpret their underlying significance or themes. If a dream contains a complex series of symbols, it might be profitable for the recipient to interpret the themes of the images individually and then to string those interpretations together in their sequential order to see the overall intended message.

The interpretation of dream symbols can be accomplished through at least four different methods. First, there is interpretation through unaided observation. Orson F. Whitney had a dream of this type around March 1877. He was serving his first mission in the state of Pennsylvania but had spent a sizable portion of his days corresponding with the Utah newspapers instead of preaching the gospel. At this time he had a vivid dream that taught him a valuable lesson about the work that he had been called to do. Brother Whitney relates that he found himself inside the Garden of Gethsemane. He watched from behind a tree as Jesus Christ and His trusted Apostles Peter, James, and John entered this place and acted out a scene that closely followed the biblical account of this event. The Savior asked His disciples to pray while He communed with the Father at a distance, but they all eventually fell asleep. The Lord shook them from their slumber, gently reproved them, and admonished them to do as He had requested. This cycle was repeated three times. As Brother Whitney watched the agony that the Savior was going through, he was deeply affected by it and felt as if he would do anything for the Lord. Suddenly the spirit of the dream changed, and, even though the location was the same, the setting was now the time of the Ascension. Jesus and His three Apostles were about to rise up into heaven because their earthly mission had now been completed. At this point Orson ran out from behind the tree where he had been watching these events and begged the Lord to take him also. The Lord gently informed the young man that he could not go with them because his work on the earth was not yet finished. Orson then asked the Lord to promise him that he would be allowed to ascend to the same place after he was through with his assignment. To this request the Lord simply responded, "That will depend entirely upon yourself." Brother Whitney (who later in life became an Apostle) recorded the interpretation of this powerful dream when he penned his autobiography. He said, "I saw the moral clearly. I had never thought of being an Apostle, nor of holding any other office in the Church, and it did not occur to me even then. Yet I know that those sleeping Apostles meant me. I was asleep at my post—as any man is who, having been divinely appointed to do one thing, does another."[19]

The next method of understanding the meaning of dreams is interpretation through inspired thought. Parley P. Pratt reports that one evening after he had finished preaching a sermon in a public location, a church minister and several other people followed him to his place of residence in order to learn more—or so they said. Some Latter-day Saints were also present on this occasion. The conversation eventually degenerated into an argument between the Saints and the visitors, and Elder Pratt could hardly get a word in edgewise. But he saw that those who had professed a desire to learn were more interested in being teachers, and so he begged his leave to retire for the night. He related what happened next in the following words.

> I fell asleep and dreamed that I was rowing and guiding a boat across a large body of water, with no other oar or helm than a walking stick. There were twelve or fifteen passengers with me in the boat, who kept continually moving from side to side and were many times near causing the boat to upset. I talked to them and tried to persuade them to sit still and keep a balance on the boat so that it might not ship water—as that was all they could do, having no oars with which they might help me to row the boat. Many times the top of the boat was about even with the surface of the water, which made it very difficult for one to manage to keep the boat erect without moving forward. But after much persuasion (though the passengers seemed not [to] be aware of the danger they were in) they were more quiet and I succeeded in bringing them all safe[ly] ashore, with the aid of my little stick.

When Parley arose from his slumber he recounted this dream to a man and woman who were there in the house. They both thought that they could interpret the dream. Said they, "[A]s you [were] conversing with those gentlemen last evening, we took the conversation away from you: we thought they were crowding upon you, and we wanted to help you: and that was the rocking of the boat by the moving from side to side of the passengers." They acknowledged that if they had been still, and kept the balance of the boat, Elder Pratt might have brought it to shore much easier—seeing as how they themselves had no paddles to assist in the situation. Parley was skeptical of what the two had to say and retorted with the paraphrase, "Interpretations belong unto the Lord" (cf. Genesis 40:8). During the course of the day, however, the Saints who lived in the neighborhood all came to visit Elder Pratt, and he was obliged to repeat his dream as each new person stopped by. Surprisingly, each of the visitors gave the very same interpretation to his dream as the first couple, though none of them knew what the others had said. The unity of these people's thoughts, said Parley, negated the necessity of inquiring of the Lord for the interpretation.[20]

Still another way to understand the meaning of dreams is interpretation through direct revelation. President Heber J. Grant provides us with an example of this type. He tells of a stake patriarch named John Rowberry who had a dream of a great vessel. He saw that he was onboard this ship and every now and then people would fall over the side. Eventually he too fell overboard and swam through the water until he arrived in the most beautiful country he had ever beheld. There he found Elder Orson Pratt and he asked him, "Where am I?" The Apostle responded, "You are in heaven, Brother Rowberry." Soon after this dream took place, the patriarch met Elder Pratt at a stake conference in Tooele, Utah, and told him the content of the dream. He did not identify the man he had met after swimming through the water, because he didn't want to tell the Apostle that it seemed he would die prior to his own demise. Elder Pratt said to him, "I will pray about [your dream], and if I get the interpretation, I will give it to you." Just before Elder Pratt left the Tooele area he told the patriarch,

> Well, I prayed about your dream, Brother Rowberry, and I got the interpretation. The people on that vessel represented the people of the world. You said that the majority of the people who fell overboard you did not know. If you will write down a list of those you did know in the order in which they fell overboard I promise you that they shall die in that exact order, and I promise you that when you shall go to heaven you shall meet the identical man that you met in your dream, and when you meet him tell him that the dream was from the Lord and the interpretation was also from the Lord through Brother Orson Pratt.

The patriarch's reply was, "Brother Pratt, I will tell him." Thirty years later Heber J. Grant was serving as the stake president in Tooele, and he received a telegram informing him that Elder Pratt was seriously ill. It was requested that the Saints in the area pray for the Apostle's recovery. As Brother Grant was going into the prayer room, Patriarch Rowberry asked him if he remembered the latter's dream, to which there was an affirmative response. The patriarch said that Elder Pratt was next on the list and it indeed proved to be that Apostle's last illness. Years later Heber J. Grant had been ordained as an Apostle, and he was present at a stake conference where he heard the aforementioned patriarch bear a vigorous testimony. And although Brother Rowberry was in good health, he asked if Elder Grant remembered his dream from years before. "Yes," was the response. The patriarch then indicated that people had died in the exact order in which they fell off the vessel in his dream, and it was his own turn next. He said that he was anxious to go to the other side and meet Brother Pratt. The next time Elder Grant visited the town of Tooele, the patriarch had passed away.[21]

The last method of interpreting dreams that we will mention is through the intervention of a heavenly guide. An example of this kind of interpretation can be seen in a story that was published in the *Millennial Star* in 1843. The widow of a man named James Grieve wrote that on the night of January 24, 1843, she dreamed that she had gone on a trip to her native village, about two and a half miles from where she presently lived. She was standing in front of a house which she intended to visit when her attention was abruptly drawn to the sun, which seemed to be somewhat eclipsed, though it was about midday. She observed a cloud passing from before the sun, and then she saw a large pendulum swinging back and forth. She steadily watched this for a few minutes when suddenly the pendulum became a key of the same size with a heavy chain attached to it. This was held by a hand located in the center of the sun. Widow Grieve drew the attention of one of her friends to this singular sight, and they both expressed their surprise. The key was then replaced by two large brooms that gradually descended from the sun. As they descended the sun grew brighter in its radiance, and by the time the brooms touched the ground, the widow thought that the day had become more beautiful than any she had ever seen. She recalled what happened next.

> I awoke from my dream, my mind being so agitated that at first I could not tell what was the matter with me; then my dream came into my mind, and with it a great fear. I slept again, and thought that I was still near the same place as when I awoke, and I saw, as it were, a person approaching me, whose appearance was that of a mortal. I told him my dream, and asked him if he could show me the meaning of the signs I had seen, and he said that he could, so I listened with attention.
>
> "The pendulum you saw extending from the sun, shows that time will soon be no more [cf. Rev. 10:6]. The hand that held the chain and key, shows that the devil is to be bound in the bottomless pit [cf. Rev. 20:1–2]; and the two brooms you saw, shows that the Lord will sweep the earth—the corn with one and

> the chaff with the other" [cf. Matt. 3:11–12]. I was much distressed to think that I was so unfit to die, and said, "Lord, what must I do to be saved" [cf. Acts 16:30]. The person to whom I was speaking at this time appeared, as I thought, as an angel and said unto me, "Believe on the Lord Jesus Christ and you will be saved" [cf. Acts 16:31]. I said, "Lord, I believe, help thou mine unbelief" [cf. Mark 9:24]. He said, "Except ye repent ye will perish—repent and be baptized in the name of the Father, and of the Son, and of the Holy Ghost" [cf. Matt. 28:19; Acts 2:38]. I think he repeated the last sentence twice or thrice over, when I awoke from my dream.[22]

Conclusion

As individuals who have received the gift of the Holy Ghost, we can be blessed from time to time with visions in the form of dreams. It can also pose a challenge because some inspired dreams may contain symbolic components, which may be difficult to interpret. This gift allows us to experience a visual element in connection with the power of God.

NOTES TO CHAPTER 10

1. Edward L. Kimball, ed., *The Teachings of Spencer W. Kimball* (Salt Lake City: Bookcraft, 1982), 455.
2. Conference Report, October 1922, 26.
3. George D. Watt, ed., *Journal of Discourses* (Liverpool, England: Samuel W. Richards and Sons, 1852–1886), 8:255; hereafter cited as *JD*.
4. *Times and Seasons,* vol. 1, no. 4, February 1840, 54.
5. *Millennial Star,* vol. 2, no. 12, April 1842, 188; hereafter cited as *MS.* The article where this classification appears is not signed, but Elder Parley P. Pratt was the editor of the issue of the *Millennial Star* in which it was published. The article may, therefore, have been authored by him.
6. Bruce R. McConkie, *Mormon Doctrine,* 2nd ed. (Salt Lake City: Bookcraft, 1966), 208 (emphasis added).
7. Parley P. Pratt, *Key to the Science of Theology* (Salt Lake City: Deseret Book, 1965), 120–22.
8. *MS,* vol. 26, no. 19, 7 May 1864, 290.
9. *JD,* 22:333.
10. Ibid., 8:255.
11. Ibid., 7:17.

12. *MS,* vol. 15, no. 19, 7 May 1853, 291. It appears that certain actions may be taken by heavenly agents if an individual is about to receive a divinely sent dream. In this same article from the *Millennial Star* we read, "The Lord does not suffer wicked spirits to foul and blot and mar a dream, when He wants to communicate His mind and will in a dream. Foul spirits are rebuked and commanded to depart when God wants to indict the truth upon anyone's mind. The angel of God guards the dreamer till a clear and a distinct impression is made. And that impression is of an unmistakable character; it cannot be misunderstood, anymore than the light of the sun can be mistaken for the darkness of midnight" (ibid.).
13. *JD,* 24:199–200.
14. See *Improvement Era,* vol. 44, no. 5, May 1941, 280–81; hereafter cited as *IE.*
15. Franklin L. West, *Life of Franklin D. Richards* (Salt Lake City: Deseret News Press, 1924), 81–82.
16. *Woman's Exponent,* vol. 9, no. 23, 1 May 1881, 178.
17. *IE,* vol. 22, no. 7, May 1919, 587.
18. *JD,* 22:333.
19. Brian H. Stuy, ed., *Collected Discourses* (Burbank, CA, and Woodland Hills, UT: B.H.S. Publishing, 1987–1992), 4:332–33; see also Orson F. Whitney, *Through Memory's Halls: The Life Story of Orson F. Whitney* (Independence, MO: Zion's Printing and Publishing, 1930), 82–83.
20. *MS,* vol. 1, no. 5, September 1840, 133–34.
21. G. Homer Durham, comp., *Gospel Standards: Selections from the Sermons and Writings of Heber J. Grant* (Salt Lake City: Deseret News Press, 1969), 297–99.
22. *MS,* vol. 3, no. 11, March 1843, 192.

GIFTS OF THE OUTWARD SENSES

CHAPTER ELEVEN
Healing

To another [is given] the gifts of healing by the . . . Spirit.
—Moroni 10:11

It is acknowledged in the seventh Article of Faith that Latter-day Saints "believe in the gift of . . . healing." We learn in the book of Mosiah that Jesus Christ possessed "power" while He was on the earth for "healing the sick, . . . causing the lame to walk, the blind to receive their sight, and the deaf to hear, and curing all manner of diseases" (3:5; cf. 3 Ne. 17:6–9). And in the book of Matthew we are informed that the Master granted the "power . . . to heal all manner of sickness and . . . disease" to His meridian disciples (10:1). This same blessing is available to the modern Saints. In Doctrine and Covenants section 35 the Savior says, "whoso shall ask it in my name *in faith* . . . shall heal the sick; they shall cause the blind to receive their sight, and the deaf to hear, and the dumb to speak, and the lame to walk" (v. 9, emphasis added).

The Prophet Joseph Smith taught that a person cannot receive the gift of healing until they first receive the gift of the Holy Ghost.[1] This preliminary step is necessary because it is the power of the Holy Ghost that acts as the healing agent. A person must have authorized access to this power before they can act as a conduit to transfer it from heaven to earth. Whenever the Lord sends the healing power down from above, it is properly classified as a gift.

It is vitally important to recognize that the gift of healing does not originate within mortal beings, regardless of the strength of their individual faith.[2] Joseph Smith reminded us that "the sick . . . [are]

raised up *by the power of God,* through the instrumentality of the Elders ministering unto them in the name of Jesus Christ."[3] Elder Orson Pratt likewise stated that persons who administer to the sick and afflicted have "power over disease, *through the Spirit of God* being poured out upon them."[4] Brigham Young made mention of this mechanism as well when he said, "When I lay hands on the sick, I expect the healing power and influence of God to pass through me to the patient, and the disease to give way. . . . [W]hen we are holy vessels before the Lord, a stream of power from the Almighty can pass through the tabernacle of the administrator to the system of the patient, and the sick are made whole."[5] It is in this context that Joseph Smith "rebuked the Elders who would continue to lay hands on the sick from day to day without the power to heal them. Said he: 'It is time that such things ended. *Let the Elders either obtain the power of God to heal the sick or let them cease to minister the forms without the power.*'"[6]

Jesus Christ informs us in the twenty-fourth section of the Doctrine and Covenants that healing the sick is a usage of the power of God that is allowable without a prior commandment from Him. But even then this power is not to be used "except it be required . . . by them who desire it" (vv. 13–14). In other words, the recipient of a healing blessing is first required to acknowledge their faith in God's power. Exceptions to this rule apply, according to Orson Pratt, in the cases of infant children and afflicted adults who do not have charge of their senses. In these two situations faith can be exercised by parents or friends in requesting the ordinance of healing on their behalf.[7]

The key to successfully administering the gift of healing is to be attuned to the will of the Lord in all matters pertaining to illness. Elder Erastus Snow gave this useful advice: "[L]et the Elders administer to the sick in faith, and let them rebuke disease *when the Spirit prompts them,* and it will be rebuked, and the sick will be healed by the power of God."[8] This recommendation is in line with the thought expressed in Doctrine and Covenants section 68, which reads: "And whatsoever [the elders] shall speak when moved upon by the Holy Ghost . . . shall be the will of the Lord, shall be the mind of the Lord, shall be the word of the Lord, [and] shall be the voice of the Lord" (v. 4).

Being attuned to the will of the Lord through the power of the Holy Ghost is also of vital importance in administering the healing ordinance because there may be times when the Lord does not desire an illness or a disease to be cured, such as a when a person has been appointed unto death (see D&C 42:48). Wilford Woodruff believed that this was the case with Elder George A. Smith. Brother Woodruff related the following: "When [Elder Smith] was almost at death's door, Brother Cannon administered to him, and in thirty minutes he was up and ate breakfast with his family. We labored with him in this way, but ultimately . . . he died. But it taught me a lesson. I felt that man was wanted behind the veil."[9]

A note on the form and order of the healing ordinance is appropriate at this point. When Jesus Christ walked the earth, He healed the sick and afflicted by the laying on of hands (see Mark 5:23; 6:5; Luke 4:40), and His disciples followed the same ritual pattern (see Acts 28:7–9). We know from a reading of the book of James that this rite, which is to be accompanied by the use of oil,[10] is to be performed by "the elders of the Church" (5:14–15). The Lord states very specifically in latter-day scripture that healing is to be done by two or more "elders of the Church" (D&C 42:43–44). It would appear from this divine directive that people who do not hold the Melchizedek Priesthood are not eligible to practice this ordinance. Such persons can, however, petition God in faith for the healing of others.

The Healing Power of God

The power of God to heal the human body of diverse maladies has been testified of in innumerable accounts. The five stories that follow are only a small representation of those that could be cited. Each bears witness to the fact that God is a merciful Father who cares about the physical welfare of His children.

The first is told by Elder N. Eldon Tanner. His great-great-grandfather, John Tanner, heard in 1832 that some Mormon missionaries were going to hold a meeting in a schoolhouse. John was a cripple who had been confined to a wheelchair by an incurable ailment. But his disability didn't dampen his spirit. He wanted to be taken to the meeting so that he could make sure that those Mormons didn't teach any false doctrine. He sat right in the front of the room and listened to the message of the two elders but didn't find any reason to heckle them. After the meeting was over he asked to be introduced to them and, when this was arranged, he invited them to stay at his home and teach him further. John listened to the missionaries that night and concluded that if he weren't a cripple, he would like to apply to be baptized. One of the elders asked him, "'Do you think the Lord could heal you?' He thought about it and said, 'I think He could if He wanted to.'" He was then pointed to James 5:14, which speaks of healing the afflicted, and was told, "'We are Elders and we hold the Priesthood of God, which is the power of God delegated to man to act in His name. Would you like us to administer to you?' He said, 'Yes.'" Elder N. Eldon Tanner explained what happened next. "They administered to him, and that very day he left his wheelchair and got up and walked three-quarters of a mile to be baptized, and never went back to his wheelchair. He had real courage, . . . courage to join the Church and to realize that the thing that meant most in his life was the gospel plan of life and salvation."[11]

Next is the remarkable story of Philo Dibble, who converted to the Church shortly after it was restored. Since it is an excellent example of healing by the power of the Spirit it will be quoted at length. Philo was in Jackson County, Missouri, in the fall of 1833, during a period of bitter persecution against the Latter-day Saints. A mob of about 150 men tore the roof off of his house. He escaped into the woods with his family, but during an altercation with the mob the next day, he was shot in the stomach with a one-ounce ball and two pieces of buckshot. Philo continues the story:

> I bled inwardly until my body was filled with blood, and remained in this condition until the next day at five p.m. I was then examined by a surgeon who was in the Black Hawk war, and who said that he had seen a great many men wounded, but never saw one wounded as I was that ever lived. He pronounced me a dead man.
>
> David Whitmer, however, sent me word that I should live and not die, but I could see no possible chance to recover. After the surgeon had left me, Brother Newell Knight came to see me, and sat down on the side of my bed. He laid his right hand on

> my head, but never spoke. I felt the Spirit resting upon me at the crown of my head before his hand touched me, and I knew immediately that I was going to be healed. It seemed to form like a ring under the skin, and followed down my body. When the ring came to the wound, another ring formed around the first bullet hole, also the second and third. Then a ring formed on each shoulder and on each hip, and followed down to the ends of my fingers and toes and left me. I immediately arose and discharged three quarts of blood or more, with some pieces of my clothes that had been driven into my body by the bullets. I then dressed myself and went outdoors. . . . From that time not a drop of blood came from me and I never afterwards felt the slightest pain or inconvenience from my wounds, except that I was somewhat weak from the loss of blood.
>
> The next day I walked around the field, and the day following I mounted a horse and rode eight miles, and went three miles on foot.[12]

Elder M. Russell Ballard recites the next account. His story is of interest because it illustrates the role that the Spirit can play in guiding others to heal those in need. Brother Ballard reports,

> Several years ago I was sitting at my desk when I suddenly felt that I needed to go to a nearby hospital to see a neighbor who had been admitted with a heart problem. At first I thought I would stop by on my way home from work, as there had been no indication that my friend's condition was serious. But the spiritual prompting was strong: I must go immediately. By this time in my life I had learned to respond to the whisperings of the Holy Spirit, so I went, though I didn't know exactly why.
>
> When I arrived at the hospital, I was told that my friend had suffered a major heart attack. Even though he was alone in his room and seemed to be asleep, I felt I should give him a blessing of health and total recovery. So I placed my hands upon his head and blessed him through the authority of the Priesthood.
>
> I have since learned that my neighbor's vital signs began changing soon after I gave him the blessing. Within five days he was out of the hospital, and he experienced a remarkable recovery within a month. . . .

> Is the age of miracles over? Not by a long shot. God continues to do miraculous things among His children through the gifts of the Spirit.[13]

The last two stories to be reported are important because they show different methods used during an administration to effect the healing process through God's power: petition and command.

Clifford E. Young, who served as an Assistant to the Quorum of the Twelve Apostles, told the following personal story during a session of general conference in 1949.

> I recall [an] occasion that came into the experience of Sister Young and me when our only boy was seriously ill. At that time peritonitis was generally fatal. This boy had had it for several days, and it appeared to be a hopeless case. The surgeon, the late Dr. George W. Middleton, who operated on the boy, removed what little of his appendix he could. He remained with us all night, and the next morning told us that we should prepare for the worst. I pay tribute to Dr. Middleton. He was a man of great faith. Those who knew him knew that he had faith. Sometimes he was regarded as too liberal in his thinking, but he did have faith in the providence and the Priesthood of the Almighty. Finally he said: "Let us administer to this boy." I anointed him, and I recall the substance of Dr. Middleton's sealing prayer. "Father," he said, "we have done all that we can for this boy. We ask Thee now with Thy divine power to touch him and to heal him and to sanctify to his good the things that we in our weak way have done." That prayer stimulated faith. The Lord healed our boy.[14]

The testimony of a man named David Richards is significant because of what it teaches about the priesthood bearer who speaks in the sacred name of Jesus Christ. The idea of functioning as a proxy is clearly implied here. The following near-contemporary account of an incident that took place in Abercanaid, Wales, was printed in the Church's British newspaper by Elder Orson Pratt. This account reads thus:

> On Friday, August the 23rd, 1850, at about eleven o'clock, while I was working among the coal, a stone fell upon me about two cwt. I was carried home and the doctor who was present said he

> could do nothing for me, and told those around me to wrap me up in a sheet that I might die. There was a lump on my back as big as a child's head. The doctor afterwards told one of my relations, about six o'clock in the evening, that I could not recover.
>
> Elder Phillips called to see me, and attended to the ordinance of the Church for the sick, and while commanding the bones in the name of Jesus, they came together, making a noise like the crushing of an old basket; my strength returned, and now I am able to go some miles to bear my testimony to this great miracle. The doctor called to see me and was astonished, and said in the hearing of witnesses that my backbone was broken; but that it now was whole, and that I was now recovering as well as any man he ever saw. Many of our greatest enemies confessed that I was healed by the power of God, and while coming here today, many who heard of my accident were struck with the greatest amazement. But I thank my Heavenly Father for His kindness towards me, hoping I shall live to serve Him more faithfully henceforth than ever.[15]

Conclusion

Healing is considered a gift of the Spirit because it is the power of the Spirit that actually causes the healing to occur—not any power inherent in man. A person who desires to perform a healing in the name of God's Son should first offer a petition to the Father, in faith, to be allowed to act as a conduit for His power and should place themselves in a state where they are considered worthy to handle that power. It is a serious responsibility to act in the stead of Deity, and so it is appropriate to make promises to the sick and afflicted only as the Spirit has prompted. This is especially important since only the Spirit can reveal the Lord's will and timetable.

NOTES TO CHAPTER 11

1. See Brigham H. Roberts, ed., *History of The Church of Jesus Christ of Latter-day Saints* (Salt Lake City: Deseret Book, 1948–1950), 4:555; hereafter cited as *HC.*
2. President George Q. Cannon: "Those who administer lay claim to no extraordinary sanctity or personal supernatural power. They simply act as ministers of

Christ, carrying out His commandments and relying upon His promise" (*Millennial Star,* vol. 39, no. 42, 15 October 1877, 675; hereafter cited as *MS).*

3. *HC,* 4:3 (emphasis added).
4. George D. Watt, ed., *Journal of Discourses* (Liverpool, England: Samuel W. Richards and Sons, 1852–1886), 16:289 (emphasis added); hereafter cited as *JD.*
5. Ibid., 14:72.
6. Parley P. Pratt, *Autobiography of Parley P. Pratt* (Salt Lake City: Deseret Book, 1985), 254 (emphasis in original).
7. See *JD,* 16:290.
8. Ibid., 25:38 (emphasis added).
9. Ibid., 22:334.
10. Zebedee Coltrin recalled an incident where some of the early Church brethren were consecrating oil and "saw visibly the finger of God enter into the mouth of the bottle" (Minutes of High Priest Quorum Meeting, Spanish Fork, Utah, 5 February 1870). If nothing else, this is a wonderful symbolic image of the oil being "touched" by the divine power of heaven. For insights on the symbolism of the consecrated olive oil in the ordinance of healing, see John A. Tvedtnes, "Olive Oil: Symbol of the Holy Ghost," in Stephen D. Ricks and John W. Welch, eds., *The Allegory of the Olive Tree: The Olive, the Bible, and Jacob 5* (Salt Lake City: Deseret Book and FARMS, 1994), 427–59.
11. Nathan Eldon Tanner, "My Experiences and Observations," in *Brigham Young University Speeches of the Year* (Provo, UT: BYU Press, 1966), 5–6.
12. George Q. Cannon, ed., *Early Scenes in Church History* (Salt Lake City: Juvenile Instructor Office, 1882), 84–85.
13. M. Russell Ballard, *Our Search for Happiness: An Invitation to Understand The Church of Jesus Christ of the Latter-day Saints* (Salt Lake City: Deseret Book, 1993), 94–95.
14. Conference Report, October 1949, 67.
15. *MS,* vol. 12, no. 20, 15 October 1850, 313.

CHAPTER TWELVE
Miracles

To some is given the working of miracles.
—DOCTRINE AND COVENANTS 46:21

A miracle, by popular definition, is any event or effect that takes place because of a supernatural power. It is generally thought of as "a deviation from the known laws of nature."[1] Orson F. Whitney held to the view that "miracles are [extraordinary results] flowing from superior means and methods of doing things." But, said he, "they are not contrary to law. They are in strict conformity therewith. It could not be otherwise. The universe is governed by law. But there are greater laws and lesser laws, and the greater have power to suspend the operation of the lesser."[2]

The Book of Mormon provides several important insights on the subject of miracles. We learn in this volume of scripture that "the God of Abraham, and the God of Isaac, and the God of Jacob" is "a God of miracles" (Morm. 9:11), and He "has not ceased to be a God of miracles" (v. 15), for He is "the same yesterday, today, and forever" (2 Ne. 27:23). We also learn from the pages of this ancient American book that "if there be no *faith* among the children of men God can do no miracle among them" (Ether 12:12; emphasis added). It is further stated that "all they who wrought miracles wrought them *by faith*" (v. 16; emphasis added). But this is a very narrowly focused faith. The book of Ether clarifies that "neither at any time hath any wrought miracles until after their *faith*; wherefore they first *believed in the Son of God*" (v. 18; emphasis added; cf. 3 Ne. 19:35). This Christ-based faith is necessary because, as pointed out in the book of 3 Nephi, authentic miracles are done "in the name of Jesus" (8:1; cf. 4 Ne. 1:5).

But this is not the only prerequisite for the performance of miracles. From the same passage in 3 Nephi we learn that a specific level of ritual purity is required before a person will be capable of performing a miracle: "And there was not any man who could do a miracle in the name of Jesus save he were cleansed every whit from his iniquity."

Even if individuals achieve a ritually pure state in this life, they still will not be able to perform miracles without another necessary ingredient—power that flows from the Godhead. "Miracles [are] wrought by the power of God," says the Book of Mormon (Alma 37:40). In the Doctrine and Covenants, Jesus Christ reveals: "Unto as many as received me *gave I power* to do many miracles" (D&C 45:8; emphasis added). And in Acts we discover that the Apostle Stephen was "a man full of faith and . . . the Holy Ghost" and was therefore able to do "great . . . miracles among the people" (6:5, 8). And this is the point where mortals make their connection with the powers of heaven—with the third member of the Godhead. Thus, Marion G. Romney pointed out that "one who has never received the gift of the Holy Ghost cannot possibly work miracles by His power."[3] Or, as Elder Bruce R. McConkie has said, "By the power of the Holy Ghost the Lord's ministers . . . work miracles. . . . Without the power of the Holy Ghost, none of these things can be done, nor should they be attempted."[4]

The ability to perform miracles is only granted to members of the household of faith for righteous reasons. They are not to be performed for selfish gain or in order to mystify others or to satisfy the curiosity of sign-seekers. Rather, a person is given the power to "work mighty miracles" so that they can become "a great benefit to [their] fellow beings" (Mosiah 8:18). A nineteenth century Saint named William Hyde had his attention focused on this concept when he received his patriarchal blessing. A pertinent passage within it reads: "Thou shalt be able to do any miracle that was ever done by man in the name of Jesus, when it is *necessary for the salvation of men or building up the Kingdom of Israel in the last days.*"[5]

Ancient and Modern Miracles

On the pages that follow there are citations of five different kinds of biblical miracles that have been paired together with some modern counterparts. The reader will notice in these examples that some miracles are produced by the power of God acting through an earthly intermediary while others occur after the Lord has been petitioned in prayer for intervention in the mortal sphere. In either case, it is the power of God that brings the miracle about.

Provision of Food

In the Old Testament book of 1 Kings we find the account of the prophet Elijah and the widow of Zarephath. It is related in this scriptural passage that Elijah was directed by revelation from the Lord to go to the town of Zarephath and there be sustained by a widow who was under the command of the Lord. Elijah obeyed, and when he got to the gate of the town he found the woman gathering sticks so that she could bake what little provisions she had left for her and her son. Elijah requested that she bring him food and drink, but she explained that her food supply was nearly exhausted, and that she expected the members of her family to die soon. But Elijah told her to fear not. If she would but fulfill his request first, he said, then the Lord would multiply her foodstuffs for a specified amount of time. The woman obeyed, and the promise was fulfilled: "The barrel of meal wasted not, neither did the cruse of oil fail, according to the word of the Lord, which He spake by Elijah" (17:8–16).

We find a counterpart to this inspiring tale of divinely provided food in an account that was related by Ted E. Brewerton of the Quorum of Seventy. Brother Brewerton tells the story as follows.

> When my grandfather James E. Fisher was set apart as a missionary in 1892, he was told, "The Lord will provide food, raiment, and shelter for you."
>
> At age 19, grandfather had traveled 160 miles by horse and wagon from Meadow, Utah, to St. George to be married in the temple to Elizabeth Stewart. They returned to Meadow where they lived as farmers for the next six years. It was then that James E. received his mission call to New Zealand. It was common at

that time to ask young married men to leave home and family to serve for two to five years. . . .

In New Zealand, Elder Fisher and his companion no doubt wondered and worried about their loved ones back home. In a new land with new customs, often relying on the kindness of others for shelter and sustenance, they must have felt out of place at times and in need of reassurance. The food commonly used by the Maori people was much different than that to which they were accustomed.

One day as the missionaries rode along on their horses, they talked about how much they missed the good, homemade bread so common back in Utah. Money from home had not yet arrived and they were, quite simply, hungry. Elder Fisher's companion suggested that they were alone and could dismount. They went into the woods and prayed. They expressed their desire to serve, as well as their love and concern for those back home.

The two Elders felt better, got back on their horses, and continued on their way. As they rode along, they noticed something just off the road. They dismounted and to their amazement found, wrapped in a white cloth, a fresh loaf of bread, the same kind of homemade bread they had talked about in their prayer. They rejoiced as they ate it, although it wasn't the bread that was so important, but the reassurance that Heavenly Father knew who they were and where they were, that they had faithful wives and that the Lord's kindness and goodness was over them all. Later, they both wrote home and told their wives of the incident.

At that time, it took six weeks for a letter to get from Utah to New Zealand, and it cost 50 cents for postage, which was then an enormous sum of money. Therefore letters were sent only about once a month.

About three months after the elders found the bread on the trail, Elder Fisher's companion received a letter from his wife. She wrote that on that same day they made their discovery, she had been baking bread.

When she opened her oven to remove it, one of the pans was empty and a white cloth that had been on the table was gone. She had been home all the time and saw no one come or go.[6]

Provision of Money

Next we have the miracle of being provided with financial means. A biblical example of this type can be found in the book of Matthew. Here we read that money was needed in order to pay an imposed tribute to the foreign power that occupied the land of Israel at the time. The Savior determined that it would be wise to comply with this demand so as not to cause offense. But in order to provide the necessary funds, he instructed Peter to go to the sea, near Capernaum, and cast a hook into the water. He told Peter that if he would look into the mouth of the first fish that he caught he would find enough money to pay tribute for the both of them. The hook was cast and the promise miraculously fulfilled (see 17:24–27).

A very similar story was told by a woman named Mary Lightner. She recalled a difficult set of circumstances in which she and a group of nineteenth-century Saints found themselves and how the issue was resolved through divine intervention. She reported the incident in this way:

> After enduring all manner of grievances we were driven from the county. While we were camped on the banks of the Missouri River waiting to be ferried over, they found there was not money enough to take all [the people] over. One or two families must be left behind, and the fear was that if left, they would be killed. So, some of the brethren by the name of Higbee thought they would try and catch some fish—perhaps the ferryman would take them. They put out their lines in the evening. It rained all night and most of the next day. When they took in their lines they found two or three small fish, and a catfish that weighed 14 pounds. On opening it, what was their astonishment to find three bright silver half dollars, just the amount needed to pay for taking their team over the river. This was considered a miracle, and caused great rejoicing among us.[7]

Calming a Storm

The calming of a storm by the Maker of heaven and earth is a familiar story to students of the New Testament. It is found in the eighth chapter of Matthew. A great tempest, we are told in the text, arose on the sea when Jesus and His disciples were traveling upon it in a ship. At one point the waves of water actually covered the vessel, and most of the occupants thought that they would perish under these conditions. But the Lord was not afraid. He arose and "rebuked the winds and the sea; and there was a great calm" (vv. 23–27).

The biographer of Elder Franklin D. Richards tells of an instance when this latter-day Apostle exercised the power of God to accomplish the same result as the Master (cf. John 14:12). He wrote as follows:

> While on one of his trips across the Atlantic, returning from the British Mission in charge of a company of Saints and Elders, the weather was very stormy, and the waves were rolling so high that the officers of the vessel were fearful of its being dashed to pieces. When the hearts of strong men were failing them, he remembered he held the holy Priesthood, which authorized him to rebuke the angry elements and command them to be still, as was done by the Savior and His Apostles in their day. Withdrawing to a part of the ship where he was unobserved, and raising his hands to high heaven, he rebuked the storm, the furious winds and waves, in the name of the Lord Jesus Christ, commanding them to cease their violence and to be calm. The tempest immediately subsided; none of the passengers were lost, and no damage was done to the vessel.[8]

Cursing

Next, we have the working of a miracle that is known as a curse. In the book of Matthew we are told about a time when the Savior verbally cursed a fig tree because it bore no fruit. Soon after this cursing took place the tree withered away (see 21:18–21). Incidentally, the Lord told His disciples that if they had unwavering faith they would be able to perform this very same miracle themselves, and even greater miracles than that.

An early LDS convert named Perrigrine Sessions recalled the issuance of a comparable curse. He remembered that when a small group of Church members were traveling in 1838 from Far West, Missouri, to Commerce, Illinois, during a heavy snowstorm they stopped at a farmhouse to try and obtain supplies and pitch their camp. The father of the Prophet Joseph Smith asked the owner of the farm if they could do these things, but when it was discovered that the petitioners were "Mormons," the man threatened them and kicked them off of his property. Once the beleaguered group reached the street, Father Smith removed his hat, raised both of his hands to heaven, and cursed the man in he name of the Lord. Brother Sessions recalled,

> When I came to travel this same road two years later, this incident was brought fresh to my mind. For behold there was nothing to mark the spot but the ruins of his home burned to ashes; his orchard [was] broken down; his farm [was] a picture of desolation; . . . I saw the power of the Priesthood manifested, for at the next farm we were received kindly and given all the comfort and assistance we needed and Father Smith left his blessing on this household as we departed. Here my eyes beheld the fulfillment of his words to the letter as there I looked upon a picture of prosperity and happiness. All this passed and the two neighbors were ignorant of the curse or the blessing placed upon them as we passed on.[9]

Invisibility

The last type of miracle addressed in this chapter is the power of invisibility or, as some would have it, the blinding of the eyes of the wicked. In the biblical book of Luke we read that Jesus Christ went into the synagogue in Nazareth on the Sabbath day and took the opportunity to vocally read a prophecy pronounced long before by the prophet Isaiah. This was a Messianic prophecy that said that the Holy One would have "the Spirit of the Lord" upon Him. This prophecy, said Jesus, was now fulfilled. After making a few more comments pertaining to His own spiritual standing and power, the people in the synagogue became "filled with wrath." They proceeded to push the Lord to the brow of a hill outside the city so that they could throw Him off, "but He, passing through the midst of them, went His way" (4:16–30).

A similar incident took place on February 8, 1886, in Salt Lake City, Utah. On this day, Wilford Woodruff, president of the Twelve, met with several members of the Quorum of the Twelve Apostles and other individuals in the Church Historian's Office. This was a time of persecution against the Church because of the practice of polygamy, and the federal government had arrest warrants out for several LDS leaders. During the meeting that Elder Woodruff was attending, about twenty federal marshals surrounded the building he was in and also the Gardo House. After the marshals had thoroughly searched the Gardo House, Lion House, Beehive House, President's Office, and the tithing headquarters, the prophet prayed for divine direction. Right after he finished petitioning the Lord, he told Andrew Jenson that he would walk with him across the street to another building. After donning some glasses, President Woodruff walked with Brother Jenson out of the door. There was a marshal standing on each side of the gate and numerous other marshals lining the sidewalk leading to the Gardo House. The street and also the area immediately in front of the President's Office were filled with people who knew the Apostle. "The eyes of all the brethren in the streets followed me from [the] time I left the Historian's Office until I entered the President's Office," said Brother Woodruff. He counteracted this attention by not looking at anyone or giving them any recognition while he was walking. "The eyes of all the marshals [were] closed by the power of God," he said. "The Saints knew me. The marshals did not." When President Woodruff reached the clerk's office safely, he closed the door behind him and thanked God for the deliverance and protection that he had received.[10]

Conclusion

We may expect to see miracles occur in our day because God has not ceased to be a God of miracles, and His power has not decreased over time. Those who petition God for miracles must meet certain qualifications: they must possess the gift of the Holy Ghost (because the miracle will be wrought through His agency); they must have faith in Jesus Christ (because the miracle will be wrought in His name); and they must be cleansed from iniquity (because they will act as a conduit for the holy power of God). With God nothing is impossible (see Luke 1:37), but the working of miracles is always subject to His will.

NOTES TO CHAPTER 12

1. Noah Webster, *An American Dictionary of the English Language* (New York: S. Converse, 1828), s.v., "miracle."

2. Orson F. Whitney, *Saturday Night Thoughts,* rev. ed. (Salt Lake City: Deseret Book, 1927), 273.
3. Conference Report, April 1956, 72.
4. Bruce R. McConkie, *Doctrinal New Testament Commentary* (Salt Lake City: Bookcraft, 1971), 2:27.
5. William Hyde, Autobiography, L. Tom Perry Special Collections Library, Brigham Young University, Provo, UT, 16 (emphasis added).
6. *New Era,* November 1990, 4, 6.
7. Mary Lightner, Autobiography, *Utah Genealogical and Historical Magazine,* Writings of Early Latter-day Saints, 196.
8. Franklin L. West, *Life of Franklin D. Richards* (Salt Lake City: Deseret News Press, 1924), 85.
9. Nels B. Lundwall, comp., *Assorted Gems of Priceless Value* (Salt Lake City: N. B. Lundwall, 1944), 316–17.
10. Scott G. Kenney, ed., *Wilford Woodruff's Journal: 1833–1898* (Midvale, UT: Signature Books, 1985), 8:375–76.

CHAPTER THIRTEEN
Prophecy

To others it is given to prophesy.

—*Doctrine and Covenants 46:22*

As with all of the gifts of the Spirit, the power of the Holy Ghost is an integral component of the gift of prophecy. The connection between the two is made explicit on the pages of scripture. In the book of Joel, for instance, the Lord pronounces a divine promise, saying, "I will pour out my Spirit upon all flesh; and your sons and your daughters shall prophesy" (2:28).[1] After the prophet Ezekiel was commanded to prophesy the fate of the wicked inhabitants of Jerusalem, the Spirit of the Lord fell upon him and told him the words which he should speak (see Ezek. 11:4–5). Another example is found in historical writings about David, who, we are told, was informed that he would prophesy after the Spirit of the Lord had come upon him (see 1 Sam. 10:6). And Lehi reports in the Book of Mormon that he prophesied according to the workings of the Spirit which was in him (see 2 Ne. 1:6). Finally, the Apostle Peter states in the New Testament that prophecy comes not by the will of man but only as men are moved upon by the Holy Ghost (see 2 Pet. 1:21).[2]

Even though there is only one man at any given time who is authorized to act as the prophet for The Church of Jesus Christ of Latter-day Saints as a whole, there is no restriction placed upon the number of people who may enjoy the gift of prophecy. President Harold B. Lee taught that "prophecy in the Church and the kingdom of God is not confined to one man. This is a nation of prophets. Every person who has the Holy Ghost has a right to . . . the gift of prophecy."[3] President Lee's teachings are in line with words found in the book of Numbers. There Moses, prophet of the Old Testament, exclaimed, "Would God that all the Lord's people were prophets, and that the Lord would put His Spirit upon them!" (11:29). President Heber C. Kimball explained how such a thing is possible. He said, "If a man . . . lets the Spirit of God dictate him, he cannot help prophesying, for the Holy Ghost is the Spirit of prophecy."[4]

In Latter-day Saint literature, Church leaders and lay commentators alike have applied a wide range of interpretations to the gift of prophecy.[5] But for the purposes of this book, prophecy is defined in the narrow sense that accords with Mosiah 5:3. There it is indicated that prophetic power is connected with "the manifestations of [God's] Spirit" and the ability to foretell "that which is to come" (cf. John 16:13; D&C 107:56). This was the definition advocated by Elder Orson Pratt, who told a gathering of Latter-day Saints that from his perspective, "the gift of prophecy" was to be equated with "foretelling future events."[6]

In Doctrine and Covenants section 130, it is made known that God—by some unspecified means—is aware of future events, and that He manifests these occurrences to the angels of the celestial sphere (see vv. 6–8). Both ancient and modern scriptures report instances where God also shares information about the future with His mortal agents who are commonly called "prophets." Heber C. Kimball taught that "by the spirit of prophecy you can become acquainted with things to come, and declare them to the Saints by the inspiration of the Holy Ghost. When men prophesy with this Spirit upon them, they will come to pass, for the Holy Ghost cannot lie."[7] By way of clarification, he also pointed out that "God does not bring to pass a thing because you say it shall be so, but because He designed [that] it should be so. . . . [I]t is the future purposes of the Almighty that the prophet foresees."[8]

Institutional and Personal Prophecies

We as Latter-day Saints are fortunate to have the opportunity to experience the gift of prophecy both indirectly (through a duly authorized messenger of God) and directly (by personal communication from Deity). Let us briefly examine each of these modes of experience in their order.

Institutional Prophecy

There are three ways whereby the gift of prophecy can be manifest as a formal, institutional function of The Church of Jesus Christ of Latter-day Saints: (1) the blessing of children, (2) patriarchal blessings, and (3) setting apart to an office or calling.

On the pages of the *Encyclopedia of Mormonism* we read that when children are named and blessed in the Church, "the blessing itself is to be given as dictated by the Spirit and may contain prophecy concerning the child's future."[9] Early Church leader George Q. Cannon instructed priesthood holders who give children their name and blessing not to check or suppress the spirit of prophecy, but to also be careful not to make statements about the future of the child that are not "prompted by the Spirit of the Lord."[10] An example of the gift of prophecy being manifest in conjunction with the blessing of children is preserved in the *History of the Church*. On March 13, 1843, when the Prophet Joseph Smith was bestowing blessings upon the heads of a group of the Saints' children, he began to turn pale and lose his strength. Jedediah M. Grant noticed this unusual circumstance and asked the Prophet why it was so. Joseph replied that while he was giving these blessings he saw that Lucifer would exert his influence to destroy these children in the future. With this prophetic knowledge of what was to come, the Church president sealed a blessing upon these children so that their lives would be secured upon the earth. It was the great exertion of the Prophet's faith and the transference of "the spirit of life" that had caused him to grow so weak, he said.[11]

Patriarchal blessings can include prophecies to bless faithful Saints. President James E. Faust made note that "the patriarchal blessing is, in essence, a prophetic blessing and utterance."[12] President Wilford Woodruff concurred with this assessment. He said that when Joseph Smith's father, who held the office of Patriarch of the Church, "laid his hands upon men's heads the spirit of blessing and of prophesy rested upon him." Wilford provided an example of the prophetic gift from his own patriarchal blessing, which was given by Father Smith. He said of the Patriarch, "He told me that I should bring all of my father's house into the Church. I dwelt upon that with a great deal of interest; and the first time I visited my father's house, although it was several years after this, I baptized him into this Church, and my stepmother, and my sisters, and everybody that was in my father's house, even a Methodist class-leader who was boarding there."[13] Likewise, when David O. McKay received his patriarchal blessing on July 17, 1887, at thirteen years of age, the patriarch prophesied unto him saying,

> Brother David Oman McKay, thou art in thy youth and need instruction, therefore I say unto thee, be taught of thy parents the way of life and salvation, that at an early day you may be prepared for a responsible position, *for the eye of the Lord is upon thee. . . .*
>
> The Lord has a work for thee to do, in which thou shalt *see much of the world,* assist in gathering scattered Israel and also labor in the ministry. It shall be thy lot to sit in council with thy brethren *and preside among the people* and exhort the Saints to faithfulness.[14]

The fulfillment of this prophecy is evident in the fact that Brother McKay was ordained as an Apostle in 1906 and as the President of the Church in 1951. After his ordination as president, he traveled approximately one million miles over the face of the earth.[15]

Elder George Teasdale of the Quorum of the Twelve Apostles said the following in regard to prophecy and being set apart to Church callings: "I know that the spirit of prophecy is in the Church. I have been on missions. I have been set apart for these missions under the hands of Apostles, and they have predicted concerning me as though they knew the work that I was about to accomplish, and those prophecies have been fulfilled. I am here today [as] a living witness to testify to that."[16] An example of a missionary being given a prophetic glimpse of his future activities comes from the pen of Elder Parley P. Pratt. In April 1836 Elder Pratt had been assigned to work as a missionary in Canada, but he had incurred a great deal of debt during the previous winter months and was pondering on whether he should stay at home to resolve this issue and provide for his family before going off to his new field of labor. One evening he was contemplating this situation when a knock came at his door. Elder Heber C. Kimball and several other persons entered his residence and "being filled with the spirit of prophecy," Elder Kimball admonished him to arise and go forward to fulfill his calling. He told Brother Pratt,

> Take no thoughts for your debts, nor the necessaries of life, for the Lord will supply you with abundant means for all things.
>
> Thou shalt go to Upper Canada, even to the city of Toronto, the capital, and there thou shalt find a people prepared for the fullness of the gospel, and they shall receive thee, and thou shalt organize the Church among them, and it shall spread thence into the regions round about, and many shall be brought to the knowledge of the truth and shall be filled with joy.[17]

After a few days, Elder Pratt was ready to depart on his mission and was informed by Brother Nickerson (his traveling companion) that he would bear Elder Pratt's expenses. After visiting Niagara Falls, Parley went to the town of Hamilton, at the head of Lake Ontario, and being destitute of funds he petitioned the Lord for assistance so that he might cross over the water to Toronto. Soon thereafter he was approached by a stranger in Hamilton who asked him if he didn't need some money and then gave him ten dollars. The man also gave Elder Pratt an introductory letter to John Taylor, who happened to be meeting with a group of religious "seekers" who had been assembling privately for two years, trying to find the true Church of Christ, with its attendant spiritual blessings. Elder Pratt met with and taught this group on three occasions and most of them requested baptism into the restored Church.[18]

Personal Prophecy

The gift of prophecy can be experienced by a person independent of any Church-related ordinances, blessings, or responsibilities. This gift can also be enjoyed spontaneously—independent of an individual actively petitioning the Lord to receive it. The following stories will serve to illustrate these two points.

Lucy Mack Smith, the mother of the Prophet Joseph Smith, said of an incident that took place in Pontiac, Michigan, in June 1831,

> Mr. Whitermore introduced me to Rev. Mr. Ruggles who was the pastor of the Presbyterian church to which . . . Mr. [Whitermore] belonged.

"And you," said Mr. Ruggles upon shaking hands with me, "are the mother of that poor, foolish, silly boy Joe Smith who pretended to translate the Book of Mormon."

I looked him steadily in the face and replied, "I am, sir, the mother of Joseph Smith. But why, may I ask, do you call him a foolish, silly boy?"

"Because," said his Reverence, "that he should imagine that he was going to break down all the churches with that simple Mormon book."

"Did you ever read that book?" I inquired.

"No," said he, "it is too far beneath me to be worthy of my notice."

[I replied,] "Then I think, sir, [that] you do not abide by that scripture which saith 'search all things.' And now, sir, let me tell you boldly that the Book of Mormon contains the everlasting gospel and it was written, for the salvation of your soul, by the gift and power of the Holy Ghost."

"Pooh," said the minister. "Nonsense, but I have no fears of any members of my church being lead away by any such [stuff] for they have too much intelligence."

"Now Mr. Ruggles," said [I]—and I spoke earnestly for the Spirit of God was upon me—"mark my words. As true as God lives, before three years we will have more than one-third of your church. And, sir, whether you believe it or not, we will take the very deacon too."

This produced a hearty laugh from the company, which was quite a large one, at the expense of the Reverend minister.

Not to be tedious, I will say that I remained in this section [of country] about three weeks after our brethren left me (making my whole stay four weeks) during which time I labored incessantly for the truth's sake and gained the hearts of many believers. . . . These [people] were anxious to have an Elder sent to them . . . [and] pledge[d] themselves that the man who came should not lack for anything. . . .

> [When I arrived home] I mentioned the state of things where I had been to Joseph. . . . [H]e seemed pleased that I had succeeded in preparing the way for a minister of the gospel and sent Brother Jared Carter to labor with them. . . . He went into the midst of Mr. Ruggles's church and converted seventy of his best member[s] and, as I said, he took the very deacon too [in January 1833]. For although I did not know anything about the situation of his church he had a very intelligent deacon by the name of [Samuel] Bent who is now a High Councilor in Nauvoo. And he told me the last time I saw him, which was not a week since, that he had never forgotten my prophecy upon his head.[19]

The next story that we will examine took place in Coventry, England, in February 1856. A man by the name of William J. Smith had been appointed by the authorities in that region to preside over the Warwickshire conference. Under his leadership this conference was the means by which many citizens of Coventry were led to the waters of baptism, and this led the clergy of the city to warn the inhabitants to stay away from the Mormons.

The Saints had been meeting regularly at the Spurn End chapel, and William decided that it would be beneficial to the work of the mission to present a series of eight lectures at this location on the first principles of the gospel. Placards were placed throughout the city, and consequently there were large crowds in attendance at the lectures.

But on the morning of the sixth lecture, William found himself gravely ill. In earnest prayer he petitioned the Lord to heal him so that he might give his lecture in the afternoon. By the time of his appointment, the Spirit of God had rested down upon him, and he felt an increased amount of strength. The story continues:

> The meeting was a very crowded one; all classes apparently were represented; scripture readers were present to take notes, while numbers, probably hundreds, were unable to obtain admission.
>
> In the rear of the chapel ran the line of railway that connected Coventry with Nuneaton, and in that portion of its road it was built upon arches high above the ground. These were so near the chapel that whenever a train passed, it not only made a great noise, but perceptibly shook the building. Elder Smith's

> audience, though so large, was a very attentive one, but shortly after he had commenced speaking a train came thundering by, causing the minds of the people to be distracted from his teachings. Feeling annoyed at the interruption, the speaker suddenly stopped talking, paused for a few moments and then exclaimed, "Babylon! Confusion! I cannot speak an hour without being interrupted by the railway." And then, stretching out his hand, he continued, "In the name of Jesus Christ, my Master, that railway arch shall fall to the ground." Elder Smith then continued his sermon. When he [was] done, he had mingled feelings; he could scarcely understand why he was prompted to utter such a prophecy; he felt that if he had left that out it would have been the best discourse he ever preached. But the words were uttered and could not be recalled; they had been heard by scores [of people], many of whom were not friends of the Saints. Still, he felt impressed that what he had prophesied was by the Spirit of God, and that gave him peace.
>
> His words were reported to nine clergymen, who made it their business to have competent judges examine the arches and discover, if possible, if there was any cause for a statement and prophecy such as his. These gentlemen declared the arches to be sound, that there were no better in England, and consequently Brother Smith was ridiculed and derided as a false prophet.
>
> Shortly afterwards Elder Smith was called away from Coventry by the presidency of the mission, and appointed to succeed Elder Henry Lunt in the presidency of the Newcastle-on-Tyne pastorate. He left Warwickshire without seeing his prophecy fulfilled; but within a few weeks a heavy rain fell and undermined the arches, and nineteen out of twenty-one fell to the ground, leaving only two standing. Through this fall much damage was done to the contiguous residences and other property. . . .
>
> Thus is the saying of the Lord corroborated, that what His servants declare by His Spirit He will fulfill.[20]

Finally, we have a unique account from a sergeant in the Mormon Battalion named Daniel Tyler. He tells of a prophecy that was uttered about him in the gift of tongues and then interpreted by himself. In 1853 Daniel had a badly broken leg and was making his way about on crutches. Because the bones in his leg had to be reset, they were taking a very long time in knitting back together, and Daniel had very little hope of being able to walk again without assistance. Daniel hobbled on his crutches to a prayer meeting that was being held within the tenth ward boundaries in Salt Lake City. After the opening exercises a woman named Sister More stood up and began speaking in tongues. "She addressed her remarks to me," said Daniel, "and I understood her as well as though she had spoken the English language. She said: 'Your leg will be healed, and you will go on a foreign mission and preach the gospel in foreign lands. No harm shall befall you, and you shall return in safety, having great joy in your labors.'"

Daniel said that the substance of this prophecy was so different from his own personal belief, and the fears of many other people, that he was tempted not to give the interpretation, "lest it should fail to come to pass." But he was impressed by the Spirit of the Lord, and so he arose on his crutches and relayed the interpretation to those who were present.

Not long after this experience, Daniel was instructed in a dream about what he should do to strengthen his fractured limb, which began to gain strength immediately after the directions were followed. In about a week he was able to walk with the help of a cane, and in the fall of 1854 he was sent to take charge of the Swiss and Italian missions of the Church. He was subsequently given responsibility for the French and German missions as well.[21]

Conclusion

The gift of prophecy is certainly one of the most personally relevant gifts that we can experience. It has the potential to guide us in decisions related to home life, relationships, employment, Church callings, and scholastic education. Righteous Latter-day Saints are eligible to enjoy the gift of prophecy on an ecclesiastical level (through the reception of different types of blessings). The Saints also have the opportunity to go before the Lord and ask Him directly for guidance in personal future events. In addition, we may be spontaneously blessed to prophesy about ourselves and about other individuals or events. We should not hesitate to take the Lord up on His generous offer to seek after this enlightening gift and thereby develop a sense of what lies before us on the path of life.

NOTES TO CHAPTER 13

1. Sometimes one of the symbols of the Holy Ghost (a cloven tongue of fire) is visible when the gift of prophecy is being exercised. Heber C. Kimball reported that during one meeting he attended, "the spirit of prophecy was poured out upon the assembly, and cloven tongues of fire sat upon them; for they were seen by many of the congregation" (Orson F. Whitney, *Life of Heber C. Kimball* [Salt Lake City: Bookcraft, 1945], 93).
2. The connection between the Spirit of God and the gift of prophecy is clearly illustrated in an important historical event. The Prophet Joseph Smith related: "No sooner had I baptized Oliver Cowdery than the Holy Ghost fell upon him and he stood up and prophesied many things which should shortly come to pass. And again, so soon as I had been baptized by him, I also had the spirit of prophecy, when, standing up I prophesied concerning the rise of the Church, and many other things connected with the Church, and this generation of the children of men. We were filled with the Holy Ghost" (*Times and Seasons,* vol. 3, no. 19, 1 August 1842, 866).
3. Clyde J. Williams, ed., *The Teachings of Harold B. Lee* (Salt Lake City: Bookcraft, 1996), 419. Elder Bruce R. McConkie asked, "Who may prophesy?" He replied that "Prophecy is for all: men, women, and children, every member of the true Church" (Bruce R. McConkie, *Doctrinal New Testament Commentary* [Salt Lake City: Bookcraft, 1971], 2:387). Elder McConkie wrote in another place, "Every member of the Church should be a prophet as pertaining to his own affairs. . . . Prophecy is one of the gifts of the Spirit to which all the Saints are entitled (1 Cor. 12:10), and faithful members of the Church are exhorted to 'covet to prophesy' (1 Cor. 14:39)" (Bruce R. McConkie, *Mormon Doctrine,* 2nd ed. [Salt Lake City: Bookcraft, 1966], 606).
4. George D. Watt, ed., *Journal of Discourses* (Liverpool, England: Samuel W. Richards and Sons, 1852–1886), 4:338; hereafter cited as *JD.*
5. See for example Daniel H. Ludlow, ed., *Encyclopedia of Mormonism* (New York: Macmillan, 1992), 3:1160–62; hereafter cited as *EM;* Hoyt W. Brewster Jr., *Prophets, Priesthood Keys, and Succession* (Salt Lake City: Deseret Book, 1991), 5–15; Brent L. Top, Larry E. Dahl, and Walter D. Bowen, *Follow the Living Prophets* (Salt Lake City: Bookcraft, 1993), 27–71.
6. *JD,* 16:291. It was the teaching of Elder Brigham H. Roberts that "knowledge of [the future] belongs to God alone, and to His servants to whom He reveals it; not to those who question His work, or challenge His power. *'Prophecy' or power to penetrate into the future, is not given to Satan or to his emissaries. For them that veil will not part.* 'For . . . prophecy came not in [old] time by the will of man; but holy men of God spake as they were moved by the Holy Ghost' [2 Pet. 1:21]. So now, prophecy, knowledge of the future, is of God, and of His servants to whom He reveals it. Prophecy, in a way, is history reversed. Prophecy is a fore-telling of that which shall be" (Brigham H.

Roberts, *A Comprehensive History of The Church of Jesus Christ of Latter-day Saints* [Salt Lake City: Deseret News Press, 1930], 6:550; emphasis added).

7. *JD,* 9:134. Elder George A. Smith declared, "A man [who] does not foresee by the Spirit of God, who does not learn things to come by it, is not living up to his privilege." He also said that there are many Latter-day Saints who can "foresee by the Spirit of the Almighty—the spirit of prophecy—things that are to come to pass, without being able to know the precise manner how it will be effected" (ibid., 10:67–68).
8. Whitney, *Life of Heber C. Kimball,* 391. It appears that there is at least one exception to this rule. The Prophet Joseph Smith said, "The Lord once told me that if at any time I got into deep trouble and could see no way out of it, if I would prophesy in His name, He would fulfill my words" (*Juvenile Instructor,* vol. 27, no. 4, 15 February 1892, 128). It is not known by the author if this was a special privilege granted only to one prophet in the dispensation of the fullness of times or if such a privilege has been granted to other servants of God in this or any other dispensation of the gospel.
9. *EM,* 1:268.
10. *Millennial Star,* vol. 24, no. 7, 15 February 1862, 106.
11. See Brigham H. Roberts, *History of The Church of Jesus Christ of Latter-day Saints* (Salt Lake City: Deseret Book, 1948–1950), 5:303.
12. *Ensign,* November 1995, 63. An excellent illustration of this concept is seen in the opening lines of a patriarchal blessing given by Hyrum Smith to Elizabeth Kirby on November 18, 1843. The Patriarch of the Church said, "Sister Elizabeth, I lay my hands upon your head in the name of Jesus of Nazareth and place and seal a blessing upon your head that shall come to pass in [the] future" (cited in Carol Cornwall Madsen, ed., *In Their Own Words: Women and the Story of Nauvoo* [Salt Lake City: Deseret Book, 1994], 181).
13. Brian H. Stuy, ed., *Collected Discourses* (Burbank, CA, and Woodland Hills, UT: B.H.S. Publishing, 1987–1992), 2:210; hereafter cited as *CD.*
14. Preston Nibley, *The Presidents of the Church,* rev. ed. (Salt Lake City: Deseret Book, 1974), 312 (emphasis added).
15. Joseph Fielding Smith, *Essentials in Church History* (Salt Lake City: Deseret Book, 1979), 540–41.
16. *CD,* 4:39.
17. Parley P. Pratt, *Autobiography of Parley P. Pratt* (Salt Lake City: Deseret Book, 1985), 110.
18. See ibid., 113–27.
19. Lavina F. Anderson, ed., *Lucy's Book: A Critical Edition of Lucy Mack Smith's Family Memoir* (Salt Lake City: Signature Books, 2001), 552–55.
20. George Q. Cannon, ed., *Early Scenes in Church History* (Salt Lake City: Juvenile Instructor Office, 1882), 68–70.
21. George Q. Cannon, ed., *Scraps of Biography* (Salt Lake City: Juvenile Instructor Office, 1883), 41–42.

CHAPTER FOURTEEN
Angels and Spirits

To another [is given] the beholding of angels and ministering spirits.
—Moroni 10:14

The Prophet Joseph Smith taught the Latter-day Saints that if they would live up to their privilege, the angels could not be restrained from being their associates.[1] He clarified this concept when he said that since God is not a respecter of persons, the Saints of the final dispensation are "entitled" to the same blessings that were received by the ancient Saints, including the visitation of angels, the spirits of the just, and even Deity. "We may come to the general assembly and Church of the Firstborn, [to the] spirits of just men made perfect, [and] unto Christ," said the Prophet. "It is our privilege to pray for and obtain these things."[2]

Even though a person can petition the Lord for the bestowal of the marvelous gift of visitations from beyond the veil, it must be kept in mind that such a blessing is only granted under certain circumstances. President Wilford Woodruff once had a conversation with a member of the Quorum of the Twelve Apostles who told him that he had a great desire for the administration of an angel and had prayed for a long time to receive one. President Woodruff informed him that even if he prayed for a thousand years for this particular gift it would never be granted "unless the Lord had a motive in sending an angel to him. . . . [T]he Lord never did, nor never will, send an angel to anybody," said President Woodruff, "merely to gratify the desire of the individual to see an angel." If the Lord sends an angel to anyone on the earth, it is only to perform a work that cannot be accomplished except through the administration of such a being.[3] There are instances in scripture where angels have appeared to mortals after prayer has been offered to God for divine intervention, but in these cases the prayers did not specifically request a visitation to occur (see Acts 12:5–10; Mosiah 27:8–14). Canonized texts reveal, rather, that messengers of God typically make appearances without any warning whatsoever and without the impetus of a mortal request (see Moses 5:6; Matt. 28:1–7; Luke 1:11).

The Lord's heavenly representatives must not only come through the veil with a definite purpose, but they must also do so with permission. Elder Orson F. Whitney reminds us that "God's house is a house of order, and the spirit world is a room in that house. This being the case, it is only reasonable to conclude that before anything important or unusual can take place there, the Master of the mansion must first give consent. Otherwise," said Elder Whitney, "confusion would prevail, and the divine purpose for which the veil was dropped between the two worlds might be thwarted." Because order is one of the hallmarks of God's kingdom, "permission from the Father of spirits would have to be obtained before one of His children, either an unembodied or a disembodied spirit, could make itself manifest to mortals."[4] This order of things precludes the possibility that angels of God and the spirits of the just can be summoned by any human being. In Charles W. Penrose's view, it is "beyond rational belief" that the servants and handmaidens of the Lord who reside beyond the veil are "subject to the will and whims of persons who know not God and whose lives and aims are of the earth." Neither is it in accordance with correct doctrine that a prophet or a prophetess of the Lord could exercise the power to call down righteous residents of the otherworldly realm to converse with them on matters of an earthly nature. Such an idea, said Brother Penrose, "ought not to be entertained by any Latter-day Saint. . . . By permission of the Lord, persons on either side of the veil may be manifest to those on the other, but this will certainly be by law and according to the order which God has established."[5]

In the Book of Mormon we learn, as a general rule, that when angels make appearances on the earth they do not show themselves to just anybody, but rather "unto them of strong faith and a firm mind in every form of godliness" (Moro. 7:30). In the words of Jedediah M. Grant, "the Latter-day Saints try to live their religion, that they may converse with angels." He specified that in order for them to "receive the administration of holy messengers from the throne of God," they must first be "sanctified in their spirits, affections, and all their desires, that the Holy Ghost may rest upon them, and their hearts be filled therewith." It is by being infused with the holiness of the Spirit, said Brother Grant, that the Saints can "become competent to bear the presence of angels."[6]

Elder John A. Widtsoe draws our attention to the fact that in scriptural texts the duties of God's messengers are many and varied. "They may announce the truths of the gospel, or convey special messages to individuals or nations. They may act as guardians to protect the righteous, or agents to inflict divine penalties upon the wicked. They may come, as at the beginning of a dispensation, with authority to bestow the priesthood or to help in the development of the organized Church. In short," said Elder Widtsoe, "they go and do as they are bidden."[7] It is revealed in Moroni 7:30 that these otherworldly beings do the bidding of the Lord Jesus Christ—ministering "according to the word of His command."

Moroni teaches further about some of the functions of angelic ministers. He says that "the office of their ministry is to call men unto repentance, and to fulfill and to do the work of the covenants of the Father, which He hath made unto the children of men" (Moro. 7:31). In other places in the Book of Mormon it is stated that angels tell mortals about the plan of salvation (see Alma 24:14) and also declare the righteousness of God (see Alma 19:34). This is closely connected with Moses 7:27, where we read that angels descend out of heaven and bear testimony of the Father and the Son.

Visitors from Beyond

Angels or spirits of the just may visit mortals under several different circumstances. First, the recipient of this gift may view these beings at a distance but have no interaction with them. Second, they may observe them in close proximity and be given some type of message. And third, they may see them face to face and engage in a verbal exchange.

The first category can be illustrated by two examples from the Bible. In 2 Samuel, King David sees an angel who has been sent by the Lord to carry out a work of destruction against the Israelites, but he receives no message from this being and does not speak to him (see 24:10–17). In the New Testament, the Lord's chief Apostles—Peter, James, and John—were allowed to see the translated prophets Moses and Elijah when they came from beyond the veil to speak with the Savior on the Mount of Transfiguration. The three Apostles saw the personages but were not spoken to (see Mark 9:2–5).

Latter-day examples of this type of event are plentiful. One such occurrence is related by Frederick G. Williams, who served as a counselor in the First Presidency of the early LDS Church. During the dedicatory sessions of the Kirtland Temple in 1836, Williams saw an angel enter through one of the windows of the building and take a seat next to him while a prayer was being given, though he did not have any interaction with this visitor.[8] President Spencer W. Kimball related a similar type of incident when he spoke of "the unusual experience told by President David O. McKay in Hawaii when a native Hawaiian brother reported that while the prayer was being offered at the spot where the first baptism had occurred, he saw George Q. Cannon and President Joseph F. Smith stand in the circle. They had long been dead."[9] Another instance of this kind is reported by Hans J. Hals, who attended the dedication of the Salt Lake Temple. In his journal he recorded the following words for the date April 6, 1893: "Angels of God were seen coming in the southeast window and sitting on the corners. Two of them moved across the large hall over the people and went out the north window."[10] A fascinating article published in an LDS publication called *The Contributor* in the latter part of the nineteenth century recites yet another occurrence that fits into the first category. It says,

> On the twenty-second of April, 1855, the ship *Samuel Curling* sailed from Liverpool with five hundred and eighty-one Saints on board, of whom three hundred and eighty-five were P[erpetual] E[migration] Fund emigrants, all under the presidency of Elder Israel Barlow, who had acted as pastor of the Birmingham and Warwickshire conferences.
>
> William Willis, on his return from a mission to India, and other prominent Elders embarked on the *Samuel Curling* which,

> after a safe and pleasant passage, arrived in New York on Tuesday the twenty-second of May. During the voyage three children were born, and as there were no deaths on board the net increase was that number.
>
> Elder Peter Reid, who emigrated to America as a passenger on the *Samuel Curling* in 1855, . . . told the writer some time ago that the ship encountered several storms in her passage across the Atlantic, but that she passed safely through them all. In the midst of one of these storms the captain got somewhat disheartened and declared to Brother Barlow, the President of the company of emigrants, that he, in his long experience as a seafaring man, had never encountered a worse one; he then added that the tempest had not reached its highest point yet, but that the next half hour would be worse still. Brother Barlow, in reply, told the captain that the storm was nearly over, and would not increase in violence. This bold remark of Brother Barlow made the captain angry, as he thought he knew more about the weather and the sea than anyone else on board; but on going into his cabin to examine his barometer and other nautical instruments, he found that Brother Barlow was right; the storm abated almost immediately. Elder Barlow afterwards told some of the Saints that while the storm was raging he saw the ship surrounded by scores of angels, who stood in a circle around it with joined hands. This was a testimony to the Saints that the Lord was watching over the ship, and that there was no danger.[11]

The second category of visitations, where heavenly messengers speak but are not spoken to, is illustrated again in the Bible. In the book of 1 Kings we read that the prophet Elijah was awakened twice by an angel who provided him with food and instructed him to eat before he took an arduous forty-day journey to the mountain of God (see 19:1–8). Similarly, the book of Matthew relates the story of an angel who descended from heaven to the garden tomb, announced to the two Marys that the Savior had arisen from the dead, and instructed them to go and tell His disciples that this miracle had occurred (see 28:1–8).

Incidents of this kind are found upon the pages of LDS historical documents. One such occurrence involved a Mormon pioneer by the name of Stephen I. Bunnell. Assistant Church Historian Andrew Jenson wrote, "Until he was forty years of age Bro[ther] Bunnell was an invalid, unable to work." But "about the year 1874 a personage appeared to him and promised that he should live to a good old age and perform a great work in the temple." From that time forward his health improved and he was never sick thereafter.[12]

Zera Pulsipher was one of the seven presidents of the Quorum of Seventy in Kirtland, Ohio. In his autobiography he recalled the great persecution against the Mormons and their leaders that took place in that town. In the year 1838, after most of the Saints had moved into the state of Missouri, Zera was still in Kirtland with about four of the quorum presidents and many poor individuals who could not afford to make the same trip. During a Sabbath day meeting inside the temple it was decided by the presidents that they would pool their resources in order to make the journey, and when they reached that decision, they "felt a great flow of the Spirit of God." But between five and six hundred other people wanted to join with them and escape persecution. After counseling together, the presidents realized that without the intervention of the power of God it would not be possible to fulfill their purpose. And so they decided to ascend into the attic story of the temple and petition the Father to provide the means for the thousand-mile trip. Zera relates, "Accordingly, one day while we were on our knees in prayer I saw a messenger apparently like an old man with white hair down to his shoulders. He was a very large man near seven feet high, dressed in a white robe down to his ankles. He looked on me then turned his eyes on the others and then to me again and spoke and said, 'Be one and you shall have enough.' This gave us great joy; we immediately advised the brethren to scatter and work for anything that they could get that would be useful in moving to a new country."[13]

Another story that fits into the second category of visitations is told by Lydia Knight. It is particularly poignant because it involves the visitation of a deceased spouse. On January 11, 1847, Lydia's husband, Newel, died of lung inflammation on the pioneer trail in Nebraska. Lydia had been given a special promise in her patriarchal blessing (by Joseph Smith Sr.) which said, "Neither distress nor death shall separate you [from your husband]. . . . Angels shall minister unto thee; thy heart shall be comforted." Sometime shortly after the fourth of February, Lydia was sitting in her home and cried out in a moment of mental anguish,

"Oh Newel, why hast thou left me!"

As she spoke, he stood by her side, with a lovely smile on his face, and said: "Be calm, let not sorrow overcome you. It was necessary that I should go. I was needed behind the veil to represent the true condition of this camp and people. You cannot fully comprehend it now; but the time will come when you shall know why I left you and our little ones. Therefore, dry up your tears. Be patient, I will go before you and protect you in your journeyings. And you and your little ones shall never perish for lack of food."

As he spoke the last words, she turned, and there appeared three ravens [cf. 1 Kings 17:1–6]. Turning again to where her husband had stood, he was not [there].

This was a great comfort and help to her, and her spirits were revived and strengthened by the promises made.[14]

One final example in this category comes from a woman named Elizabeth G. MacDonald. She was living in Liverpool, England, in May 1853 when she fell down a flight of stairs and was so seriously injured that she became bedridden. But then a marvelous, prophetic occurrence took place one Saturday afternoon. She recalled it in the following words:

I was feeling especially depressed and sorrowful and while my neighbor, Mrs. Kent, who had just been in, was gone to her home for some little luxury for me, as I turned in my bed I was astonished to behold an aged man standing at the foot. As I somewhat recovered from my natural timidity he came towards the head of the bed and laid his hands upon me, saying, "I lay my hands upon thy head and bless thee in the name of the God of Abraham, Isaac and Jacob. The Lord hath seen the integrity of thine heart. In tears and sorrow thou hast bowed before the Lord, asking for children; this blessing is about to be granted unto thee. Thou shalt be blessed with children from this hour. Thou shalt be gathered to the valleys of the mountains, and there thou shalt see thy children raised as tender plants by thy side. Thy children and household shall call thee blessed. At present thy husband is better than many children. Be comforted. These blessings I seal upon thee, in the name of Jesus. Amen." At this

> moment Sister Kent came in, and I saw no more of this personage. His presence was so impressed upon me that I can to this day minutely describe his clothing and countenance.

The next Church conference after this visitation took place, Sister MacDonald's husband "was released to go to the [Salt Lake] valley," and they departed on their journey in March 1854. She and her husband eventually settled in St. George, Utah, and raised their family there "in the midst of good influences."[15]

The scriptures illustrate instances of the third category—where conversations are carried out between beings from behind the veil and mortal personages. The book of Moses (which is part of the Joseph Smith Translation of the book of Genesis) preserves the tale of Adam having a conversation with an angel about his motivation for offering sacrifices unto the Lord and the deep meaning behind his ritual actions (see Moses 5:4–8). And in the New Testament book of Luke the account is told of a temple priest named Zacharias, who encountered an angel in the House of the Lord at Jerusalem. In these sacred precincts, the two of them had a conversation about Zacharias's earnest desire to be blessed with posterity (see Luke 1:5–20).

Many examples of this type of encounter can be found in LDS sources. One of them comes from the pen of Elder Russell M. Nelson. He recorded a sacred experience that took place in conjunction with the dedication of the Washington D.C. Temple in 1974. He was told this story by Elder Hugh B. Brown and wrote it down with permission. Elder Nelson states,

> On the morning of the temple dedication, President Brown greeted me with the news that he had been visited during the night by President Harold B. Lee (President Lee had died the year before). Elder Brown described it as a glorious visit, one that meant much to him, for President Lee had been aware of some of the difficulties encountered by President Brown in the decisions that led to the construction of the temple in Washington, D.C.
>
> Later that morning, as we took President Brown to breakfast, Sister Harold B. (Freda Joan) Lee approached us. As we exchanged greetings, President Brown said to her, "I had a glorious visit with Harold last night. He is just fine. It was so good to visit with him."

> This was such a moving experience for us all. We felt the presence of President Lee's spirit in the temple through the witness of President Brown.[16]

An additional example of this type of visitation comes from an account by John Parry. This man had joined the Church in England in 1846 and shortly thereafter had been appointed to preside over the Birkenhead branch. Brother Parry found that he was often troubled in his sleep by evil spirits, and so on one occasion he took the time to discuss his problem with the leader of the Liverpool branch. He wanted to know why he was being annoyed by these agents of the devil. The Liverpool branch president informed him that some people were troubled more than others by these wicked beings and advised him to say the following prayer before retiring for the night:

> "O God, the Eternal Father, I ask Thee in the name of Thy Son, Jesus Christ, to give Thine angels charge concerning me this night, and allow not the powers of darkness to molest my spirit nor body."
>
> He did this, and was troubled with evil spirits no more, until one night, feeling very sleepy, he uttered a hasty, formal prayer and went to bed. During the night he was almost overcome by the power of evil spirits, which were visible. Unable to utter a word, he prayed fervently in his mind to the Lord to release him. In an instant the heavens appeared to him to open, and he saw an angel descend towards him. The personage took hold of him and raised him up a little, and immediately the powers of darkness disappeared.
>
> Elder Parry asked the angel why it was that the Lord permitted the evil one to abuse him in such a manner, to which he replied: "Because thou didst not pray from the heart, but with thy lips."[17]

Finally, we have a visitation from beyond the veil as related by Elder Parley P. Pratt. In his autobiography he writes of the time when he was confined to a prison in Richmond, Missouri, after a mock trial had been convened by the enemies of the Saints. The conditions of his confinement were almost unbearable. Not only did he have to stay in a dark, cold, filthy room, but he also had to share his quarters with a set of unprincipled guards and one very obnoxious apostate from the faith. Under these most unpleasant conditions, Elder Pratt fasted and prayed for several days and asked the God of heaven, with a determined focus, to answer him this one question: would he ever be free again in mortality to enjoy the society of his family and preach the gospel to the inhabitants of the earth? He reports what happened next.

> [S]uddenly I seemed carried away in the spirit, and no longer sensible to outward objects with which I was surrounded. A heaven of peace and calmness pervaded my bosom; a personage from the world of spirits stood before me with a smile of compassion in every look, and pity mingled with the tenderest love and sympathy in every expression of the countenance. A soft hand seemed placed within my own, and a glowing cheek was laid in tenderness and warmth upon mine. A well known voice saluted me, which I readily recognized as that of the wife of my youth, who had for near two years been sweetly sleeping where the wicked cease from troubling and the weary are at rest. I was made to realize that she was sent to commune with me, and answer my question.
>
> Knowing this, I said to her in a most earnest and inquiring tone: "Shall I ever be at liberty again in this life and enjoy the society of my family and the Saints, and preach the gospel as I have done?" She answered definitely and unhesitatingly: "Yes!" I then recollected that I had agreed to be satisfied with the knowledge of *that one* fact, but now I wanted more.
>
> Said I: "Can you tell me how, or by what means, or when I shall escape?" She replied: "That thing is not made known to me yet." I instantly felt that I had gone beyond my agreement and my faith in asking this last question, and that I must be contented at present with the answer to the first.
>
> Her gentle spirit then saluted me and withdrew. I came to myself. The doleful noise of the guards, and the wrangling and angry words of the old apostate again grated on my ears, but heaven and hope were in my soul.[18]

Detecting Visitors

The Prophet Joseph Smith informed the adherents of the restored faith in his day that they could "look for angels and receive their ministrations, but [they were] to try the spirits and prove them, for it is often the case that men make a mistake in regard to these things." He also gave the reason for why the testing of otherworldly visitors is so vitally important. He informed the Saints that "lying spirits are going forth in the earth. There will be great manifestations of spirits, both false and true."[19]

The prospect of being deceived by the spirits of wicked individuals who have died or the evil spirits who were cast out with Lucifer in premortal times is greatly reduced if a person understands the keys whereby they may be detected. On the following pages are nine keys that may be employed if a person finds himself or herself face to face with a being from beyond the veil who claims to be sent by the Father.

Key 1: Divine Confirmation

It was the teaching of Joseph Smith that even though "the devil [or his followers] may appear as an angel of light" there is a sure way to determine their true identity. The Prophet said that any person who experiences a visitation can "ask God to reveal it. If it be of the devil, he will flee from you." But if the messenger is "of God he will manifest himself or make it manifest." We may go to the Lord and ask Him in regard to any such appearance, said President Smith, because "He will know all about it," especially if He is the one who sent the messenger in the first place.[20]

A good example of divine confirmation can be seen in the episode of the transfiguration of the Savior. As He stood upon a high mountain with Moses and Elijah, His face shone like the sun and His clothing became white, like that of a heavenly being. Then the voice of God the Father confirmed to Peter, James, and John that Jesus Christ was an authentic messenger sent from the heavenly realm. He said to them, "This is my beloved Son, in whom I am well pleased; hear ye Him" (Matt. 17:1–8).

Key 2: Physical Appearance

"Angels are beings who have bodies and appear to men in the form of man," explained the Prophet Joseph Smith.[21] In fact, said the

Prophet, "Angels are Saints with their resurrected bodies."[22] Orson F. Whitney taught, "Gods, angels and men are of one and the same species, in different spheres and stages of development."[23] And Elder Parley P. Pratt said much the same thing: "Gods, angels and men are all of one species, one race, one great family."[24] It follows, therefore, that "an angel of God never has wings."[25] Charles W. Penrose of the First Presidency said in 1912, "The popular notion that angels are winged beings, because it is stated by some scripture writers that they saw them 'flying through the heavens,' is a fallacy. . . . [A]ngels are of the same race and descent as men, whether in body or in spirit, and do not need wings for locomotion, nor do they appear in birdlike form." Furthermore, said President Penrose, "they are of the family of Deity in different degrees of progression and are 'in the image and likeness' of the Most High."[26] It follows that anyone who has an encounter with a personage not appearing completely human is not in the presence of a holy being.

Key 3: Clothing

We are fortunate to have an incident related by Joseph Smith that points to another key whereby a person can distinguish between true and false visitors. The Prophet said, "A man came to me in Kirtland, and told me he had seen an angel, and described his dress. I told him he had seen no angel, and that there was no such dress in heaven."[27] In trying to determine the difference between authorized and unauthorized messengers, then, it would seem appropriate to enquire into the type of clothing that is worn by angels.

It is evident from a variety of scriptural passages that the typical dress of God's kingdom is a long, pure white robe (see 1 Ne. 8:5; Rev. 3:5; D&C 20:6). In Joseph Smith's published history, however, he mentions an instance where a false messenger appeared to a Latter-day Saint "arrayed in white,"[28] and so it is important to point out that there are other pieces of clothing worn by some of the citizens of the upper realm which can serve to identify them as personages of high standing and authority.

For instance, a sash of white linen[29] or even one of a golden color (Rev. 1:13; 15:6) is sometimes worn on the outside of a true messenger's white robe. In addition, Brigham Young reported that he,

Truman O. Angell, and William W. Phelps saw a group of about forty angels hovering inside the Kirtland Temple, and they were all wearing whites robes and white caps.[30] Similarly, David O. McKay saw in a nighttime vision a great multitude of people in heaven, each of them dressed in "a white flowing robe, and a white headdress."[31] On one occasion when New York native Elam Cheney was sitting inside the Kirtland Temple listening to Joseph Smith deliver a sermon, he saw a group of six angels wearing white clothing, white caps, and white moccasins.[32] Elizabeth Tyler described an angel that she had seen to the Prophet Joseph Smith. She said that this being wore "a white robe, underclothing, and moccasins." He also "had on a peculiar cap, different from any she had ever seen." The Prophet confirmed to her that she had seen a genuine angel of the Lord.[33] Thus we come to understand that if a genuine messenger from God makes an appearance, they may be expected to wear things such as white underclothing, a white flowing robe, a white sash, white headgear, and white moccasins.

Key 4: Radiance or Glory

In Doctrine and Covenants section 129, attention is drawn to the fact that the spirits of the just have no body within which they can contain or hide their natural glory, and so they cannot help but shine when they appear unto mortals (see v. 6). Joseph Smith restated and expanded upon this idea when he said that these godly "spirits can only be revealed in flaming fire or glory. Angels [or resurrected beings] have advanced further, their light and glory being tabernacled; . . . [But] the spirits of the just . . . must be revealed in fire" or glory.[34]

Evil spirits are inherently dark beings. But we learn in the book of 2 Nephi that they have the ability to somehow transform themselves "*nigh unto* an angel of light" (9:9, emphasis added; see also D&C 128:20). But the difference in luminescence is detectable. We learn from a passage in the Pearl of Great Price that the light which accompanies the deceptive spirits of the infernal realm is dim in comparison to the glow of authentic celestial glory. When Satan appeared to Moses on a mountain and tried to lie to him about his identity, Moses was able to "judge between [Satan] and God," because when he was face to face with the Almighty he had been transfigured by His glory in order to be able to endure His presence. And he was also not able to look upon God with his "natural" sight. Yet when Moses was face to face with Satan he could look upon the adversary with his "natural" vision, which caused him to ask the impostor who stood before him, "Where is thy glory, for it is darkness unto me?" (Moses 1:1–2, 11–18).[35]

Key 5: Message

Another way to determine the difference between authorized messengers from the Lord and unlawful impostors is to understand the kind of things that a true envoy would be expected to say. We learn from Moroni chapter 7 that when "angels . . . minister unto the children of men" they are "subject unto [Christ], to minister according to the word of His command." It is further stated that "the office of their ministry is to call men unto repentance, and to fulfill and to do the work of the covenants of the Father, which He hath made unto the children of men, [and] to prepare the way among the children of men, by *declaring the word of Christ*" (vv. 29–31; emphasis added). Orson Pratt informs us that "false spirits have taught those who have listened to them, that there is no efficacy in the atonement" of the Redeemer.[36] Any messenger from the spirit world who rejects Jesus Christ or the established doctrines connected with Him is, therefore, definitely not an emissary sent from God and should be cast out of one's presence immediately—in the name of Jesus Christ.

President Joseph F. Smith notifies us about another aspect of messages that originate with the Lord. He said, "Spiritual light comes . . . through messengers of the Lord. . . . When spirits of just men made perfect are sent with a message from on high . . . [t]hey deliver their message in light, and that message tends to the practical uplifting, progress and advancement of men."[37] A heavenly message is thus distinguished by its useful and worthy purpose.

The Prophet Joseph Smith presented the Saints with two separate precepts that are related to communications that messengers may bring from beyond the curtain that divides the worlds. First, he said, "It is contrary to the economy of God for any member of the Church . . . to receive instructions for those in authority, higher than themselves," and he specified that "if any person [has] . . . a visitation from a heavenly messenger, *it must be for his own benefit and instruction.*"[38] The second precept provided by the Prophet has to do with the accepted doctrines of the Church. He revealed that a false messenger can be detected if they contradict a revelation that has formerly been given by God.[39]

Key 6: Actions

There are some things that messengers from the Lord simply will not do. For instance, "no true angel from God will ever come to ordain any man, because they have [already] been sent to establish the priesthood by ordaining [Joseph Smith] thereunto." Since the priesthood has already been established upon the earth, and it is possible to ordain many people to it, "no heavenly messenger will ever come to interfere with that power by ordaining any more" individuals. Therefore, "if any man comes to you professing to be ordained by an angel, he is either a liar or has been imposed upon in consequence of transgression by an angel of the devil, for [the] priesthood shall never be taken away from [the] Church."[40]

According to President Brigham Young there is a "system of laws by which the Gods and the angels are governed . . . [and] there is no being in all the eternities [who is not] governed by law."[41] Even the "wicked spirits," said Joseph Smith, seem to have "bounds, limits, and laws by which they are governed" or controlled.[42] From Wilford Woodruff we learn that "as a general thing, angels do not administer to anybody on the earth unless it is to . . . perform a work that men cannot do for themselves."[43] Indeed, we are informed by Joseph Fielding Smith that "it is contrary to the law of God" for heavenly messengers to "do anything for man that man can do for himself."[44] Therefore, it must be concluded that if a personage comes from behind the veil and executes acts for an individual that they can do independently, then that personage has not been sent from above.

Key 7: The Sign of the Dove

The Prophet Joseph Smith spoke of an infallible key connected with the discernment of angels when he taught that "the sign of the dove [was] instituted before the creation" and the "devil could not come in sign of a dove."[45] Why is it that the adversary cannot come in this particular sign? Because, said the Prophet, "the dove [is] an emblem or token of truth."[46] It was decided by Deity in premortal times that "the father of all lies" (2 Ne. 2:18; Ether 8:25; Moses 4:4) would not be allowed the ability to utilize this significant sign as a tool of deception. Joseph Smith could, therefore, confidently teach the Latter-day Saints that "any spirit or body that is attended by a dove you may know to be a pure spirit [or embodied personage]. Thus you may in some measure detect the spirits [or embodied personages] who may come unto you."[47]

Key 8: The Test of Deception

Doctrine and Covenants section 129 teaches of "keys whereby you may know whether any administration is from God." This revelation, which refers directly to the appearance of beings from beyond the veil, teaches,

> When a messenger comes saying he has a message from God, offer him your hand and request him to shake hands with you. If he be *an angel* he will do so, and you will feel his hand. If he be *the spirit of a just man made perfect* . . . he will not move, because it is contrary to the order of heaven for a just man to deceive; but he will still deliver his message. If it be *the devil as an angel of light,* when you ask him to shake hands he will offer you his hand, and you will not feel anything; you may therefore detect him (vv. 4–9, emphasis added).

In elaborating upon these instructions, the Prophet Joseph Smith said that the "spirit of a good man . . . from heaven, who has not a body, will never undertake to shake hands with you for he knows you cannot perceive his touch and never will extend his hand."[48] Furthermore, said President Smith, this particular class of spirit "will not offer . . . his hand for this is against *the law given him.*"[49] However, if the spirit is "from the devil, he will either shrink back from you [because he fears detection] or offer his hand, which if he does you will feel nothing, but be deceived."[50]

Key 9: The Keys of the Priesthood

It was the viewpoint of Elder Orson Pratt that only personages who are under a celestial law have the "right and legal authority to minister to the Saints" who dwell on the earth. Why? Because the Latter-day Saints are governed and administered by a celestial law and priesthood, said Elder Pratt, and "no beings or angels under an inferior law or priesthood, can administer unto any beings or Saints under a superior law and priesthood, for this would be a violation of the order of heaven." He also informs us that even though beings of an inferior class may indeed make appearances on the earthly side of the veil, the Saints "have no right to receive their teaching; for they hold not the keys of authority, neither understand the celestial law, and are without the priesthood; therefore they who hearken to their visions or their teaching are captivated and brought in[to] bondage to the inferior or lower kingdoms."

How, then, are the Saints to "distinguish between angels of authority, and such as have no authority, seeing there are so many different classes?" The only way to "distinguish correctly," said Elder Pratt, is to utilize "the keys of the priesthood, obtained through the ordinances of endowment."[51] The Prophet Joseph Smith referred to these items as "the keys of the kingdom" and explained that these "keys are certain signs and words by which false spirits and personages may be detected from true." One of their functions, said the Prophet, is to enable endowed men and women to "prevent imposition."[52]

Conclusion

The gift of beholding angels and the spirits of the just is one of the only spiritual blessings available to the Saints that will most likely not be granted if it is sought after through prayer. This is a gift bestowed only when the Lord deems it necessary to perform some work that mortals cannot perform for themselves. If it so happens that a person sees a being from beyond the veil, it is vitally important that they properly identify their visitor and thereby prevent impostors from leading them astray.

NOTES TO CHAPTER 14

1. See Andrew F. Ehat and Lyndon W. Cook, eds., *The Words of Joseph Smith: The Contemporary Accounts of the Nauvoo Discourses of the Prophet Joseph* (Orem, UT: Grandin Books, 1991), 117; hereafter cited as *WJS;* cf. 3 Ne. 7:18.

2. *WJS,* 14–15.
3. Brian H. Stuy, ed., *Collected Discourses* (Burbank, CA, and Woodland Hills, UT: B.H.S. Publishing, 1987–1992), 5:233; hereafter cited as *CD.* President Woodruff mentions in this source that he had, in fact, received the ministration of angels during his lifetime though he never prayed for that particular spiritual gift to be bestowed upon him (see ibid., 234).
4. *Improvement Era,* vol. 23, no. 3, January 1920, 231–32; hereafter cited as *IE.*
5. Ibid., vol. 1, no. 7, May 1898, 498, 500.
6. George D. Watt, ed., *Journal of Discourses* (Liverpool, England: Samuel W. Richards and Sons, 1852–1886), 2:279; hereafter cited as *JD.*
7. John A. Widtsoe, *Evidences and Reconciliations* (Salt Lake City: Bookcraft, 1987), 108.
8. See Brigham H. Roberts, ed., *History of The Church of Jesus Christ of Latter-day Saints* (Salt Lake City: Deseret Book, 1948–1950), 2:427; hereafter cited as *HC.* David Whitmer—who was one of the witnesses to the divine authenticity of the Book of Mormon—saw several angels inside this same consecrated building, but there is no indication that there was any communication between them (see ibid.).
9. Spencer W. Kimball, *Faith Precedes the Miracle* (Salt Lake City: Deseret Book, 1972), 39.
10. Hans Jensen Hals, Journal 1829–1910, 6 April 1893, LDS Church Archives, Salt Lake City, Utah.
11. *The Contributor,* vol. 13, no. 12, October 1892, 547–48.
12. Andrew Jenson, *Latter-day Saint Biographical Encyclopedia* (Salt Lake City: Deseret News Press, 1914), 2:600.
13. Zera Pulsipher, Autobiography, L. Tom Perry Special Collections Library, Brigham Young University, Provo, UT, 7.
14. Susa Young Gates, Lydia Knight's History (Salt Lake City: Juvenile Instructor Office, 1883), 71–72. The text of Lydia Knight's patriarchal blessing can be found in chapter 5 of this same volume.
15. Edward W. Tullidge, *The Women of Mormondom* (New York: Tullidge and Crandall, 1877), 458–59.
16. Russell M. Nelson, *The Gateway We Call Death* (Salt Lake City: Deseret Book, 1995), 100–101.
17. George Q. Cannon, ed., *Early Scenes in Church History* (Salt Lake City: Juvenile Instructor Office, 1882), 45.
18. Parley P. Pratt, *Autobiography of Parley P. Pratt* (Salt Lake City: Deseret Book, 1985), 204–205 (emphasis in original).
19. *HC,* 3:391–92.
20. *WJS,* 12.
21. Ibid., 44.
22. Ibid., 6.
23. *The Contributor,* vol. 8, no. 3, January 1887, 85.

24. Parley P. Pratt, *Key to the Science of Theology* (Salt Lake City: Deseret Book, 1965), 40.
25. *WJS,* 12.
26. *IE,* vol. 15, no. 10, August 1912, 951.
27. *HC,* 5:267.
28. Ibid., 4:581.
29. *Kansas City Times,* 11 April 1895. This is a statement by Katherine Smith (the Prophet's sister) regarding the angel Moroni.
30. See Scott G. Kenney, ed., *Wilford Woodruff's Journal: 1833–1898* (Midvale, UT: Signature Books, 1985), 5:120.
31. Clare Middlemiss, comp., *Cherished Experiences from the Writings of President David O. McKay* (Salt Lake City: Deseret Book, 1955), 102.
32. See Aaron Lindon Cheney, "History of Elam Cheney"; copies in private family possession.
33. *Juvenile Instructor,* vol. 27, no. 3, 1 February 1892, 93.
34. *HC,* 6:51.
35. Parley P. Pratt made the same point when he said:

"Good spirits, in the superlative sense of the word, are they who, in this life, partook of the Holy Priesthood, and of the fullness of the gospel.

"This class of spirits minister to the heirs of salvation, both in this world and in the world of spirits. They can appear unto men, when permitted, but not having a fleshy tabernacle, they cannot hide their glory. Hence, an unembodied spirit, if it be a holy personage, will be surrounded with a halo of resplendent glory or brightness above the brightness of the sun.

"Whereas spirits not worthy to be glorified will appear without this brilliant halo; and although they often attempt to pass as angels of light, there is more or less [an appearance] of darkness about them" (Pratt, *Key to the Science of Theology,* 116).

Pratt, in a fictional story that he composed during the Nauvoo period of Church history (and read in the presence of Joseph Smith), writes of seeing God seated upon a white throne with "a pillar of light above His head" (Parley P. Pratt, *The Angel of the Prairies* [Salt Lake City: Deseret News Printing and Publishing Establishment, 1880], 13–14). According to early LDS dissident Ezra Booth, the Prophet Joseph Smith made a very similar remark around 1831. Joseph reportedly said that when he saw an angel there was "a bright pillar upon his head" whereas when he saw the devil there was a "black pillar" upon his head. Booth reported that it was by this mark that the Prophet was able to distinguish between the two types of otherworldly beings (*Ohio Star,* vol. 2, 27 October 1831, 3). It is interesting to note a parallel provided by a man named John Butler who, in a vision shown to him in November 1857, saw "a personage filled with light, except for a dark circle over his head. John knew this personage was the devil transformed into an angel of light" (William G. Hartley, *My Best For the Kingdom: History and Autobiography of John Lowe Butler, A Mormon Frontiersman* [Salt Lake City: Aspen Books, 1993], 304).

36. *JD,* 15:253.
37. *IE,* vol. 13, no. 4, February 1910, 366.
38. *HC,* 1:338 (emphasis added).
39. See ibid., 4:581.
40. *Millennial Star,* vol. 8, no. 9, 20 November 1846, 139; hereafter cited as *MS.* This statement is attributed to the Prophet Joseph Smith.
41. *JD,* 14:280.
42. *HC,* 4:576.
43. *CD,* 1:218.
44. Joseph Fielding Smith, *Doctrines of Salvation* (Salt Lake City: Bookcraft, 1954), 1:196.
45. *WJS,* 160.
46. Ibid., 163.
47. Ibid., 66.
48. Ibid.
49. Ibid., 6 (emphasis added).
50. Ibid., 44.
51. *MS,* vol. 7, no. 2, 15 January 1846, 31–32.
52. *WJS,* 119–20. On another occasion the Prophet told a gathering of Relief Society sisters that they and the elders were going to receive these "keys" that they might "be able to detect everything false" (ibid., 117). George Laub noted in his Nauvoo, Illinois, journal that when he received his endowment, he was taught "how to detect false spirits or deceivers who profess to be apostles [i.e., sent ones] and are none" (*BYU Studies* 18.2 [winter 1978]: 165). An article written in a late nineteenth-century LDS publication says, "It is a duty we owe to ourselves to take on trust nothing whatever, but to put all things to [the] test before we accept them. Our first parents, after their banishment from the Garden of Eden, being then subject to evil as well as good, were instructed not to accept a message even though brought by what seemed [to be] an angel of light, unless that messenger should give a certain required signal. This is what [the Apostle] Paul meant when he said, 'Though any man, though an angel from heaven shall teach any gospel than that which [Christ] had taught, let him be accursed.' Thus spiritual teachers are required to show their credentials even as, in military life, he who approaches a sentinel on duty is required to give the countersign" (*The Contributor,* vol. 1, no. 4, January 1880, 88).

CHAPTER FIFTEEN
Tongues

It is given to some to speak with tongues; and to another is given the interpretation of tongues.

—*Doctrine and Covenants 46:24–25*

In the books of the New Testament we find that the gift of tongues is a two-pronged sign from God. The Lord Jesus Christ referred to the ability to "speak with new tongues" as one of the "signs [that] follow them that believe" (Mark 16:17), while the Apostle Paul said that "tongues are for a sign . . . to them that believe not" (1 Cor. 14:22). An illustration of both of these concepts can be found in the book of Acts. On the day of Pentecost, cloven tongues of fire sat upon the Twelve Apostles of the Savior, and, being filled with the Holy Ghost, they spoke "the wonderful works of God" in other tongues as the Spirit gave them utterance. The Gentiles who witnessed this extraordinary linguistic display "were all amazed" and, after being told by the Apostle Peter that the manifestation came by the Spirit of God, they were inclined to listen to his testimony and exhortations (2:1–40).

The Prophet Joseph Smith confirmed that "the gift of tongues [comes] by the power of the Holy Ghost."[1] When the Prophet dedicated the temple in Kirtland, Ohio, in 1836 he directly petitioned the God of heaven to repeat the New Testament pattern by pouring out the gift of tongues upon His covenant people, "even cloven tongues as of fire" (D&C 109:36). Oliver Cowdery verified that this request was granted for, on one occasion when he was in the midst of more than 300 Latter-day Saints, "the Spirit was poured out" and he "saw cloven tongues, like as of fire rest upon many" of them "while they spake with other tongues."[2] In the early part of the twentieth century the First Presidency of the LDS Church (consisting of Joseph F. Smith, Anthon H. Lund, and Charles W. Penrose) taught that the cloven tongues of fire were a visual sign of the coming of the Holy Ghost[3] or, as Elder B. H. Roberts put it, this was His "insignia" (cf. Matt. 3:11; 3 Ne. 9:20; D&C 19:31).[4]

Bridging the Language Gap

President Joseph Smith placed emphasis on the idea that "the ultimate design of [the gift of] tongues is to speak to foreigners."[5] "It was particularly instituted for the preaching of the gospel to other nations and languages," he said.[6] The Lord refers to this notion in Doctrine and Covenants section 90 where He says, "For it shall come to pass . . . that every man shall hear the fullness of the gospel in his own tongue, and in his own language, through those who are ordained unto this power, *by the administration of the Comforter*" (v. 11, emphasis added)—thus hinting that the preaching of the gospel may be accomplished at times through the employment of a spiritual gift.

Elder Orson Pratt pointed out that the great benefit of the gift of tongues is that the Lord's servants can more profitably spend their time preaching the doctrines of salvation rather than laboring in the ordinary way to learn the languages of the earth (which could take years). "If [these servants] could be endowed immediately by the power of the Holy Ghost to speak in any language necessary," said Elder Pratt, "how much laborious study would be avoided! How much time would be saved that could be occupied more usefully in the spread of the gospel! How much more accurately would principles be expressed when not only the ideas, but the language itself, is given by the Holy Ghost!"[7] It was maintained by George Q. Cannon that if he were called on a foreign-speaking mission, he would pray constantly for the gift of tongues and the gift of interpreting tongues. He also encouraged missionaries who are sent to foreign-speaking missions to seek for these two distinct gifts "with all earnestness and faith."[8]

Examples of missionaries being blessed with the gift of tongues abound. For example, Alonzo A. Hinckley (President Gordon B. Hinckley's uncle) reports that when he was called to serve as a missionary in the Netherlands he could not speak a word of the Dutch language but had a yearning to bear testimony to these people of the truthfulness of the gospel. He fasted and prayed as part of his regimen to learn this tongue but could only master a few simple sentences. With these rudimentary skills at his command he went through one neighborhood gathering missionary tracts that had earlier been handed out. At the first place he stopped, the power of God rested upon him, and he was able to understand every word of a lady who proceeded to say many vile things against the Church. Alonzo bore the following witness of what happened at that time: "I did receive upon that occasion, through the power of the Lord, the gift of tongues sufficiently to bear testimony to the divinity of the work of God, and to defend an innocent people, so much so that the woman herself was impressed by the Spirit of the Lord, for she broke down in tears and said, 'There may be bad people among the Latter-day Saints, but I know that you are a servant of the Lord.'"[9]

Next we have the recital of a story by Elder Rudger Clawson. This latter-day Apostle told the tale of two young elders who were laboring among the Boers of South Africa. He said of one of their teaching experiences,

> They came into a home where the wife could speak English, but the husband could not speak it, so these young men engaged in conversation with the wife. All at once the husband spoke up, he spoke in Dutch, and addressed his remarks to the elders, who were unacquainted with the language, and they both clearly understood what he said; and when they answered him in English, although he was not familiar with the English language, he understood them. But the remarkable thing about it was that when the Boer addressed the first elder in Dutch, the second elder could not understand him, but the first elder understood; and when the Boer addressed the second elder and asked him a question, he understood him, but the first elder could not understand it.[10]

As President Joseph Fielding Smith reiterated, the gift of tongues is closely connected with the work of spreading the gospel among the nations of the earth. "It is a remarkable fact," he admitted, "that the elders of the Church going forth to foreign lands have had the gift of tongues by which they have learned to speak these foreign tongues within very brief periods of time."[11]

It must be understood, however, that the gift of tongues is not restricted to preaching the gospel to potential converts. It can also be utilized by the Lord in the case of Saints preaching to other Saints. President Thomas S. Monson related one such occurrence. He said that he accompanied President Hugh B. Brown to Apia, Western Samoa. During a talk given by President Brown, a messenger came forward and handed the interpreter a note that read: "It is not necessary for you to interpret the remainder of President Brown's talk, for we are hearing him in our native tongue."[12] Harold B. Lee noted a similar incident in his diary. He wrote of a talk that he gave on October 4, 1959, in Montevideo, Uruguay: "In the morning session it was evident that as I spoke the audience was understanding and reacting to what I said before the interpreter had repeated it, even though they knew no English. It was a veritable evidence of the gift of tongues to many there."[13] A third witness to the gift of tongues comes from David O. McKay. He prayed directly to God the Father for the gift of tongues to be manifest among an LDS audience in Huntly, New Zealand, and as he delivered his sermon in English, some of the Maori nodded that they understood his words. Brother McKay asked that the interpreter repeat a summary of his remarks just in case some in the audience had not enjoyed the gift. While the talk was being summarized, however, some of the people who had understood the sermon (but did not understand English) arose and corrected the interpretation of the interpreter.[14]

Edifying the Saints

It is clear from a reading of the book of 1 Corinthians that the gift of tongues is given of God to mankind for the purpose of edification (see 14:5). Orson Pratt focused on this aspect of the gift when he stated that the Saints who lived in the Savior's time "were confirmed and strengthened in their faith by the enjoyment of this gift. Jesus had promised this miraculous sign, among many others, to believers; if they had failed to receive the blessings," noted Elder Pratt, "they would have had reason to doubt whether they were true believers; but when they received tongues, together with all other promised blessings, they were no longer in doubt, but were assured, not only of the truth of the doctrine, but that they themselves were accepted of

God."[15] German-born Karl G. Maeser (who later in life became one of the founders of Brigham Young University) was one person who was confirmed in the faith through the reception of the gift of tongues. On the night after he was baptized as a convert to the Church, he looked up into heaven and prayed, saying,

> Oh, God, I have found, as I believe, the gospel of thy Son Jesus Christ. I have rendered obedience to it by going down into the waters of baptism. Give to me a manifestation, give to me an absolute witness of the Spirit that I have found the truth, and I pledge to you if necessary my life for the advancement of this cause.

That night Brother Maeser was walking from the place of his baptism to his home in company with Elder Franklin D. Richards, who was then acting as the president of the European mission. These two men had an interpreter with them (William Budge) and through him Brother Maeser expressed his desire to converse with Elder Richards upon the principles of the gospel. Brother Maeser did not understand English, and Elder Richards did not understand German. After a few questions had been asked and answered, Elder Richards told the interpreter he did not need to have the questions relayed anymore since he was able to understand them. In turn, Brother Maeser told the interpreter that he did not need the answers to be relayed because he could understand them. The two men conversed in this condition as they walked for several miles. But when they reached a river and crossed over it they were separated from each other's company. When they regrouped the gift was gone; they needed the help of the interpreter once again. Karl asked, "How was it, Apostle Richards, that we understood each other, and now we cannot understand?" Elder Richards responded that "one of the fruits of the gospel of Jesus Christ was the gift of tongues and the interpretation. Then he said: 'God has given to you and to me this night the privilege of partaking of one of the fruits of the gospel by having the interpretation of tongues. Brother Maeser, you have received a witness from God that you have found the truth.'"[16]

The gift of tongues has been given by a gracious Heavenly Father on countless occasions to edify His Latter-day Saints. Historical records, periodicals, books, journals, and diaries record numerous instances of this blessing's bestowal. What is surprising is the diversity of ways whereby this gift can be exhibited. Tongues can be spoken or sung; they can occur during prayer, preaching, or ordination; they can happen spontaneously or after a heartfelt petition. No less surprising are the kinds of things that are spoken of or revealed during the manifestation of this gift. They include the following:

– Proclamations of blessings for faithfulness[17]

– Declarations of patriarchal lineage[18]

– Announcements of future trials and rewards[19]

– Exhortations for renewed hope and trust[20]

– Warnings about the results of actions[21]

– Promises for obedience[22]

– Prophecies of future callings[23]

– Revelations concerning present events[24]

– Songs that offer praise;[25] describe the various gospel dispensations;[26] refer to the coming of Christ;[27] speak of the redemption of Zion;[28] portray the travels, toils, and tribulations of the Nephites;[29] mention the blessings Adam bestowed upon his family at Adam-ondi-Ahman;[30] detail Enoch's visions;[31] admonish the Saints to keep covenants, follow Christ, pray, and live by faith and the word of God[32]

Cautionary Notes

There are a few words of caution that those who experience the gift of tongues should take special note of. They are centered on how one should react to the reception of this gift, what one should do after experiencing this gift, and what limitations are placed upon this gift.

Quenching the Spirit

It is obvious from the material discussed in this chapter that the gift of tongues can be manifest in many different ways and also with little or no warning. If a person is unfamiliar with the various dimensions and aspects of this gift, it may naturally cause some hesitancy or even distress. Joseph F. Smith gave the following counsel in regard to this blessing: "[I]f the Lord gives you the gift of tongues, *do not despise it, do not reject it*. For if it comes from the Spirit of God, it will come to those who are worthy to receive it, and it is all right."[33]

A man by the name of Benjamin Brown (who converted to the restored gospel after being assured of its authenticity through the visitation of angels) remembered the time of the Kirtland Temple dedication and how the Saints were blessed with a veritable latter-day Pentecost. He recalled that the Spirit of the Lord was profusely poured out, and hundreds of brethren spoke in tongues. But because many of them were young in the Church and had never witnessed such a manifestation before, they felt alarmed. This situation caused Joseph Smith to pray to the Lord to withhold the Spirit while he explained its operations in general and the gift of tongues in particular.[34]

Benjamin recorded another incident where the opportunity for a spiritual experience was lost through hesitancy—only this time the loss was his own. He was giving the opening prayer at a Sabbath day meeting when suddenly the gift of tongues fell upon him. But because he mistakenly thought that there wasn't anybody present who could interpret what he would say he quenched the Spirit, and it left him. Immediately thereafter one of the other men in the room arose and began to deliver a message in tongues.[35]

Yet another example of spiritual loss through inaction comes from Zina D. Huntington. Soon after her baptism on August 1, 1835, the gift of tongues rested upon her with what she referred to as "overwhelming force." She was "somewhat alarmed at this strange manifestation, and so checked its utterance." But then she discovered that as a result the gift had left her entirely, and she felt that she had offended the Holy Spirit. Zina suffered a great deal in her feelings over this matter and so she decided to do something to rectify the situation. Her report reads as follows:

> I walked down to a little spring in one of the meadows, and as I walked along I mused on my blessing and how I had turned away the Spirit of God. When I reached the spring, I knelt down and offered up a prayer to God and told Him if He could forgive my transgression, and give me back the lost gift, I would promise never to check it again, no matter where or when I felt its promptings.
>
> I have kept this vow, but it has been a heavy cross at times, for I know that this gift is the least of all gifts, and it is oftentimes misunderstood and even treated lightly by those who should know better. Yet it is a gift of God, and should not be despised by him who receives it, but magnified to its extent.[36]

Seeking Interpretation

During the dedication services of the Kirtland Temple on March 27, 1836, the Prophet Joseph Smith prayed not only for the Latter-day Saints to receive the gift of speaking in tongues, but he also petitioned God the Father for the gift of interpreting tongues (see D&C 109:36). According to Elder Orson Pratt, unknown tongues are interpreted "by the gift and power of the Holy Ghost."[37] Testimony from Zina Huntington confirms this fact. She said that once after she heard a manifestation of the gift of tongues, she "interpreted the talk by the help of the Spirit of God."[38]

It was one of Joseph Smith's steadfast rules that a person was to "speak not in the gift of tongues without understanding it, or without interpretation."[39] The primary reason for this rule is that without an interpretation there cannot be any edification for those who hear the words that are being spoken. In 1 Corinthians the Apostle Paul informed the Saints of his day that if there was no interpreter of an unknown tongue, then the Church as a whole could not be benefited because only God would understand what was being said (see 14:1–28).

The interpretation of tongues can be manifest in a variety of circumstances. "The gift of interpretation may be possessed by the one speaking in tongues," said Elder James E. Talmage, "though more commonly the separate powers are exercised by different persons."[40] A few examples of different situations may prove instructive here. A woman named Margrette W. Young recalled an incident where a brother in the Church who was present at a baptismal service spoke in tongues and then gave the interpretation himself.[41] A Mormon pioneer by the name of Millen Atwood once received the gift of tongues and at the same time the gift of interpretation rested upon his wife.[42] Sometimes the interpretation must be deliberately sought after. President Heber J. Grant reported that his wife once spoke in tongues to him but neither one of them was given the interpretation, and so they both knelt before the Lord and asked Him to reveal it.[43] Mary Lightner, who was baptized into the restored Church the same year that it was formally organized, was another person who petitioned the Lord for the gift of interpreting tongues. She had heard Oliver Cowdery, John Whitmer, and Thomas B. Marsh each speaking in tongues in great power during Sunday meetings and desired to understand what they were saying. She asked Heavenly Father for the privilege of understanding their words. On another occasion when these men were filled with the Spirit and manifesting their gift, she was called upon to interpret and was immediately able to do so.[44]

One vital reason for always seeking the interpretation of tongues is to prevent imposition by the adversary. It was the view of President Joseph F. Smith that "there is perhaps no gift of the Spirit of God more easily imitated by the devil than the gift of tongues."[45] As the Prophet Joseph Smith pointed out, if any person "were under the influence of [the devil's] spirit, they of course could speak Hebrew, Latin, Greek, Italian, Dutch or any other language that the devil knew."[46] Helen Mar Whitney (the eldest daughter of Heber C. Kimball) related an incident where the gift of interpreting tongues was actually used to detect an attempted imposition by the powers of evil. She recollected this event with the following words:

> At an evening meeting held at my mother's, one of the sisters, who had met with us but little, feeling the spirit resting upon her to speak in tongues, arose and began talking—at first very quietly. In a moment her voice changed, as did also her countenance, and her movements were such that there was no mistaking the spirit which was operating upon her. Two or three who were present had the gift of interpretation, and they said with one accord that she uttered nothing but the most wicked blasphemy. But this lasted only an instant as sister Laura Pitkin, who came into the Church at the beginning, arose and took hold of her arm, and in a quiet but commanding tone bade her sit

> down. She dropped into her chair as suddenly as though she had received a blow, and covering her face with her hands groaned aloud, as though realizing what she had done.[47]

Limitations on the Gift of Tongues

Like with any of the other gifts of the Spirit, the Lord will never bestow the gift of tongues upon an individual for the purpose of transcending the bounds of their stewardship. The Prophet Joseph Smith gave instructions to the Saints specifying that "the gift of tongues . . . was not given for the government of the Church."[48] President Brigham Young taught the very same principle saying, "the gift of tongues was given for a blessing to the Saints, but not to govern them, nor to control the Elders, or dictate the affairs of the Church."[49] Just the opposite was true, said Brother Brigham. "All gifts and endowments given of the Lord to members of the Church are not given to control the Church; but [rather the members] are under the control and guidance of the priesthood, and are judged of by it. Some have erred upon this point, and have been led captive by the devil."[50]

"Revelations for the Church and callings of individuals come not by the gift of tongues, but through the priesthood" leaders, noted Reuben Hedlock during one of the sessions of an 1846 general conference in Britain. "Revelations come from God through the head and not through the limbs," meaning (in reference to the Apostle Paul's analogy of the body and the gifts of the Spirit) that lay members with spiritual gifts do not trump the authority of the ordained authorities.[51] In this light, one of Joseph Smith's seemingly restrictive statements on the gift of tongues is both logical and wise. He insisted that "if anything is taught by the gift of tongues it is not to be received for doctrine."[52] Only certain high-ranking Church officials have been entrusted with the responsibility of determining doctrinal issues, not the average Saint—no matter how gifted they may be.

An editorial published in the *Messenger and Advocate* in the mid-1830s sums up the foregoing ideas well. It cites a modern revelation and then provides a brief, but pointed, comment. It reads:

> "Thou shalt take the things which thou has received which have been given unto thee in my scriptures for a law, [. . .] to govern my Church" [D&C 42:59]. . . .

> Here we learn that we are to be governed by the laws of God, and not by the gifts of tongues, or whims and caprices of men.[53]

Conclusion

The gift of tongues is a surprisingly diverse blessing of the Spirit, which can be manifest in many different ways. In the early days of the Restoration it was common to witness this dramatic gift among the Latter-day Saints, today, however, it is less publicly visible yet popularly linked with the Church's missionary program. Still, there are some modern-day instances where a person is given the ability to spontaneously, but temporarily, speak or understand a foreign language that they know nothing about. When the Lord restores the Adamic language to the earth, the gift of tongues will no longer be necessary because there will be unity in communication. But until then, the gift of tongues is useful in spreading the message of the gospel and building God's kingdom among the various nationalities of the earth.

NOTES TO CHAPTER 15

1. Brigham H. Roberts, ed., *History of The Church of Jesus Christ of Latter-day Saints* (Salt Lake City: Deseret Book, 1948–1950), 4:485; hereafter cited as *HC.*
2. Leonard J. Arrington, "Oliver Cowdery's Kirtland, Ohio, 'Sketch Book,'" *BYU Studies* 12.4 (summer 1972): 426.
3. See *Improvement Era,* vol. 19, no. 5, March 1916, 461; hereafter cited as *IE.*
4. Brigham H. Roberts, *Seventy's Course in Theology* (Salt Lake City: Deseret News, 1907–1912), 5:79.
5. *HC,* 5:31.
6. Ibid., 2:162; see also ibid., 3:379.
7. Orson Pratt, *Orson Pratt's Works on the Doctrines of the Gospel* (Salt Lake City: Deseret News Press, 1945), 83–84.
8. Jerreld L. Newquist, ed., *Gospel Truth: Discourses and Writings of George Q. Cannon* (Salt Lake City: Deseret Book, 1987), 155–56.
9. Conference Report, October 1904, 22–23; hereafter cited as CR.
10. Ibid., April 1909, 94–95.
11. Joseph Fielding Smith, *Church History and Modern Revelation* (Salt Lake City: The Church of Jesus Christ of Latter-day Saints, 1947), 2:152; hereafter cited as *CHMR.*
12. *Church News,* 2 September 1989, 8; hereafter cited as *CN.*

13. L. Brent Goates, *Harold B. Lee: Prophet and Seer* (Salt Lake City: Bookcraft, 1985), 283.
14. *CN,* 18 October 1952, 2.
15. Pratt, *Orson Pratt's Works on the Doctrines of the Gospel,* 84–85.
16. CR, April 1927, 16–17.
17. See James B. Allen, Ronald K. Esplin, and David J. Whittaker, *Men with a Mission: The Quorum of the Twelve Apostles in the British Isles* (Salt Lake City: Deseret Book, 1992), 109, 116.
18. See Journal of Wandle Mace, LDS Church Archive, Salt Lake City, Utah, 21.
19. See William Holmes Walker, Autobiography, L. Tom Perry Special Collections Library, Brigham Young University, Provo, UT, 3.
20. See Edward W. Tullidge, *The Women of Mormondom* (New York: Tullidge and Crandall, 1877), 431.
21. See CR, April 1900, 33; *IE,* vol. 8, no. 2, December 1904, 109–11.
22. See Jacob Hamblin, Autobiography, L. Tom Perry Special Collections Library, Brigham Young University, Provo, UT, 7.
23. See CR, April 1935, 13.
24. See Tullidge, *Women of Mormondom,* 207; George Q. Cannon, ed., *Gems for the Young Folks* (Salt Lake City: Juvenile Instructor Office, 1881), 67.
25. See *The Contributor,* vol. 3, no. 5, February 1882, 157–58.
26. See Andrew Jenson, *Latter-day Saint Biographical Encyclopedia* (Salt Lake City: The Andrew Jenson History Company, 1901–1936), 3:564.
27. See *Millennial Star,* vol. 27, no. 9, 4 March 1865, 133; hereafter cited as *MS.*
28. See *IE,* vol. 2, no. 6, April 1899, 447.
29. See Donald Q. Cannon and Lyndon W. Cook, eds., *Far West Record: Minutes of the Church of Jesus Christ of Latter-day Saints, 1830–1844* (Salt Lake City: Deseret Book, 1983), 66.
30. See Tullidge, *Women of Mormondom,* 474–75.
31. See Kirtland Revelation Book, February 1833, LDS Church Archives, Salt Lake City, Utah.
32. See Lorenzo Brown, Journal, L. Tom Perry Special Collections Library, Brigham Young University, Provo, UT, 5.
33. CR, April 1900, 41 (emphasis added).
34. See Cannon, ed., *Gems for the Young Folks,* 65.
35. Ibid., 67.
36. *Young Woman's Journal,* vol. 4, no. 7, April 1893, 318–19.
37. George D. Watt, ed., *Journal of Discourses* (Liverpool, England: Samuel W. Richards and Sons, 1852–1886), 7:178; hereafter cited as *JD.*
38. Zina Diantha Huntington Diary, LDS Church Archives, Salt Lake City, Utah.
39. *HC,* 3:392.
40. James E. Talmage, *The Articles of Faith* (Salt Lake City: Deseret News Press, 1901), 227.

41. See Autobiography of Margrette W. Pierce Whitesides Young, LDS Church Archives, Salt Lake City, Utah.
42. See Tullidge, *Women of Mormondom,* 431.
43. See *IE,* vol. 30, no. 1, November 1926, 19–20.
44. See Mary Lightner, Autobiography, *Utah Genealogical and Historical Magazine,* 195.
45. Joseph F. Smith, *Gospel Doctrine* (Salt Lake City: Deseret Book, 1949), 201.
46. *HC,* 4:579.
47. Jeni Broberg Holzapfel and Richard Neitzel Holzapfel, eds., *A Woman's View: Helen Mar Whitney's Reminiscences of Early Church History* (Provo, UT: BYU Religious Studies Center, 1997), 461–62.
48. *CHMR,* 3:46.
49. Elden J. Watson, ed., *Manuscript History of Brigham Young: 1801–1844* (Salt Lake City: Smith Secretarial Service, 1968), 60.
50. *JD,* 11:136.
51. *MS,* vol. 7, no. 12, 15 June 1846, 193.
52. Andrew F. Ehat and Lyndon W. Cook, eds., *The Words of Joseph Smith: The Contemporary Accounts of the Nauvoo Discourses of the Prophet Joseph* (Orem, UT: Grandin Books, 1991), 119.
53. *Messenger and Advocate,* vol. 2, no. 15, December 1835, 240.

CHAPTER SIXTEEN
Visions

I will pour out my Spirit . . . [and you] shall see visions.

—*Joel 2:28*

Those who examine LDS historical documents will discover that the nineteenth-century Saints included visions in catalogs of the spiritual gifts of the gospel.[1] "A vision from God," explains the *Encyclopedia of Mormonism,* "is a form of revelation whereby God discloses Himself and His will. It is a visual mode of divine communication, in contrast with hearing words spoken or receiving impressions to the mind." Visions are "perceptions, aided by the Spirit, of something ordinarily invisible to human beings."[2]

Examples of God-given visions are scattered throughout scriptural texts, and the mechanism by which they are delivered is clearly identified. In the book of Acts, the Apostle Stephen, "being full of the Holy Ghost," saw the heavens open and witnessed "the Son of Man standing on the right hand of God" (7:55–56). The book of Ezekiel teaches that Ezekiel was enabled to see a vision through the instrumentality of "the Spirit of God" (11:24). And the seventy-sixth section of the Doctrine and Covenants relates an instance where the Lord touched the eyes of the understanding of two of His servants "by the power of the Holy Spirit" so that they could simultaneously see representations of things that were normally hidden from their view (vv. 19, 116). Lastly, in the Book of Mormon, when the prophet Nephi was allowed to see a vision of things that his father had previously seen, he was prepared for the experience by being "caught away in the Spirit of the Lord" (1 Ne. 11:1).

Visions may be straightforward in their presentation and message, such as when the Apostle Paul was warned by the Savior to depart from the city of Jerusalem (see Acts 22:17–18), or they may be constructed of multiple symbolic elements, like the one that was shown to the Apostle Peter to convince him to take the gospel to the Gentiles (see ibid., 10:10–16). Wilford Woodruff teaches us the important precept that when a symbolic vision is represented before our eyes, "it is [designed] to teach us a principle. We may never see anything take place exactly as we see it in . . . a vision, yet it is intended to teach us a principle," he said.[3] Thus, as with the interpretation of inspired dreams, it is profitable to look beyond the visual symbols themselves and to identify the overall themes which they represent. The Prophet Joseph Smith taught that in the case of symbolic visions we can always turn to the Lord for assistance in understanding their elements. He said that if "God ever gives a vision of an image or beast or figure of any kind, He always holds Himself responsible to give a revelation or interpretation of the meaning thereof."[4] Therefore, said the Prophet, "when you see a vision pray for the interpretation. If you get not this [interpretation from the Lord], shut it up [i.e., put the vision aside, end it; cf. Dan. 8:26; D&C 76:47]. There must be certainty in this matter."[5]

Seership is a specialized form of the visionary gift and, as represented in the writings of Mosiah in the Book of Mormon, it is the greatest gift that God can bestow upon one of His mortal children. The recipient of this "high gift from God" is granted the ability to see as God sees, which means that "all things" can be revealed to their view, including matters pertaining to the past, the present, and the future (8:14–17). Elder Orson Pratt offered some interesting comments on how this incomparable gift of sight operates. He said,

> Among the choice blessings of the kingdom of God, may be mentioned the seer's gift or the gift of seeing with the Urim and Thummim.
>
> This gift is a peculiar manifestation of the Spirit to the natural eyes, as well as to the mind. The Urim and Thummim is a stone or other substance sanctified and illuminated by the Spirit of the living God, and presented to those who are blessed with the gift of seeing.

> [Not] all Saints [can] see by the illuminations of the Urim and Thummim.[6]

Seership is the power to see as God sees. Heber C. Kimball expanded our understanding when he said that the Urim and Thummim operate by the same "spirit, element, and power" that enables angels to "look" and also whereby God "sees all things."[7] And the Prophet Joseph Smith pointed us to a significant connection between these earthly instruments and a heavenly counterpart when he stated that the Urim and Thummim stones are symbolic representations of the planet or globe where God resides, which is itself a great Urim and Thummim, having the capacity to reveal "things past, present and future."[8] In addition, we have the significant insight from Orson Pratt that it was only necessary for Joseph Smith to use his personal seerstone until he had become "thoroughly endowed with the inspiration of the Almighty and the spirit of revelation." It was then no longer necessary for him to use a special stone to exercise the gift of seership.[9] He had learned how to become infused with the power of the Spirit of God to such a degree that he could tap into the visions of eternity with his own body; he became a larger version of the earthly Urim and Thummim.

Visionary Experiences

The blessing of visions is available to all righteous Latter-day Saints. Elder Bruce R. McConkie advocated the idea that "every member of the Church, independent and irrespective of any position that he may hold, . . . is entitled to view the visions of eternity."[10] An event in the life of President Woodruff illustrates this point well. By April 1837 Brother Woodruff had only been a member of the restored Church of Jesus Christ for a little more than three years and three months and held the office of a Seventy. On the seventh day of April, he and two other men went to the Kirtland Temple with the intent of attempting to "enter into the visions of heaven." They knelt in prayer within the veils that covered the pulpits, but Satan strove against them with great power in order to try and deprive them of the privilege that they sought. Brother Woodruff was overcome by the adversary at one point and had to leave the pulpits. On reaching the outer court of the building, he found Freeman Nickerson, a faithful father in the house of Israel. Brother Woodruff asked Freeman to join his group of brethren in prayer so that they might "gain a victory over Satan and get a blessing at the hand of God." The four men knelt together before the Lord in His holy house and being "united in heart," with "faith through Jesus Christ," they overcame Satan's power, and he departed from them. The Spirit of God then descended upon these faithful brethren until it felt like fire shut up in their bones, and they were shown "many great things" in vision.[11]

Visions can be utilized by the Lord to accomplish many different types of tasks. For instance, a vision might be shown to an individual as a notification of divine approval. An unidentified Scotsman who embraced the gospel in the latter part of the nineteenth century said that "while the Elder's hands were on his head, during the ordinance of confirmation, his mind seemed to be caught away from his surroundings and he beheld a glorious vision. . . . Among many other things he seemed to see three personages, whose appearance was very glorious. One of these held a large book, which seemed to be the book of life. This book he opened and after turning to a particular page, he said to the other two personages—pointing to the brother who was being confirmed—'This man's sins are remitted.'" The Scotsman professed that because of this spiritual experience he knew in his own mind that his newfound religion was indeed the work of God.[12]

Another use to which a visionary experience can be put is to help a mortal to understand their place in the grand scheme of things. During one of the sessions of general conference in April 1910, Elder Orson F. Whitney of the Quorum of the Twelve recalled an occasion when, by vision, he viewed the wide span of earthly history and saw his own place within it. He indicated in his remarks that his personal testimony that the LDS Church was God's truth came to him while he was laboring as a missionary in Kirtland, Ohio. He was walking up a hill toward the temple one evening when suddenly his mind was illuminated and expanded until it seemed as if he could comprehend all of human history from the time of Adam down to the end. The whole plan of redemption was opened before his mind, and he saw why the LDS Church had been established. He saw why prominent men had been placed on the earth in the past, during the various gospel dispensations. And in the future he could see events for which the great work of the latter days was preparing. Elder Whitney said of this event, "I saw nothing with my natural eyes, but from that moment I recognized my place in history; I saw what God required of me. I knew where I came from, why I am here, and where I am going. And that conviction has never left me; it is the greatest thing the Lord ever gave to me."[13]

Another way a vision can be utilized by the Lord is in teaching a person something about the circumstances of their mortal probation. Eliza R. Snow recorded that after her baptism into the restored Church of Jesus Christ, she received a baptism of the Spirit as sensibly as her submersion in water. She related the following: "I had retired to my bed, and as I was reflecting on the wonderful events transpiring around me, I felt an indescribable, tangible sensation, if I may so call it, commencing at my head and enveloping my person and passing off at my feet, producing inexpressible happiness. Immediately following, I saw a beautiful candle with an unusual long, bright blaze directly over my feet. I sought to know the interpretation, and received the following, 'The lamp of intelligence shall be lighted over your path.'"[14]

A vision may be shown to a person if they are in need of reassurance during trying circumstances. This was the case with Amasa Lyman. In the winter of 1845–46, Amasa was living in Nauvoo, Illinois. It was a time of great disturbance as the Saints were being hounded by their enemies to leave the city that they had built up and cherished. At this time Amasa was confined to bed because of an illness. He was awake in his bed one morning when suddenly the objects that surrounded him disappeared, and he found himself standing outside in a vacant lot near the printing office. He then heard a rumbling noise such as is made by a large group of people who are on the move. He looked down Main Street and saw a mass of humanity coming toward him, but as they approached he saw that they were not walking on the ground. Rather, they were moving through the air at the height of the top of the buildings. At the front of this group Amasa saw Joseph Smith, Hyrum Smith, and Don Carlos Smith, each wearing white robes with golden sashes and each carrying a sword in his hand. These three deceased Church leaders stopped the large company of people in front of Amasa and faced west (the direction the body of the Church was about to go in the mass exodus). Brother Lyman reported, "After contemplating the scene a few moments, I was again in my bed as before, and the vision had disappeared. This was my assurance, in the commencement of our troubles there, that I received of the guardianship that was around us and the protection that we were receiving from the hosts of heaven."[15]

Visions are sometimes employed by the Almighty to comfort those who grieve in their time of loss. Lorenzo Snow wrote to Parley P. Pratt about a manifestation of this type. He said that on October 28, 1841, Elizabeth Morgan of London, England, had passed away with her family and friends at her bedside. Before Elizabeth's passing she asked Elder Snow to pray for her, and then she would depart in peace. Lorenzo complied with this request but noted that while he was praying, the Holy Spirit rested down upon him in power, and he felt moved upon to ask for the comfort of Elizabeth's grieving husband, "even if it was by the ministering of Sister Morgan's departed spirit, that he might thereby have consolation and fullness of hope." At the same hour that this prayer was being offered, another sister in the Church, living in the same city, had an open vision displayed before her. She "saw Sister Morgan standing in full view before her, clothed in robes beautiful and white, and around about her head were clouds of glory, surpassing in splendor and brilliancy, the sun at noonday." This sister rejoiced in her vision and immediately informed her husband of its occurrence. When word of this event reached Elizabeth's husband, "he lifted up his head and rejoiced in sorrow, receiving consolation in the valley of grief." He had no doubt that his companion now rested "in mansions of peace and glory."[16]

Moses Thatcher reported seeing an interesting vision that assisted him in fulfilling his missionary responsibilities. Moses was baptized on December 29, 1856, in California. He was ordained an elder the following March, and only one month later, he was called to serve a mission—at the age of fifteen. The very thought of trying to preach made Moses ill, and when he attempted to speak about the Restoration in public he found himself unable to utter a single word. Moses pleaded with his missionary companion not to call upon him to preach or pray in public; a request that was mercifully complied with. But on one occasion he found himself alone in another denomination's meeting where the religion of the Latter-day Saints was being vilified. "Moses was profoundly moved and in humble, earnest, inward prayer besought the Lord to manifest to him his duty and give him strength to perform it. In answer he was impressed to reply. Securing permission to speak, the Spirit of God came upon him powerfully and, without the least hesitation or manifestation of timidity, he disproved many of the assertions" that had been made about his faith. Then he began having visions. He testified that on some occasions he was wrapped "in the Spirit [and] sometimes spoke for an hour, often correctly quoting scripture he had never read, the words and sentences, as he declared, appearing before his spiritual eyes." He simply read what he saw "as from an open book."[17]

Some visions from God can contain prophetic and symbolic elements, and it is evident from examples of these manifestations that the symbolism can range from the simple to the complex. An instance where a simple set of symbols was used to convey a message can be seen in a story published in 1838 in the *Elders' Journal*. James G. Marsh—the nine-year-old son of Elder Thomas B. Marsh—declared that he had been shown in vision that the daughter of Hezekiah Peck, who was his neighbor, was going to die, and he saw angels escorting her spirit to paradise. The Lord explained to young James that this vision was vouchsafed to "show him that there is no bitterness in the death of the righteous." This young girl did in fact pass away a short time later.[18]

An example of a more intricate symbolic vision comes to us from Zera Pulsipher. He relates that in March 1837 he and some other people were out working in the woods about one mile south of the Kirtland Temple. A rattling sound like a dozen wagons going over cobblestones caught his attention, but as it drew nearer he discovered that there were no wagons approaching. The sound came from the air, and as it passed directly over his head, Zera heard the distinct sound of a steamboat whistle. Then he actually saw a steamboat moving through the air, filled with passengers. At the bow of this ethereal boat was Alva Beaman, who had served as the president of the Kirtland elders quorum but had recently passed away. He was swinging his hat and singing. When the steamboat came to the front of the Kirtland Temple, Zera saw it split in half; one part was white and the other black. The black part of the boat went off to the north while the white part traveled west. The interpretation of this vision became clear to Brother Pulsipher when a bitter apostasy was instigated by some Church leaders in Kirtland just a few months later and the main body of the Church went west and settled in Missouri.[19]

Finally, Ezra Thayre tells of a symbolically complex vision. Around October 1830, Ezra was not a member of the restored Church but was "in the Spirit" at his home when a representation of Oliver Cowdery appeared before him carrying a scroll and a trumpet. In the vision, Oliver presented the scroll to Ezra. This scroll represented Doctrine and Covenants section 33, and Oliver stated that it was a revelation from God (this revelation was given through Joseph Smith just a short time later). Oliver then told Ezra to blow the trumpet, and Ezra reports that upon his blowing this instrument, "it made the most beautiful sound" that he had ever heard (in D&C 33:2 the Lord commands Ezra to declare His gospel "as with the sound of a trump"). This vision passed away and another vision was then opened to Ezra's view. He saw himself driving down an unfamiliar road. He saw houses, a green meadow, a grist mill, horses, and six people—one of whom was Parley P. Pratt. Ezra saw Parley pull two large fish and one small fish out of the water that was next to the grist mill. He was made to understand that the two large fish represented himself and Keziah Cowdery (who was Oliver Cowdery's mother), while the small fish represented Northrop Sweet. Ezra recognized all of the objects from this vision on the day of his baptism at the mill; Northrop Sweet left the Church soon after he was baptized.[20]

Conclusion

A vision is a gift of the Spirit that enables us to view things by the power of the Holy Spirit—not only with an enhanced physical faculty but also with a broader inner perspective. We may be shown simple scenes that are easy to understand or complex images that require interpretation. We may see something concerning others or something about ourselves. We may even be granted the great privilege of seeing things from God's eternal perspective and thereby gain knowledge of the past, the present, and the future. Regardless of what we see, if we experience the gift of visions, our perception will change, and we will never view our lives, purpose, or possibilities in quite the same way. And that is precisely why we as Latter-day Saints should earnestly seek after this gift.

NOTES TO CHAPTER 16

1. See *Times and Seasons,* vol. 2, no. 14, 15 May 1841, 410; see also ibid., vol. 3, no. 1, 15 November 1841, 579; *Millennial Star,* vol. 2, no. 12, April 1842, 188; hereafter cited as *MS;* George D. Watt, ed., *Journal of Discourses* (Liverpool, England: Samuel W. Richards and Sons, 1852–1886), 3:298; hereafter cited as *JD;* Article of Faith 7.
2. Daniel H. Ludlow, ed., *Encyclopedia of Mormonism* (New York: Macmillan, 1992), 4:1511.
3. *JD,* 22:333.
4. Andrew F. Ehat and Lyndon W. Cook, eds., *The Words of Joseph Smith: The Contemporary Accounts of the Nauvoo Discourses of the Prophet Joseph* (Orem, UT: Grandin Books, 1991), 185.
5. Ibid., 12.
6. Nels B. Lundwall, comp., *Masterful Discourses and Writings of Orson Pratt* (Salt Lake City: N. B. Lundwall, 1946), 552.
7. *JD,* 4:2.
8. George D. Smith, ed., *An Intimate Chronicle: The Journals of William Clayton* (Salt Lake City: Signature Books and Smith Research Associates, 1995), 96; see also D&C 130:6–11.
9. Letter, Orson Pratt and Joseph F. Smith to John Taylor, published in *Deseret News,* 23 November 1878.
10. *New Era,* June 1980, 48.
11. Dean C. Jessee, "The Kirtland Diary of Wilford Woodruff," *BYU Studies* 12.4 (summer 1972): 392–93.
12. *Juvenile Instructor,* vol. 13, no. 11, 1 June 1878, 129–30.
13. Conference Report, April 1910, 59–60.
14. Nicholas G. Morgan Sr., ed., *Eliza R. Snow: An Immortal* (Salt Lake City: Nicholas G. Morgan Sr. Foundation, 1957), 6.
15. *JD,* 5:58–59.
16. *MS,* vol. 2, no. 7, November 1841, 109–10.
17. Andrew Jenson, *Latter-day Saint Biographical Encyclopedia* (Salt Lake City: Deseret News Press, 1901), 1:128–29.
18. *Elders' Journal,* vol. 1, no. 3, July 1838, 48.
19. Zera Pulsipher, Autobiography, L. Tom Perry Special Collections Library, Brigham Young University, Provo, UT, 9.
20. *Saints' Herald,* vol. 3, October 1862, 79–80, 82–84.

CHAPTER SEVENTEEN
Casting Out Evil Spirits

I cast out devils by the Spirit of God.

—MATTHEW 12:28

In premortal times Lucifer offered himself for the role of the Redeemer of mankind but was not chosen to act in that capacity (see Abr. 3:22–28; Moses 4:1–4). He did not accept this decision but instead became angry and was able to convince a third part of the Father's spirit children to join him in an open rebellion against their King. This group of spirits was punished for their treason by being permanently cast out of their Progenitor's presence and relocated to the earth. Here they have made war with those who did not transgress like them (see Rev. 12:1–17; D&C 76:28–29; cf. 1 Pet. 5:8). In the Book of Mormon it is made known that the ultimate aim of Lucifer is to make all of mankind as miserable as he is (see 2 Ne. 2:27).

Fortunately for Latter-day Saints, they are not left defenseless against the arch enemy of God and against his malevolent cohorts. One of the "spiritual gifts" of the gospel that the Father has granted to the disciples of Jesus Christ is that of "casting out devils."[1] This gift is available to both men and women[2] who have formally allied themselves with the Savior.

The passage found in Matthew where the adversary tempts the Savior clearly demonstrates that the Lord Jesus Christ possesses authority to command Satan to depart from His presence (see 4:10–11). In other New Testament scriptures it is also apparent that those who follow Satan acknowledge that Jesus Christ is the Son of God, and they understand that He possesses the power to command their departure and bring about their destruction (see Luke 4:36; Mark 1:23–27, 34; Matt. 8:16). From the combination of these texts we can surmise that Satan and his followers are compelled to acknowledge both the power and the authority of the Master.

The godly power that is utilized in expelling evil spirits is explicitly identified in Matthew 12:28, where the Messiah Himself says, "I cast out devils by the Spirit of God." The casting out of evil spirits is, therefore, considered a gift of the Spirit. Ancient scriptures tell us that Jesus Christ grants His disciples the authority to use His name (in the manner of a proxy) to cast out devils (see Mark 16:17; Moses 1:18–22; 3 Ne. 7:19). The Lord specifies, however, in Doctrine and Covenants section 84 that it is only after individuals are baptized and "receive the Holy Ghost" that they will be granted the privilege of using His name to "cast out devils" (vv. 64, 67).[3] Thus, the disciples of Christ are armed with the very same power whereby He casts out evil spirits—they are armed with the Spirit of God.

Casting out devils is a miracle that the Savior allows His disciples to perform without first receiving a direct command from Him to do so (see D&C 24:13–14). But the person who desires to perform this type of miracle is directed to first ask God the Father, in faith, and in the name of Jesus Christ, for the power necessary to perform it (see ibid., 35:9). Proper acknowledgment of the source of this miracle is important lest the person through whom it is wrought gets carried away with an improper sense of their role in the matter. Joseph Smith once said, after he had cast an evil spirit out of a person, "It was done not by man, nor by the power of man; but it was done by God, and by the power of godliness; therefore, let the honor and the praise, the dominion and the glory, be ascribed to the Father, Son and Holy Spirit."[4]

Elder Orson Pratt provided valuable insight into why the Lord grants individual members of His earthly kingdom the ability to cast evil spirits out of their presence. He said the following about New Testament history:

> Devils and unclean spirits frequently took possession of the human tabernacle, tormenting individuals in various ways. Jesus promised believers that they, in His name, should cast them out.

> Now one object which Jesus had in view in granting this power, was to benefit the one possessed. Another object was to confirm the believers, that they by having power over the devil in this life, might be more fully assured that they should obtain a complete victory and final triumph over him in the world to come. That person who cannot obtain power in the name of Jesus to cast out devils in this life, has great reason to fear lest the devil shall obtain power over him in the next life. What assurance has anyone that he shall obtain a complete salvation from the power of the devil, when his spirit shall leave the body, if he cannot claim the promise of Jesus, and cast him out while his spirit dwells in the body? One of the purposes, then, which Jesus had in view in bestowing this blessing was that believers might learn to prevail against the devil before they should enter the invisible world of spirits.[5]

There are a number of mythical ideas that are associated with the gift of casting out evil spirits. An exploration of these myths may prove to be profitable for students of the gospel as well as those who may happen to have unpleasant personal encounters with unholy visitors from the unseen realm.

Myth 1: Using the Name of Jesus Christ Is All That Is Required in Expelling Evil Spirits

The basic pattern for casting out unclean entities, as outlined in scripture, is to verbally command them to depart in the name of Jesus Christ (see 3 Ne. 7:19). It is evident that the denizens of hell fear the use of this holy name against them,[6] but, as mentioned in the paragraphs above, the power of heaven needs to accompany the use of this name (see Matt. 12:28). The following stories will illustrate several other ingredients necessary for a successful exorcism of these foul beings.

Wilford Woodruff reported an instance where he was requested to assist in casting an evil spirit out of a sister in the Church who resided in Manchester, England. She was in a terrible rage and had to be restrained by three men. When Wilford arrived to attend to this task, he found that a crowd had gathered—consisting of Saints and also unbelievers who wanted to see a miracle performed. Elder Woodruff wished that the crowd would be dispersed so that faith could prevail, but seeing as how he was a stranger in the place, he made no such request. He and William Clayton laid their hands upon the afflicted woman's head and administered to her. "But the unbelief of the wicked present was so great," said Elder Woodruff, "we could not cast the devil out of her, and she raged worse than ever." He then ordered the room cleared of everyone except a few of the woman's personal attendants, and then he laid his hands upon her head once again, along with Brother Clayton, and commanded the devil to depart in the name of the Son of God. This time the desired effect was achieved. Then only a few days later an evil spirit tormented the woman's little child (which was only a few months old), and Wilford and others had to cast it out also. Elder Woodruff, ever careful to give proper credit, maintained that all this was done "by the power of God, and not of man."[7]

Fasting and prayer are closely tied to the concept of faith. Indeed, they demonstrate and strengthen it. Elder James E. Talmage noted that "the Savior's statement concerning the evil spirit that the Apostles were unable to subdue—'Howbeit this kind goeth not out but by prayer and fasting' [Matt. 17:14–21]—indicates gradation in the malignity and evil power of demons, and gradation also in the results of varying degrees of faith." Brother Talmage drew attention to the fact that "the apostles who failed on the occasion referred to had been able to cast out demons at other times." But they needed something more in their present circumstance. "Fasting, when practiced in prudence, and genuine prayer are conducive to the development of faith with its accompanying power for good," said Elder Talmage.[8] The effectiveness of prayer in dealing with malignant forces is seen in the story of Niels Eskildz, a native of Denmark. He converted to the restored gospel of Jesus Christ and was baptized on November 1, 1862. But on the night following his baptism,

> evil spirits seemed to fill the room in which he had retired to sleep. They were not only terribly visible, but he heard voices also, taunting him with having acted foolishly in submitting to baptism and joining the Latter-day Saints. He was told that he had deserted the only friends he ever had, and would find no more among the "Mormons," who would allow him to die of starvation rather than assist him; that he had no means of earning a livelihood in the far western land to which the Saints all hoped to migrate, and he would never cease to regret it if he ever went there.

> This torment was kept up incessantly until he sought relief in prayer, and three times he got out of bed and tried to pray before he succeeded in doing so. Then his fervent pleading unto the Lord for power to withstand the temptation of the evil one, and to hold fast to the truth, brought relief to him. The evil spirits gradually, and with apparent reluctance, withdrew, and peace came to his soul, with the assurance that the Lord approved of his embracing the gospel, and that he could safely rely upon the Lord for future guidance.[9]

Myth 2: Evil Spirits Cannot Have an Effect upon Physical Objects

As a member of the Quorum of the Twelve Apostles, Joseph Fielding Smith wrote that "it may seem strange to us, but it is the fact that Satan exercises dominion and has some control over the elements. This he does by powers which he knows, but which are hidden from weak mortal men." As evidence for this belief he pointed to a passage of scripture in Ephesians where Satan is called the "prince of the power of the air" (2:2).[10]

There are several Church-related historical records that preserve stories of evil spirits exercising power over physical objects. For instance, the Prophet Joseph Smith recalled a time when Sidney Rigdon was pulled out of his bed three times in one night.[11] The Prophet was also present when Leman Copley (a man who weighed two hundred and fourteen pounds) was sitting on a window sill during a Church meeting and was thrown through the air in somersault fashion, landing with his back across a bench.[12] Elder Wilford Woodruff had the unpleasant experience of being choked almost to death by a malignant entity,[13] and Heber C. Kimball stated that once while he was attempting to cast a foul spirit out of a missionary he was "struck with great force by some invisible power, and fell senseless on the floor."[14] Elder Parley P. Pratt assures us that evil spirits can cause convulsions, cramps, and contortions in the human body.[15] John Pulsipher, whose family converted to the LDS Church less than two years after it was organized, records one incident where a wicked spiritual personage not only caused physical suffering to a human body, but also manipulated and destroyed other physical objects. He relates the following:

> Our enemies had threatened never to let us go out of Kirtland two wagons together, but when we got ready to start, the largest

> company of Saints that had ever traveled together in this generation started out in good order without an enemy to oppose us. We traveled along in fine order and after a few hundred miles we [ran] out of money and stopped and worked about a month at Dayton, Ohio and got means to pay our way thru to Missouri.
>
> While at Dayton the devil entered our camp and got possession of one of the Sisters. She was in awful pain and talked all the time and some of the time in rhyme. The Elders administered to her. The evil spirits left her and entered another person and on being rebuked again would enter another and so continued a good part of the night. But when the devil was commanded in the name of Jesus Christ to leave the camp, he went and was very mad. He went thru the whole camp, made a roaring noise, knocked over chairs, broke table legs and made awful work.[16]

Myth 3: Evil Spirits Only Afflict Sinful People

This particular myth is effectively discounted through the examination of stories from the lives of well-known Latter-day Saints. Following are three examples that should serve to make the point.

Lorenzo Snow was called to build up the kingdom of God in London, England, in 1840. One night while sleeping in his apartment he was awakened by a clamor. A menacing spiritual essence filled the chamber where he was located, and he said "it seemed as though every piece of furniture in the room was put in motion, back and forth against each other in such terrible fury that sleep and rest were utter impossibilities." This nuisance continued to occur for several nights in a row, and so Brother Snow held a special fast. After scripture study and prayer he commanded the foul spirits to leave the house and wasn't bothered again.[17]

Both Boyd K. Packer and A. Theodore Tuttle were imperiled by a terrifying evil force that came upon them separately while on a Church business trip in the state of Idaho. Brother Packer said that for his part it felt as if the motel room where he was staying was "filled with demons," and he had to call upon God in mighty prayer and exercise the power of the priesthood until the darkness departed.[18]

When Spencer W. Kimball was serving as a member of the Quorum of the Twelve Apostles in 1946, "President George Albert

Smith gave him the responsibility of working with Indians. Soon afterward, he awoke sensing a horrible enemy, unseen but very real, trying to destroy him. After a struggle, he rebuked the evil spirit and obtained relief. He concluded that perhaps the work he had just begun presented a special threat to the powers of darkness."[19]

There is some indication that good people are bothered and attacked by evil entities from the spirit world because of the good works that they either try to accomplish on their own or are assigned to perform. Joseph Smith's experience immediately before the First Vision is a good illustration of this point. In describing what happened right before the opening of the final dispensation of the gospel he said, "I was seized upon by some power which entirely overcame me, and had such [an] astonishing influence over me as to bind my tongue so that I could not speak. Thick darkness gathered around me, and it seemed to me for a time as if I were doomed to sudden destruction."[20] Wilford Woodruff once asked the Lord why he had been harassed all of his life by the force of evil, and the answer he received was that the devil knew that if he lived he would continue to write—a prospect which evidently annoyed the arch enemy of God's kingdom.[21] When Heber C. Kimball questioned the Prophet Joseph Smith as to whether there was anything wrong with him that caused an entire legion of evil spirits to attack him when he was serving a mission for the Church, he was assured by the Prophet that there was nothing amiss. And the Prophet provided Heber with a very valuable insight. He said, "the closer we observe the celestial law, the more opposition we shall meet."[22]

Myth 4: Evil Spirits Will Permanently Leave Once They Are Cast Out

While it is true that in many cases where evil spirits are cast out by authority they never return, there are other instances where they put up a fight until a decisive victory is gained against them. Although several of the encounters mentioned previously include the phenomenon, the following histories provide additional insight.

The first example of this type comes from the pen of Wandle Mace. He was a resident of Nauvoo, Illinois, in October 1840, when his young son John became stricken with great pain and distress. For several days and nights the boy would petition his father to give him priesthood blessings and would be relieved of the symptoms of his illness, but they would always return after a short interval. Brother Mace thought this situation was peculiar and decided to enlist the help of Lyman Whitney (whose family shared the Mace's home) to bless his child. While Brother Whitney offered the prayer, Wandle felt a sinking, deathlike feeling come over him, and he struggled to keep his hands upon his son's head. The boy benefited from this administration and recovered from his illness, but Brother Whitney's family shortly became affected by the same influence. Then each member of both families became sick. More blessings were given, but the illness always returned after a brief reprieve. The unusual nature of this situation brought depression to the hearts of both fathers. Wandle's wife, who was a staunch believer in the restored gospel, resisted the reception of a blessing and made the strange remark that the two men had no power to cast out the illness. After some conversation with his spouse, Wandle became convinced that the powers of darkness were the source of their troubles, and he asked Brother Whitney to take a walk with him. They went to a secluded place in the woods to pray and supplicated God for power to cast out the "unclean spirits and devils" who were distressing their families. Upon their return to the house they found Wandle's wife with a terrible and defiant look in her eyes. Brother Mace reports: "Together [we] administered by laying our hands on her head and with all the power we held by virtue of the priesthood of the Son of God we rebuked the devil and every evil spirit and power in the name of Jesus Christ. When we had ceased praying and took our hands off her head, she had fainted. When this passed off she was extremely weak, almost lifeless but in her right mind." The two brethren then went through the house and laid their hands upon each member of their families and rebuked the evil spirits in the name of Jesus Christ and commanded them to depart from the house and trouble them no more. Their prayers were answered, and they praised God for delivering them from their great affliction.[23]

Another example of this type is found in an LDS Church periodical. On March 4, 1851, a ship called *Olympus* sailed from Liverpool, England, with Mormon immigrants onboard. Before leaving the dock, Elder John Taylor prophesied that among the trials the Saints would encounter during their voyage would be trouble from evil spirits. After the ship set sail this prediction was verified. A twelve-year-old boy named Mackenzie awoke in the dead of night and started shouting out the name of one of the Saints. It was apparent to those around him that this boy was possessed by an entity that was highly enraged. They labored to exorcise this spirit "but this proved effectual only for a short time, as the evil one returned bringing others of his companions with him and again entered into the lad. This was repeated several times, until there were seven of them who called themselves legion and bid defiance to all who were on the ship, declaring that they would be subject to no one but Brigham Young." A passenger named Thomas Smith could actually see these denizens of hell through the power of God's Spirit and finally cast them out one by one.[24]

Sometimes the reason for repeated assaults by evil spirits is to prevent the growth and progress of God's kingdom. Such was the case with a young lady who was seeking to be baptized into the Church in North Carolina. Before the ordinance could be attended to she was tormented and abused in a fearful manner. A Latter-day Saint named Ezra C. Robinson said of this incident, "For three hours we stood over her exercising the authority of the Priesthood in rebuking the evil spirits who stubbornly resisted us and returned at short intervals after being rebuked, struggling for the mastery. She pointed toward the ceiling, crying, 'Can't you see them?' When we placed our hands upon her head she rose from her prostrate position with such violence as to throw me upon my back. Finally, impressed by the Spirit of the Lord, we anointed her with oil and she was relieved from that time until she was baptized a few hours later. When taken to the water she was very weak, unable to walk without assistance, but when baptized she was restored. The glow of health returned to her cheeks and she walked home without the least assistance."[25]

Finally, there is the account of a veritable horde of demons who tried to prevent Brother Richard Currell from being ordained to an office in the priesthood in 1847. After Richard expressed his desire to be ordained to the office of a priest, he was possessed by some evil spirits who declared that he should not receive the ordination, and they also said that if he attempted to go to Coventry, England, to receive the ordinance they would follow him there. Brother Currell took the journey anyway, which was about twenty miles in all. By the time he and a group of elders reached the town of Warwick, he had been infested by bad spirits on several occasions, and each time they were rebuked and cast out. Once the travelers reached Leamington Spa—where they planned to stay at a house for the night—"the devils began to rage and swear." One witness to the surreal affair tells the rest of the account.

> I got to the house about nine o'clock in the evening. I had scarcely got in before they began to swear at me. I rebuked them, and they came out of him; but as fast as one lot went another came, declaring Currell should not go to Coventry, each party tearing him and trying to kill him: thus they continued until one o'clock, when we lay down, until five—when another party came swearing that we should not take him to conference, and tried to choke him. We cast out several lots until eight o'clock when five of us started to take [Brother Currell] with us to Coventry, ten miles distant.
>
> Several times we cast them out on the road, but in coming to Stoneleigh the struggle was fearful. However, we rebuked them in the name of Jesus. . . . As we drew near to the city. . . the devils came oftener and stronger, swearing by the God that made us [that] we should not take [Brother Currell] to conference. By this time a number of the brethren from Coventry met us. I got them to carry Brother Currell while I walked by his side and rebuked the devils as fast as they came. We arrived at the room about half past eleven o'clock, a great crowd following us into the room. I endeavored to speak to them but the foul spirits came so often, and what with the noise and confusion of the people, I thought it best to close the meeting.

While this witness and several other Saints were preparing to eat their lunch, some stronger evil spirits took possession of Brother Currell, and they were expelled also. Then in walked two policemen who arrested the poor man, who was suffering so much at the hands of sinister powers. The narrator of the story went to the police station with him while a mob hooted and hurled insults their way. And when they got to their destination both men were arrested without bail; one for having a devil and the other for casting it out and thereby causing a public disturbance. About two hours elapsed before the authorities realized that they were wrong in denying these men bail. Soon they were free, and by three o'clock they were back at the room where the Church conference was being held. The attendees voted on the transaction of various items of business, one of which was to ordain Richard Currell to the office of a priest. Our chronicler continues his tale: "When we laid our hands upon him the devil entered him and tried to prevent us from ordaining him; but the power of Jesus Christ in the holy priesthood was stronger than the devil. And after all the endeavors of the powers of darkness to prevent us, in the name of Jesus Christ we ordained Brother Richard Currell to the office of a priest in The Church of Jesus Christ of Latter-day Saints."[26]

Conclusion

The ability to cast out evil spirits is one of the gifts of the Spirit used by the Saints in all ages, and it is accomplished through the power of the Holy Ghost. It is a gift a worthy Saint can exercise by acting in the name of the Savior. This gift is useful for all Latter-day Saints because they are each potential targets for Satan and his followers. The great value of this gift is that it allows individuals to gain a partial victory over Satan here and now and assures complete power to overcome the adversary in the hereafter. It would be well for each of us to educate ourselves on the myths that surround evil spirits so that we are not deceived either by them or by our fellow men who may misunderstand how and why they operate.

NOTES TO CHAPTER 17

1. *Times and Seasons,* vol. 3, no. 1, 15 November 1841, 579; hereafter cited as *T&S;* see also George D. Watt, ed., *Journal of Discourses* (Liverpool, England: Samuel W. Richards and Sons, 1852–1886), 9:324; hereafter cited as *JD.*
2. Joseph Smith: "No matter who believeth, these signs, such as . . . casting out devils . . . should follow all that believe, whether male or female" (Brigham H. Roberts, ed., *History of The Church of Jesus Christ of Latter-day Saints* [Salt Lake City: Deseret Book, 1948–1950], 4:603; hereafter cited as *HC).* Orson Pratt indicated that women, as well as men, could "cast out devils" (*JD,* 18:42). One woman's patriarchal blessing confirmed this gifted ability. It read: "Thou shalt have power given unto thee . . . to cast out evil spirits" (Dawn Hall Anderson

and Marie Cornwall, eds., *Women Steadfast in Christ* [Salt Lake City: Deseret Book, 1992], 55).

3. The Prophet Joseph Smith echoed this teaching. He said, "Until [a person] obeyed these ordinances and received the gift of the Holy Ghost, by the laying on of hands, according to the order of God, he could not have . . . commanded an evil spirit to come out of a man, and it obey him" (*T&S,* vol. 3, no. 12, 15 April 1842, 752; see also *JD,* 7:37; 8:218). One nineteenth-century Saint wrote: "By laying on hands for the gift of the Holy Spirit, the authority to . . . cast out devils, is conferred" (Orson Spencer, *Letters Exhibiting the Most Prominent Doctrines of The Church of Jesus Christ of Latter-day Saints* [Salt Lake City: George Q. Cannon and Sons, 1891], 68).
4. *HC,* 1:83.
5. Parker P. Robison, comp., *Orson Pratt's Works on the Doctrines of the Gospel* (Salt Lake City: Deseret News Press, 1945), 83.
6. For a story that illustrates this point see Conference Report, April 1926, 125.
7. Preston Nibley, comp., *Three Mormon Classics* (Salt Lake City: Stevens and Wallis, 1944), 87–88. This story demonstrates the need for unity in vanquishing the forces of darkness. Another story of casting out evil spirits that shows the need for unity can be found in Andrew Jenson, *Latter-day Saint Biographical Encyclopedia* (Salt Lake City: Deseret News Press, 1901), 1:345.
8. James E. Talmage, *Jesus the Christ* (Salt Lake City: Deseret Book, 1962), 395 n. 2.
9. George Q. Cannon, ed., *Treasures in Heaven* (Salt Lake City: Juvenile Instructor Office, 1914), 22–23.
10. Joseph Fielding Smith, *Church History and Modern Revelation* (Salt Lake City: The Church of Jesus Christ of Latter-day Saints, 1946), 1:207. It is apparent from a number of scriptural sources that Satan has a limited ability to manipulate each of the elements of creation: Earth (Moses 1:19–21), Air (Eph. 2:2), Fire (Rev. 13:13), and Water (ibid., 12:15).
11. See *JD,* 3:229–30.
12. Levi Ward Hancock, Autobiography, L. Tom Perry Special Collections Library, Brigham Young University, Provo, UT, 33–34.
13. See Brian H. Stuy, ed., *Collected Discourses* (Burbank, CA, and Woodland Hills, UT: B.H.S. Publishing, 1987–1992), 5:199.
14. George Q. Cannon, ed., *President Heber C. Kimball's Journal* (Salt Lake City: Juvenile Instructor Office, 1882), 20.
15. See Parley P. Pratt, *Key to the Science of Theology* (Salt Lake City: Deseret Book, 1965), 117.
16. John Pulsipher, Autobiography, L. Tom Perry Special Collections Library, Brigham Young University, Provo, UT, 3.
17. Francis M. Gibbons, *Dynamic Disciples: Prophets of God* (Salt Lake City: Deseret Book, 1996), 112–13.
18. Lucile C. Tate, *Boyd K. Packer: A Watchman on the Tower* (Salt Lake City: Bookcraft, 1995), 119–20.

19. Daniel H. Ludlow, ed., *Encyclopedia of Mormonism* (New York: Macmillan, 1992), 2:786; hereafter cited as *EM.*
20. *T&S,* vol. 3, no. 11, 1 April 1842, 748.
21. See *EM,* 4:1581.
22. *JD,* 3:263.
23. Wandle Mace, Autobiography, L. Tom Perry Special Collections Library, Brigham Young University, Provo, UT, 63.
24. *The Contributor,* vol. 13, no. 8, June 1892, 345–46.
25. *Improvement Era,* vol. 3, no. 1, November 1899, 30–31.
26. *Millennial Star,* vol. 9, no. 15, 1 August 1847, 231–33.

BY THEIR FRUITS

CHAPTER EIGHTEEN
Determining the Source of Manifestations

Prove all things; hold fast [to] that which is good.
—1 THESSALONIANS 5:21

Once Latter-day Saints step over the threshold between earthly and spiritual experience there arises the possibility of becoming targets of unseen, unfriendly forces. The devil, said Elder Wilford Woodruff, "is a personage of great power; he has great influence and knowledge. He understands that if [the Lord's] kingdom, which he rebelled against in heaven, prevails on the earth, there will be no dominion here for him." And he is not alone. There are "a vast number of fallen spirits, cast out with him, here on the earth," and together "they labor to overthrow the Church and kingdom of God."[1] Elder James E. Talmage spoke about one of the ways whereby the adversary and his minions go about their nefarious work. He stated that "Satan from the first has been a great imitator; he is an experienced strategist. Never has the Lord set His hand to do a specific thing for the good of His people upon the earth, of outstanding feature, but that Satan has attempted to imitate it in some degree."[2] And this tactic applies to the gifts of the Holy Spirit also for, as Elder John A. Widtsoe states, "The evil one, ever vigilant in his work of destruction, tries to simulate with an evil purpose every gift of God."[3] Indeed, as John Taylor acknowledged, "Satan has the power to transform himself into an angel of light; he can give visions and revelations as well as spiritual manifestations."[4]

Since "nothing is a greater injury to the children of men than to be under the influence of a false spirit when they think they have the

Spirit of God,"[5] it would be advisable to the Saints, as those who have taken sides with the Lord, to learn how to tell the difference between His manifestations and those of the devil. The following nine general keys of detection have been gleaned from the scriptures and also from the counsel of General Authorities who have served throughout the dispensation of the fullness of times. They are offered here in the hope that they will prove advantageous to those who need them most.

Key 1: Spiritual Credentials

When Marion G. Romney was serving as an Apostle, he stood before a general conference audience and made the straightforward and uncompromising remark that if a person who works miracles has not "received the gift of the Holy Ghost through the prescribed ordinances . . . then his works, whatever they may be, are not the manifestations of the Holy Spirit. This is a key test," he said, "because . . . the gifts of the Spirit are given by the power of the Holy Ghost. Without the gift of the Holy Ghost, the manifestations of His gifts may not be enjoyed."[6]

Key 2: Spiritual Standing

If we have received the gift of the Holy Ghost through the proper method and at the hands of those who possess authentic authority, then we are eligible for the reception of spiritual gifts, unless we disqualify ourselves in some way. Joseph Fielding Smith taught how this can happen. He said that there is "a danger confronting all those who yield to temptation; who violate covenants, speak evil of authorities, etc. When a man does any of these things he becomes subject to deception and inspiration from an evil source."[7] In the words of President George A. Smith, "No man need be led astray [by false spirits] only as he suffers himself to lose the Holy Spirit, which is the result of sin, wickedness, neglect or transgression."[8]

Key 3: Character of the Manifestation

No matter what kind of otherworldly event is manifested among mortals, its source can be determined fairly easily by examining its overall character. We read in Moroni chapter 7 that "that which is of

God inviteth and enticeth to do good continually; wherefore, everything which inviteth and enticeth to do good, and to love God, and to serve him, is inspired of God" (v. 13). On the other hand, "the devil is an enemy unto God, and fighteth against him continually, and inviteth and enticeth to sin, and to do that which is evil continually" (v. 12). The Lord has instructed all Latter-day Saints to "put [their] trust in that Spirit which leadeth to do good . . . to do justly, to walk humbly, [and] to judge righteously" because that is His Spirit (D&C 11:12).

In one modern scriptural text we read, "That which doth not edify is not of God, and is darkness" (D&C 50:23). The Apostle Paul touched upon this subject when he stated in the fourteenth chapter of the book of 1 Corinthians that if a person exercised the gift of speaking in tongues and there was no interpretation available then nobody would receive edification; confusion would reign (see vv. 2,5,7,9,11). President Brigham Young was a personal witness to a manifestation that produced no obvious edifying results. He said, "I have seen the effects of . . . anomalous sleep . . . many a time in my youth. I have seen persons lie on the benches, on the floor of the meeting house, or on the ground at their camp meetings for ten, twenty, and thirty minutes, and I do not know but an hour, and not a particle of pulse about them." When these people arose from their experience, "they called it the power of God." But when Brother Young got old enough he asked these people what had taken place during their trances, and they responded that nothing happened at all. They did not learn anything, neither did they see any spiritual personage while in their state of unconsciousness. So Brigham asked them, "Then what is the use or utility of your falling down here in the dirt?"[9]

President Young explained to a group of LDS ward members, "No man gets power from God to raise disturbance in any branch of the Church," and he specified that "such power is obtained from an evil source."[10] The scriptures support this view; they teach that rebellion (see Mosiah 2:37) and contention or anger (see 3 Ne. 11:29; see also Mosiah 2:32 and Moro. 9:3) are characteristics of Satan and his followers. Any manifestations, therefore, that produce or foster these traits are not from the Lord.

Key 4: Focus of the Manifestation

When a person is trying to determine the source of any given spiritual manifestation they must take into consideration the focus of the event; is it on God or man? President George Q. Cannon reiterated the principle that "the Lord has chosen the weak things of the world, that they might not glory in themselves nor in their own strength; and the man that does claim the glory takes steps to destroy his influence and to lose his power and gifts." And he stated emphatically that "the Lord will not bless men who seek to take the glory to themselves."[11]

We gain a related insight from Elder James E. Talmage, who informs us that "to be valid as a testimony of truth, miracles must be wrought in the name of Christ, and to His honor, in furtherance of the plan of salvation." Miracles, he said, "are not given . . . as a means of gaining notoriety for him through whom they are accomplished. [The] gifts of the true Spirit are manifested in support of the message from heaven."[12]

Key 5: Harmony with Revealed Truth

One sure way to prevent imposition by the devil and his cohorts is to be thoroughly conversant with the word of God and to use it as a gauge for measuring the ideology of others. In the Joseph Smith Translation of the Bible the Savior is reported as saying, "And whoso treasureth up my word shall not be deceived" (JST, Mark 13:43).

In expounding upon this principle, the First Presidency of the Church—consisting of Joseph F. Smith, Anthon H. Lund, and Charles W. Penrose—wrote the following in a letter to the general body of the Saints. This communication is dated August 2, 1913. It reads,

> When visions, dreams, tongues, prophecy, impressions or any extraordinary gift or inspiration conveys something out of harmony with the accepted revelations of the Church or contrary to the decisions of its constituted authorities, Latter-day Saints may know that it is not of God, no matter how plausible it may appear. . . . [A]nything at discord with that which comes from God through the head of the Church is not to be received as authoritative or reliable. . . . [R]evelation . . . is not to be accepted when contrary to Church covenants, doctrine or discipline, or to

> known facts, demonstrated truths, or good common sense. . . . Be not led by any spirit or influence that discredits established authority, contradicts true scientific principles and discoveries, or leads away from the direct revelations of God for the government of the Church. The Holy Ghost does not contradict its own revealings. Truth is always harmonious with itself.[13]

"Wherever miracles are wrought by the power of God," said Elder Orson Pratt, "*there* will be found a true and righteous doctrine, unmixed with error: wherever miracles are wrought by the power of the devil," however, "*there* will be found more or less false doctrine. . . . Those who do miracles by the power of God," explained Pratt, "generally have a message to publish to the people by authority from God." On the other hand, "those who do miracles by the power of the devil, pretend to no message whatever; or if they pretend to have a message to deliver to the people, it will be found, on inspection, to be mixed with error."[14]

Key 6: Boundaries of Stewardship

This next key is critically important in the task of detection. Spencer W. Kimball has taught that "if one does receive revelations [from God], which one may expect if he is worthy, . . . they will always be within his own jurisdiction and never beyond."[15] This is what Elder Dallin H. Oaks of the Quorum of the Twelve called "stewardship in revelation." This principle can be understood in simple terms: "Only the president of the Church receives revelation to guide the entire Church. Only the stake president receives revelation for the special guidance of the stake. The person who receives revelation for the ward is the bishop. . . . Individuals can receive revelation to guide their own lives. But when one person purports to receive revelation for another person outside his or her own stewardship . . . you can be sure that such revelations are not from the Lord."[16]

A good illustration of the stewardship principle is presented in a story that was told by Elder Charles C. Rich. He related the following: "[W]hen I was presiding in California, evening meetings were established. . . . On one occasion I had been away for a short time, and on my return I found a large crowd on the water's edge, some of whom were being baptized. I think brother Hopkins was there, and I asked him, subsequently, what induced the people to turn out so suddenly. He replied that some sister had received a revelation the night before, commanding them to be baptized. I told him that if any revelation had been given on that subject, I should have known it." Elder Rich would have been made aware of such a command because he was the presiding authority. His advice was that Latter-day Saints "should seek to be governed by these principles, and learn to discern the spirits, and discriminate between that which is from God and that which is from beneath. If we seek unto the Lord," said Elder Rich, "He will give us wisdom to lead us into all truth." And he made this sobering observation: "It is a serious thing to say the Lord has spoken through us if He has not. . . . If we receive revelations we should be sure they are not leading us outside of our duties, but tend to our instruction and improvement, and lead us to perform those duties devolving upon us."[17]

Key 7: Presence or Testimony of the Spirit

Another key for detecting the source of a spiritual manifestation is the testimony or confirmation of the Holy Spirit. Again, we turn to the Elder Orson Pratt for insight. He noted that a person might see all of the signs promised to Christ's believers being exercised among the Latter-day Saints. And he chose the gift of tongues to illustrate a point saying, "[A person] may see [the Saints] speak in different tongues . . . but how is he to judge or know whether they do speak in another tongue or not? It is true he hears sounds put together which resemble languages he has heard foreigners speak; but it is not a testimony that imparts a knowledge to his mind: he wants something greater than this." Suppose that "he hears others, who are ignorant and unlearned, by the gift and power of the Holy Ghost interpret these tongues, and unfold the things spoken by the power of the Spirit of God in another language: . . . [H]ow does [the observer] know that they give the true interpretation?" Since the individual's own understanding will not testify of such a thing the spectator needs "a testimony independent of this—a higher [testimony], a greater testimony—even that of the Holy Spirit."[18] This is only logical for, as Elder Pratt stated in another place, "The Spirit knows its own revelations and can testify of them."[19] Jedediah M. Grant, who held office as a counselor in the First Presidency, had practical experience in this area. He recalled a time when he heard Brigham Young speak in tongues. He said, "the effect it produced I shall never forget; *I could feel the Spirit,* although I did not fully understand the tongue. I have heard others speak in tongues, but it had not the same effect, and I have marked the different impressions received under different individuals."[20]

Both scriptural and historical sources preserve descriptions of what the Spirit of God feels like when it is present, and thus they provide us with even more refined keys of detection. A person under the influence of the Spirit may feel a kind of energy or power either surrounding them or within them (see Moro. 10:4–5; D&C 111:8). This power is sometimes so intense that it is manifest as a warm or burning feeling (see D&C 9:8; cf. Luke 3:16; 3 Ne. 19:13–14).[21] It is not uncommon for persons who are under this heavenly influence to also feel a sense of sanctity. In scriptural texts restored through the Prophet Joseph Smith, God is referred to as the "Man of Holiness" (Moses 6:57; 7:35), and if a portion of His Spirit were to rest upon an individual, it would only be natural that they would experience some degree of His fundamental nature. In addition, some people have noted that the Spirit of God produces a sensation of "sweetness" within them,[22] while other effects of the Spirit include enlightenment (see D&C 11:13), joy (see Mosiah 4:3), comfort (see Alma 17:9–10), and peace (see D&C 111:8).

Key 8: Direct Revelation

As Latter-day Saints, we each have a potent option available to us in the fight against devilish deceptions. If the authenticity of any spiritual gift is in question we can go straight to our omniscient Father and obtain a revelatory judgment from Him regarding it.

This type of approach was used by the Prophet Joseph Smith. In 1842 the Church's official Nauvoo, Illinois, newspaper (*Times and Seasons*) ran the following notice:

> We have lately seen a pamphlet written and published by James C. Brewster; purporting to be one of the lost books of Esdras; and to be written by the gift and power of God. We consider it a perfect humbug, and should not have noticed it, had it not been assiduously circulated in several branches of the Church.
>
> This said Brewster is a minor; but has professed for several years to have the gift of seeing and looking through or into a stone.[23]

Brewster showed President Smith his manuscript but the Prophet decided to take the step necessary to resolve the issue of its origin. Joseph wrote, "I inquired of the Lord, and the Lord told me the book was not true—it was not of Him. If God ever called me, or spake by my mouth, or gave me a revelation, he never gave revelations to that Brewster boy."[24]

Elder Orson Hyde relates an interesting incident, when a divine revelation was issued to detect false spiritual gifts even though such a judgment had not been sought after. Elder Hyde recalled that on the morning of March 14, 1846, the Spirit of the Lord came upon him, and he was moved to write down a revelation from the Lord Jesus Christ. This heavenly communication concerned an apostate by the name of James J. Strang. This man claimed that he had received revelations from God and also claimed that he had been visited by an angel. The Lord specifically denied to Elder Hyde that Strang had been guided by His voice or the voice of one of His angels. Rather, said the Lord, Strang went about to deceive the people and "Satan helpeth him."[25]

Key 9: Duplicate Manifestation

The final key of detection that we will examine in this chapter is mentioned in modern-day scripture. In Doctrine and Covenants section 50 we learn that if a spiritual manifestation is not understood by observers, nor shared by them, then they should take the matter up with God in the name of His Son. Verses 31 through 33 read:

> If you behold a spirit [i.e., spiritual power] manifested that you cannot understand, and you receive not that spirit [i.e., do not experience the same thing yourself], ye shall ask of the Father in the name of Jesus; and if he give not unto you that spirit, then you may know that it is not of God. And it shall be given unto you, power over that spirit [or manifestation]; and you shall proclaim against that spirit with a loud voice that it is not of God—Not with [a] railing accusation, that ye be not overcome, neither with boasting nor rejoicing, lest you be seized therewith.

An example of this method being employed can be found in the writings of Jared Carter. He reports that he and another man found themselves in an uncertain situation and so they applied the instructions in the scriptural passage just cited. He says,

> On a certain occasion I attended a meeting together with Sylvester Smith . . . where, just as we were about to administer the sacrament, a young woman was taken with an exercise that brought her to the floor. I doubted the propriety of such an experience in a public meeting and suggested to Bro. Sylvester that we should try that spirit according to the revelation that God had given. Complying with my suggestion, we kneeled down and asked our Heavenly Father in the name of Christ, that if that spirit which the sister possessed was of Him, He would give it to us. We prayed in faith, but we did not receive the spirit. After Bro. Sylvester had made some communication, which was not proclaiming against the spirit, I arose and proclaimed against it with a loud voice. . . .[26]

A duplicate manifestation may also be requested of God if we are granted a spiritual gift, but we desire to make sure of its source. Such was the case with Elder Parley P. Pratt. After the martyrdom of Joseph and Hyrum Smith, Elder Pratt found himself burdened by the weight of his new responsibility to be a director of the Saints. He prayed aloud to God for guidance, and the Spirit suddenly came upon him, filling his heart with joy and gladness. Specific instructions were then relayed to him through the gift of revelation, and he was "comforted above measure." The change that overcame Parley was so sudden, however, that he scarcely believed the reality of his own experience, and so he prayed that the Lord would repeat the occurrence. As Elder Pratt was praying, the same Spirit descended upon him and the message was repeated.[27]

Conclusion

It is imperative that even as we petition the King of heaven for the gifts of the Spirit, we remain on guard against counterfeit manifestations from the opposing power. We never know when the prince of darkness may take note of our pleas to the Father and attempt to answer them himself. Or his plan to destroy us spiritually may be accomplished if we believe in the false manifestations of other people. That is why the preceding keys of detection are so crucial to our spiritual health and well-being. If we keep in mind at all times that the Lord's house is a house of order, and we are diligent in weighing that truth against the manifestations that we or others may experience, then we are much more likely to keep ourselves in the good graces of God and continue to receive His blessings.

NOTES TO CHAPTER 18

1. George D. Watt, ed., *Journal of Discourses* (Liverpool, England: Samuel W. Richards and Sons, 1852–1886), 13:163; hereafter cited as *JD.* Joseph Smith revealed that "in relation to the kingdom of God, the devil always sets up his kingdom at the very same time in opposition to God" (Brigham H. Roberts, ed., *History of The Church of Jesus Christ of Latter-day Saints* [Salt Lake City: Deseret Book, 1948–1950], 6:364; hereafter cited as *HC).*
2. Conference Report, April 1931, 27; hereafter cited as CR.
3. John A. Widtsoe, *Evidences and Reconciliations* (Salt Lake City: Bookcraft, 1987), 98. Elder Widtsoe also states that legitimate "spiritual gifts are properly enjoyed by the Saints of God under the direction of 'such as God shall appoint and ordain over the Church'—that is, the Priesthood and its officers. Such gifts, when found outside of the Priesthood, are often dangerous, and usually are manifestations of evil spirits" (John A. Widtsoe, *Program of The Church of Jesus Christ of Latter-day Saints,* 2nd ed. [Salt Lake City: Department of Education of The Church of Jesus Christ of Latter-day Saints, 1937], 129).
4. *Millennial Star,* vol. 19, no. 13, 28 March 1857, 197; hereafter cited as *MS.* Joseph Smith taught that manifestations produced by evil spirits are "calculated to bring disgrace upon the Church of God; to cause the Spirit of God to be withdrawn; and to uproot and destroy those glorious principles which [have] been developed for the salvation of the human family" (*Times and Seasons,* vol. 3, no. 11, 1 April 1842, 747; hereafter cited as *T&S).* People who are under the influence of these spirits will have experiences that "neither edify nor instruct" (Parley P. Pratt, *Key to the Science of Theology* [Salt Lake City: Deseret Book, 1965], 118). Manifestations in this category include strange ecstasies, strange visions, strange revelations (not congenial to the doctrine and spirit of the gospel), strange noises and utterances (unnatural or muttering), swooning or fainting, shouting or screaming, unusual dancing or whirling on the heels, running, jumping, suspended animation, trembling or shaking, twitching or jerking, tumbling or falling down, wallowing on the ground, odd actions, frothing at the mouth, entertaining wild and enthusiastic notions, making unseemly gestures, having a distorted body or countenance, experiencing cramps, going into fits, making accusations against others, insanity, disorderly

prayer or singing, loss of strength, helplessness or being physically but invisibly bound, loss of memory, loss of understanding, and engaging in immoral conduct (see *HC,* 1:325; ibid., 2:225; *JD,* 11:2, 4, ibid., 16:288; *T&S,* vol. 3, no. 11, 1 April 1842, 743–48; Lavina F. Anderson, ed., *Lucy's Book: A Critical Edition of Lucy Mack Smith's Family Memoir* [Salt Lake City: Signature Books, 2001], 506–508; Parley P. Pratt, *Autobiography of Parley P. Pratt* [Salt Lake City: Deseret Book, 1985], 48; *BYU Studies* 12.3 [spring 1972]: 310–11; Alfred D. Young, Autobiography, L. Tom Perry Special Collections Library, Brigham Young University, Provo, UT, 17–18). The foregoing types of manifestations can only originate from evil or unholy sources for, as John Taylor said, "there [is not] anything unnatural in the gifts of the Spirit" (*Messenger and Advocate,* vol. 3, no. 9, June 1837, 514; see also *HC,* 4:580).

5. Ibid., 4:573. This statement was made by the Prophet Joseph Smith.
6. CR, April 1956, 72. Though it is possible for some people outside of the LDS Church to be given authentic spiritual gifts on a temporary basis (see appendix 2), it is not possible for them to enjoy those gifts in perpetuity because they have not obeyed the divine laws that would grant them such a privilege—they have not been baptized by proper authority nor have they received the gift of the Holy Ghost.
7. Joseph Fielding Smith, *Church History and Modern Revelation* (Salt Lake City: The Church of Jesus Christ of Latter-day Saints, 1949), 4:47.
8. *JD,* 17:196.
9. Ibid., 14:113.
10. Ibid., 9:93.
11. *CR,* April 1898, 34.
12. James E. Talmage, *The Articles of Faith* (Salt Lake City: Deseret News Press, 1901), 235.
13. James R. Clark, comp., *Messages of the First Presidency of The Church of Jesus Christ of Latter-day Saints* (Salt Lake City: Bookcraft, 1970), 4:285–86. An article found in an early LDS Church periodical mentions that "it behooves every disciple to watch that they are not deceived. . . . [And in order that they may not be] deceived, we beseech all the disciples to search diligently the revelations, and learn the order of the kingdom of our Heavenly Father. In this way we shall be preserved from evil, and delivered from seducing spirits and doctrines of devils, and the commandments and precepts of men. Everything in the Church of God must be conducted in order, according to the authority of the offices which He has given; for these all were given for the perfecting of the Saints, for the work of the ministry, for the edifying of the body of Christ" (*Evening and Morning Star,* vol. 1, no. 12, May 1833, 90).
14. Parker P. Robison, comp., *Orson Pratt's Works on the Doctrines of the Gospel* (Salt Lake City: Deseret News Press, 1945), 233–34 (emphasis in original).
15. Edward L. Kimball, ed., *The Teachings of Spencer W. Kimball* (Salt Lake City: Bookcraft, 1982), 458.

16. Dallin H. Oaks, "Revelation," *Brigham Young University 1981–82 Fireside and Devotional Speeches* (Provo, UT: University Publications, 1982), 25. Brigham Young similarly said, "If a person asks for a thing that does not concern him, such as governing the Church, as a member of the Church inquiring concerning the duty of a presiding Elder, what the prophet or the Twelve [Apostles] ought to do, etc. he will not get an answer. If he does it will not be from God" (*HC,* 5:527). Elder James E. Talmage explicated the same truth. He said, "When you hear . . . of men who are receiving revelations concerning the conduct of this Church, and those men are not such as you have sustained by the uplifted hand before the Lord as your representatives with the Lord, and as His prophets and revelators unto you, you may know that those men are not speaking by the power of God" (CR, April 1931, 29).
17. *JD,* 19:163.
18. Ibid., 7:178.
19. Robison, comp., *Orson Pratt's Works on the Doctrines of the Gospel,* 69.
20. *JD,* 3:8 (emphasis added).
21. In the *History of the Church* Joseph Smith is quoted as saying, "The quorum of the Seventy enjoyed a great flow of the Holy Spirit. Many arose and spoke, testifying that they were filled with the Holy Ghost, which was like fire in their bones" (*HC,* 2:392). Samuel Smith (the Prophet's younger brother) taught that when God provides "a testimony of the truth" to an individual they "will feel a burning sensation in [their] breast which is the Spirit of God" (Anderson, ed., *Lucy's Book,* 499). William Smith (another brother of the Prophet) said of his confirmation as a Church member, which took place on 10 June 1830, "I felt the Spirit of God like a burning fire shut up in my bones" (William B. Smith, *William Smith on Mormonism* [Lamoni, IA: Herald Steam Book and Job Office, 1883], 16). Wilford Woodruff reports, "The power of God rested upon us and we were baptized with the Holy Ghost and the Spirit of God was like fire shut up in our bones" (Dean C. Jessee, "Kirtland Diary of Wilford Woodruff," *BYU Studies* 12.4 [summer 1972]: 393). Benjamin Brown states, "The Spirit of the Lord was again upon me, like fire in my bones" (George Q. Cannon, ed., *Gems for the Young Folks* [Salt Lake City: Juvenile Instructor Office, 1881], 56). George A. Smith relates, "The Spirit seemed to burn in my bones" (*JD,* 5:221).
22. In a letter written by Joseph Smith and Hyrum Smith on 4 June 1844, they spoke of "the sweet influences of the Holy Ghost" (*HC,* 6:427). Ezra T. Benson referred to "the sweet and benign influences of the Holy Ghost" (*JD,* 3:62). President George Q. Cannon said, "You who have received the Holy Spirit; you who have felt its power; you whose hearts have been gladdened under its heavenly influence, you know how sweet it has been; you know that there is nothing on earth so sweet as the outpouring of the Spirit of God on a human being. No matter what experience you may have had in riches and in all that earth desires, there is nothing that compares with the heavenly sweetness and

joy of the Spirit of God. This is a foretaste of that which is to come" (Brian H. Stuy, ed., *Collected Discourses* [Burbank, CA, and Woodland Hills, UT: B.H.S. Publishing, 1987–1992], 2:185). Brother Cannon asked on another occasion, "Did you ever taste anything that equals the taste of the Spirit of God—the sweetness, the heavenly joy and the peace which it brings to the soul? You who have partaken of it know that there is nothing so sweet. Honey to the natural taste is not to be compared to the sweetness of the Holy Spirit to the spirit of man" (*JD,* 22:132).

23. *T&S,* vol. 4, no. 2, 1 December 1842, 32.
24. *HC,* 5:214.
25. *MS,* vol. 7, no. 10, 15 May 1846, 157; originally published as a broadside in Nauvoo, Illinois.
26. Cited in Max H. Parkin, "The Nature and Cause of Internal and External Conflict of the Mormons in Ohio between 1830 and 1838" (master's thesis, Brigham Young University, 1966), 74–75.
27. Pratt, *Autobiography of Parley P. Pratt,* 293–94. A man by the name of David John was given a revelatory dream in January 1856 wherein he saw an angel and was shown several visions. After awaking from this dream, David bowed before the Lord and asked that if the messenger had been sent by Him, that it might be confirmed by the appearance of the same messenger. Upon falling asleep again David saw the same angel who repeated some of the things he had previously said (see Andrew Jenson, *Latter-day Saint Biographical Encyclopedia* [Salt Lake City: Deseret News Press, 1901], 1:489–90).

CONCLUSION

The gifts of the Spirit are blessings given by a loving Heavenly Father to His children who have received the gift of the Holy Ghost. Through ancient and modern scripture and through living prophets and apostles, the Lord has taught His people about the nature of spiritual gifts and of their place in the gospel of Jesus Christ.

This book opened with a short story that merits repeating as it draws to a close. The Prophet Joseph Smith once told an investigator that if he chose to join himself with the Lord's restored Church but decided to ignore its intrinsic spiritual gifts, his action would be comparable to a person requesting nourishment but then refusing to partake of it once it had been placed before him. This is a metaphor that should not be forgotten. The children of God are not expected to starve spiritually while they are seated at His table. Neither is their dining privilege restricted to only the first stage of a seven-course meal. The invitation that has been offered to them is to participate in a feast until they have become satisfied.

The responsibility to feast on the gifts of the Spirit is explicitly referred to by all three of the scriptural personalities who provide detailed discourses on these blessings. The Apostle Paul encourages us to "desire spiritual gifts" (1 Cor. 14:1); the prophet Moroni exhorts us to "lay hold upon every good gift" (Moro. 10:30); the Lord Jesus Christ commands us to "seek . . . earnestly the best gifts" (D&C 46:8). Developing spiritual gifts is a matter of actively using them in a way that builds the kingdom of God and edifies the Saints.

The desire for spiritual gifts must be coupled with faith. The Savior expounded upon this principle when He spoke to Hyrum

Smith in May 1829. He told the brother of the Prophet, "Thou shalt have a gift if thou wilt desire [it] of me in faith, with an honest heart, believing in the power of Jesus Christ, or in my power" (D&C 11:10). It is evident from this statement by the Son of God that personal desire for heavenly endowments is not enough; desire for the gifts of the Spirit must be intertwined with honest faith in the almighty power of God.

We can have complete confidence that God will fulfill all of His words, for He has issued the decree that His words cannot return unto Him void (see Moses 4:30). He will, therefore, assuredly bestow spiritual gifts upon those who worthily seek for them according to His holy will. Once we do what is required of us to receive the gifts of the Spirit, our lives will be richly blessed, and we will be given the chance to bless the lives of others. Our confidence in God, His ways, and His truths will increase. And most importantly, we will experience the power of the Lord through the gifts of the Spirit. In striving for the these gifts, we will qualify for the greatest of all of God's gifts—eternal life (see D&C 14:7).

APPENDIX ONE
A Multitude of Gifts

While the main text of this book has focused attention on spiritual gifts that are found in three scriptural lists, and a few others that were mentioned in early LDS writings, it appears that there are a multitude of additional gifts that are available to Latter-day Saints. Elder Bruce R. McConkie held the view that "spiritual gifts are endless in number and infinite in variety." And he asserted that "those listed in the revealed word are simply illustrations of the boundless outpouring of divine grace that a gracious God gives those who love and serve Him."[1]

Some additional spiritual gifts are brought to the attention of individuals when they receive their patriarchal blessings. Spencer W. Kimball, for instance, learned during his blessing that he had been granted a desirable and very useful gift. He was told: "You will preach the gospel to many people, but more especially to the Lamanites, for the Lord will bless you with the gift of language and power to portray before that people the gospel in great plainness."[2] Joseph Fielding Smith was informed in his blessing that he had received a similar gift, but one which had a distinct purpose. He heard the patriarch say, "The blessings of the Lord shall rest upon thee. His spirit shall direct thy mind and give thee word and sentiment, that thou shalt confound the wisdom of the wicked and set at naught the counsels of the unjust."[3] Finally, we have an example from the blessing of Lyman R. Sherman, who served on the high council both in Kirtland, Ohio, and Far West, Missouri, in the days of Joseph Smith. Lyman's father had passed away before Lyman received his patriarchal blessing in April 1835. His special gift was tied directly to interaction with the

Spirit of God. He was assured with these words: "God shall be thy father and He shall comfort thee."[4]

Some adherents to the faith of the restored gospel may not believe that they have been blessed with any of the gifts that are enumerated in the scriptures, and that they may not have had any gifts formally identified through the reception of a patriarchal blessing either. Elder Carlos E. Asay of the Quorum of the Seventy acknowledged that "some people wonder where they were when the spiritual gifts were distributed. Perhaps some even feel that they were completely overlooked." Brother Asay admitted that at times he had envied the gifts that were made apparent in the lives of those around him and occasionally wondered why he had not received more of a spiritual endowment himself. But he also pointed out that it is much more important, and productive, to look within ourselves instead of casting a distracted glance around us. "Is it possible that certain gifts lie dormant within you?" he asked. "Perhaps," he said, "you haven't mined deeply enough within your own soul to discover the golden gifts that reside there. Maybe you haven't heeded sufficiently the subtle intimations of the Spirit that provide clues to the inner powers."[5] Bishop Glen L. Pace, who served as a counselor in the Presiding Bishopric of the Church, reminds us of the scriptural teaching that "not everyone has every gift," and he therefore admonishes us "not [to] feel inadequate when we see that others possess gifts we have not experienced. We all have need of each other, and we each have some gifts and talents unique to us."[6] This is the accepted teaching of holy writ. The Apostle Paul states, "Every man hath his proper [Greek: *idios*—meaning "own," "private," "separate"] gift of God, one after this manner, and another after that" (1 Cor. 7:7). It may be that some people do not recognize their gifts simply because they have not considered the subject with a broad enough perspective. Several leaders of the Lord's Church have identified spiritual gifts that may be manifest in a person's life but which may not at first be recognized as such.

– Harold B. Lee speaks of "the great gift of understanding" in the task of raising children and also "intuition" to be able to safeguard the sanctity of the home.[7]

– George Q. Cannon draws attention to charity, patience, and the power to subdue one's temper.[8]

– Marvin J. Ashton mentions listening to others, seeking after righteousness, bearing a mighty testimony, having an agreeable disposition, being able to ponder, avoiding contention, and being a disciple.[9]

– Charles W. Penrose includes joy, peace, longsuffering, gentleness, goodness, meekness, and temperance among the gifts of the Spirit.[10]

– Marion G. Romney acknowledges gifts such as judgment, virtue, diligence, humility, composure, kindness, and godliness.[11]

It is the privilege of every Latter-day Saint to approach Heavenly Father in prayer and to ask Him to help them identity the gift that they have had bestowed upon them, to ask for His assistance in cultivating it throughout their lives, and to petition Him to receive additional gifts for the benefit of themselves and the rest of His children.

NOTES TO APPENDIX 1

1. Bruce R. McConkie, *A New Witness for the Articles of Faith* (Salt Lake City: Deseret Book, 1985), 371. An article printed in the *Encyclopedia of Mormonism* likewise maintains that "the Spirit can grant any gift that would fill a particular need; hence, no exhaustive list is possible" (Daniel H. Ludlow, ed., *Encyclopedia of Mormonism* [New York: Macmillan, 1992], 2:544).
2. Conference Report, April 1947, 144.
3. Francis M. Gibbons, *Joseph Fielding Smith: Gospel Scholar, Prophet of God* (Salt Lake City: Deseret Book, 1992), 49.
4. Book of Patriarchal Blessings Index, Archives Division, Church Historical Department, The Church of Jesus Christ of Latter-day Saints, Salt Lake City, Utah.
5. Carlos E. Asay, *In the Lord's Service: A Guide to Spiritual Development* (Salt Lake City: Deseret Book, 1990), 125–26.
6. Glenn L. Pace, *Spiritual Plateaus* (Salt Lake City: Deseret Book, 1991), 144–45.
7. Clyde J. Williams, ed., *The Teachings of Harold B. Lee* (Salt Lake City: Bookcraft, 1996), 285.

8. Brian H. Stuy, ed., *Collected Discourses* (Burbank, CA, and Woodland Hills, UT: B.H.S. Publishing, 1987–1992), 2:249.
9. *Ensign,* November 1987, 23.
10. George D. Watt, ed., *Journal of Discourses* (Liverpool, England: Samuel W. Richards and Sons, 1852–1886), 22:161.
11. Marion G. Romney, *Learning for the Eternities* (Salt Lake City: Deseret Book, 1977), 126.

APPENDIX TWO
Questions and Answers

There are several questions about spiritual gifts that are commonly asked by students of the scriptures and that are worthy of investigation. This appendix will attempt to provide substantial and reliable answers to six of these inquiries.

1. Can a person who is not a member of the Lord's restored Church, and who has thus not received the gift of the Holy Ghost by an authorized priesthood bearer, be the recipient of authentic spiritual gifts?

Yes, they certainly can. Numerous instances have been reported in LDS literature where non-members have been blessed with genuine gifts of the Spirit.[1] President Willard Richards even prayed on one occasion that the Lord would give "dreams and visions and revelations by [the] Spirit" to those who were outside the bonds of His covenant, so that they would see their true spiritual condition and the blessings that were in store for them if they would seek out the servants of God and obey the principles of the restored gospel.[2] And that is the key to understanding this phenomenon: authentic spiritual gifts, when experienced by non-members, will always lead the recipient to the truth, never away from it.

There are some Christian denominations that claim they have the gifts of the Spirit in their midst, and this may indeed be true for individual members of these congregations since God can bless whomever He chooses to. But, as President Brigham Young has taught, even though there are people "out of the Church who possess great gifts . . . yet these gifts belong to the Church, and those who are faithful in the kingdom of God inherit them and are entitled to them."[3] It cannot be forgotten, as Elder Matthias F. Cowley reminds us, that God will not sanction unauthorized acts by any means. If baptism and confirmation are administered outside of the true Church of Jesus Christ, then "visions, dreams, healings, prophecies, tongues, etc." cannot be secured as a perpetual inheritance. Those who claim such an inheritance presumptuously can only reap the condemnation of the Lord.[4]

2. Since the gifts of the Spirit are sacred in nature, should manifestations associated with them ever be shared with other individuals?

There are actually two different answers to this question. The Prophet Joseph Smith is reported in the *History of the Church* as saying to a gathering of brethren that if any of them obtained "a prophecy or vision" during their meeting, they were to "rise and speak that all may be edified and rejoice together."[5] It is apparent from the numerous descriptions of spiritual experiences in official LDS newspapers, books, and periodicals that leaders of the Church have felt in times past that it is completely appropriate to publicly share some accounts of this type.

On the other hand, there are times when the Lord may place restrictions upon the recipient of a particular gift. For example, the Lord commanded Joseph Smith and Sidney Rigdon to write down parts of the vision commonly referred to as section 76 of the Doctrine and Covenants, but there were certain portions of the vision that these two men were forbidden to record or to share even with the Latter-day Saints (see vv. 113–116). The Prophet reported that he and Elder Rigdon saw a hundred times more than they were allowed to reveal.[6]

3. What precautions should be taken by those who have been blessed with the reception of spiritual gifts?

First, we have the suggestion of Lorenzo Snow. He said, "It is very easy to understand when a conversation is attended with profit. We then feel our minds enlightened, and feel the power of God resting upon us through the Holy Spirit. . . . Conversation, conducted in this Spirit, proves highly profitable, not only to ourselves, but the persons with whom we converse." But not all participants in a conversation are willing or able to cultivate the Spirit of the Lord. Indeed, some of them are inclined to foster a "bad, wrangling, and contentious spirit." Brother Snow reminds us about the Savior's directive not to cast pearls before swine (see Matt. 7:6), and in equating spiritual gifts to pearls, he warns that "we too frequently engage in conversation concerning things of the kingdom of God with individuals of a wrong and bad spirit; and feeling ever anxious to make them see, understand, and acknowledge our light, we urge on and persist in the conversation, until we fall into an unpleasant state of mind, and finally catch the spirit of the person with whom we are conversing."[7]

Next, we have some advice from Elder Parley P. Pratt. He observed that some of the Saints—especially those who are newly initiated into the world of spiritual happenings—become overzealous to share their experiences with all around them lest they "grieve the Spirit" by their silence. Elder Pratt admonished members of the Church not to be overcome by such enthusiasm for two reasons.

Reason 1: Overenthusiastic behavior can lead into the realm of sign-seeking (either the Saint seeking to provide a sign to others in demonstration of the power of their gift or an unbeliever calling for the manifestation of a sign to satisfy their curiosity). Such activity is forbidden by the Lord in Doctrine and Covenants section 46 verse 9.

Reason 2: If a person gets the notion that they must announce their spiritual experiences to the public then Satan might find an opportunity to ensnare them. As an extreme example, Elder Parley P. Pratt wrote that the adversary could give someone a revelation concerning an upcoming murder or an arson and if the person was not able to successfully detect the source of these messages, they might announce it publicly, and the civil authorities could suspect them of being the perpetrator.[8]

4. How can it be determined with certainty that the spiritual gifts enjoyed within the LDS Church are not simply the counterfeits of the devil?

Elder Orson Pratt turned to the Bible when confronted with this question. He acknowledged the idea that "Satan was to come with all power, signs, and lying wonders, and with all deceivableness of unrighteousness in them that perish, because they had pleasure in unrighteousness." This concept can be found in 2 Thessalonians chapter 2 verses 7 through 12. But he answered the charge that the Saints were partaking of the adversary's "strong delusions" by saying, "[P]rove to us that we have had pleasure in anything contrary to the gospel of Jesus Christ—that this people have not obeyed the scriptures of eternal truth. Those signs that were to come, and these lying wonders, etc., were to be practiced by individuals that had pleasure in unrighteousness and who rejected the gospel of Jesus Christ." He then drew attention to the story of Moses and the magicians of Egypt. How was anybody in their day supposed to distinguish between the two powers being manifested by them when both sides were able to perform the same exact miracles? Elder Pratt explained that the distinction was clear because "Moses believed and obeyed the words of the Most High God, and the magicians . . . did miracles . . . not in the name of God, but by their enchantments; and so it is with all wicked miracle-workers."[9] Only the true followers of the Lord will be granted the privilege of handling His power on the earth while imposters will have to garner their abilities from some other source.

5. When, and under what circumstances, were the gifts of the Spirit introduced in the dispensation of the fullness of times?

The subject of spiritual gifts was evidently first brought to the attention of Joseph Smith during the spring of 1820 when he went to pray in what is now known as the Sacred Grove. According to Orson Pratt, Charles W. Penrose, and Lorenzo Snow, the Father and the Son explained the loss of these blessings through the process of apostasy and told the young prophet of their impending reestablishment.[10]

This idea becomes even more intriguing when the text of Moroni's discourse on spiritual gifts is compared with the words that Jesus Christ reportedly spoke during the First Vision. Moroni admonishes his brethren to *"deny not the power of God"* and *"deny not the gifts of God"* (Moro. 10:7–8, emphasis added). He states that these two things will only be done away among mortals because of unbelief. He then offers this sober thought:

> And wo be unto the children of men if this be the case; for there shall be *none that doeth good* among you, *no not one.* For *if there be one among you that doeth good, he shall work by the power and gifts of God.* (Moro. 10:25, emphasis added)

The parallel between these Book of Mormon texts and Deity's declarations in the grove is clear. In the Prophet's 1832 account of his experience, he represents the Savior as saying, "the world lieth in sin . . . at this time and *none doeth good, no not one.* They have turned aside from the gospel and keep not my commandments. They draw near to me with their lips while their hearts are far from me."[11] And in the Prophet's 1838 account, he continues this dialogue: "They draw near to me with their lips but their hearts are far from me. They teach for doctrines the commandments of men, having a form of godliness but *they deny the power thereof.*"[12]

Three years after the First Vision took place, the Prophet Joseph Smith was again reminded of the restoration of spiritual gifts. When the angel Moroni visited Joseph in September 1823 he not only quoted Joel 2:28–29—which is a prophecy of the gifts of the Spirit being enjoyed in the latter days (cf. Acts 2:17–18)—but also reportedly said, "with signs and with wonders, with *gifts* and with healings, with the manifestations of *the power of God,* and with the Holy Ghost, shall the hearts of the faithful be comforted."[13]

6. Where can a person find more material to read on the gifts of the Holy Spirit?

At the end of the selected bibliography in this book there is an extensive reading list on spiritual gifts. It includes articles published by members of the First Presidency, Quorum of the Twelve Apostles, Quorum of the Seventy, Church Education System teachers, a research historian, and a Church magazine editor. The publication dates among these papers range from 1899 to 2005.

NOTES TO APPENDIX 2

1. See H. Dean Garrett, ed., *Regional Studies in Latter-day Saint Church History: Illinois* (Provo, UT: Department of Church History and Doctrine, 1995), 233 [dreams]; George Q. Cannon, ed., *Early Scenes in Church History* (Salt Lake City: Juvenile Instructor Office, 1881), 42–43 [prophecy]; Edward W. Tullidge, *The Women of Mormondom* (New York: Tullidge and Crandall, 1877), 161–62 [visions]; James Henry Rollins, Autobiography, L. Tom Perry Special Collections Library, Brigham Young University, Provo, UT, 2; *Saints' Herald,* vol. 3, October 1862, 79–80, 82–84 [angels/spirits]; Anthon L. Skanchy, Autobiography, translated and edited by John A. Widtsoe, *Improvement Era,* vol. 18, no. 2, December 1914, 123 [casting out evil spirits]; Parley P. Pratt, *Autobiography of Parley P. Pratt* (Salt Lake City: Deseret Book, 1985), 129–31; Matt. 8:5–13; 15:21–28 [faith to be healed].
2. George D. Watt, ed., *Journal of Discourses* (Liverpool, England: Samuel W. Richards and Sons, 1852–1886), 6:305; hereafter cited as *JD.*
3. Ibid., 11:325.
4. Matthias F. Cowley, *Cowley's Talks on Doctrine* (Chattanooga, TN: Benjamin E. Rich, 1902), 60–61.
5. Brigham H. Roberts, ed., *History of The Church of Jesus Christ of Latter-day Saints* (Salt Lake City: Deseret Book, 1948–1950), 2:391.
6. See ibid., 5:402.
7. *Millennial Star,* vol. 2, no. 3, July 1841, 37–38.
8. See ibid., vol. 1, no. 5, September 1840, 128.
9. *JD,* 7:37–38.
10. See ibid., 12:354–55; ibid., 22:93; Eliza R. Snow, *Biography and Family Record of Lorenzo Snow* (Salt Lake City: Deseret News, 1884), 137.
11. Milton V. Backman Jr., *Joseph Smith's First Vision: Confirming Evidences and Contemporary Accounts,* 2nd ed. (Salt Lake City: Bookcraft, 1980), 155.
12. Ibid., 162.
13. *Messenger and Advocate,* October 1835, vol. 2, no. 13, 199 (emphasis added).

APPENDIX THREE

Directory and Harmony of Scriptural Lists

There are three main lists of spiritual gifts in the LDS canon. They are found in the New Testament (1 Cor. 12:3–10), the Book of Mormon (Moro. 10:6–16), and the Doctrine and Covenants (D&C 46:13–25). Each of these lists name the same group of spiritual gifts in the exact same sequence. A casual reading of the Doctrine and Covenants list might give the impression that "faith" is the subject both in verses 19 and 20, but a careful look at these passages reveal that verse 19 is speaking of a power within oneself to *receive* while verse 20 has reference to a power within oneself to *give*. In any case, the subject matter of the section 46 verses follows in perfect sync with the content and sequence of the other scriptural lists. The D&C list should, therefore, be interpreted with that perspective in mind.

Directory of Lists

1 Corinthians 12:3–10

Testimony of Jesus (v. 3)
Differences of Administrations (v. 5)
Diversities of Operations (v. 6)
Word of Wisdom (v. 8)
Word of Knowledge (v. 8)
Faith (v. 9)
Healing (v. 9)
Miracles (v. 10)
Prophecy (v. 10)
Discerning of Spirits (v. 10)

Speaking in Tongues (v. 10)
Interpreting Tongues (v. 10)

Moroni 10:6–16
Testimony of Jesus (vv. 6–7)
Different Ways of Administration (v. 8)
Manifestations of the Spirit (v. 8)
Word of Wisdom (v. 9)
Word of Knowledge (v. 10)
Faith (v. 11)
Healing (v. 11)
Miracles (v. 12)
Prophecy (v. 13)
Angels and Spirits (v. 14)
Speaking in Tongues (v. 15)
Interpreting Tongues (v. 16)

D&C 46:13–25
Testimony of Jesus (v. 13)
Differences of Administration (v. 15)
Diversities of Operations (v. 16)
Word of Wisdom (v. 17)
Word of Knowledge (v. 18)
Faith (v. 19)
Healing (v. 20)
Miracles (v. 21)
Prophecy (v. 22)
Discerning of Spirits (v. 23)
Speaking in Tongues (v. 24)
Interpreting Tongues (v. 25)

Even though all three of the gift lists follow the exact same pattern in naming the gifts of the Spirit (and they share a number of other common themes as well), they still have a unique overall structure, audience, and purpose—as seen by the following outlines. The specific gifts listed in the three chapters are omitted in this summary to emphasize the main points of commentary about spiritual gifts.

1 Corinthians 12: Paul attempts to educate his fellow Saints

The Saints should not be ignorant of spiritual gifts.
There are a variety of gifts.
The manifestations of the Spirit are given to profit every man.
The Spirit divides His gifts among mortals according to His will.
Analogy of body parts and gifts.
God has set the gifts among His Church members as it has pleased Him.
Even gifts that seem to be feeble are necessary.
Covet earnestly the best gifts.

Moroni 10: Moroni exhorts unbelieving Lamanites who may have access to his writings in the future.

Deny not the power of God.
God works by power according to the faith of mortals.
God is the same yesterday, today, and forever.
Deny not the gifts of God.
There are many gifts.
Gifts are given by the manifestations of the Spirit in order to profit mortals.
Gifts come by the Spirit of Christ.
Gifts come according to the will of Christ.
Every good gift comes from Christ.
Christ is the same yesterday, today, and forever.
Gifts will never be done away unless it is through the unbelief of mortals.

D&C 46: The Lord educates and gives instructions in connection with the Joseph Smith Translation of the Bible.

Gifts will prevent deception.
Earnestly seek after the best gifts.
Gifts are a benefit for the obedient.
Don't seek gifts for signs.
There are many gifts.
Not everyone has every gift.
Each Saint receives at least one gift.
Gifts are distributed so that all may be benefited.

Gifts are distributed according to the Lord's will, mercy, and pleasure, and also according to the conditions of the children of men.
The manifestations of the Spirit are for the profit of everyone.
All these gifts come from God and are for the benefit of His children.
Some Church leaders are given the ability to tell whether manifestations originate with God.
Those who ask for spiritual gifts in prayer, by the Spirit, will receive those gifts by the Spirit.
It is possible for some individuals to receive all of the gifts that are available.
Those people who ask in the Spirit ask according to God's will and their petition is therefore granted.
Everything done in the Spirit must be done in the name of Jesus Christ.
When blessings are received from God, thanks must be offered to Him in the Spirit.
The Saints must practice virtue and holiness continually.

Harmony of Lists

The following harmony demonstrates how each of the three canonical lists correspond to each other. It should be noted that the gift of "operations" is not specifically named in the Book of Mormon list even though it becomes clear by comparing it to the other two lists that the same meaning is intended. It is not known why the explicit reference is missing. It possibly could have been omitted during an editing procedure.

"no man can say that Jesus is the Lord, but by the Holy Ghost" (1 Cor. 12:3)
"ye may know that [Christ] is, by the power of the Holy Ghost" (Moro. 10:7)
"To some it is given by the Holy Ghost to know that Jesus Christ is the Son of God" (D&C 46:13)

"there are differences of administrations" (1 Cor. 12:5)

"there are different ways that these gifts are administered" (Moro. 10:8)
"to some it is given by the Holy Ghost to know the differences of administration" (D&C 46:15)

"there are diversities of operations . . . [by] God . . . [through] the manifestations of the Spirit" (1 Cor. 12:6–7)
"the gifts of God . . . are given by the manifestations of the Spirit" (Moro. 10:8)
"it is given by the Holy Ghost to some to know the diversities of operations, whether they be of God" (D&C 46:16)

"to one is given by the Spirit the word of wisdom" (1 Cor. 12:8)
"to one is given by the Spirit of God, that he may teach the word of wisdom" (Moro. 10:9)
"to some is given, by the Spirit of God, the word of wisdom" (D&C 46:17)

"given . . . the word of knowledge by the . . . Spirit" (1 Cor. 12:8)
"teach the word of knowledge by the . . . Spirit" (Moro. 10:10)
"given the word of knowledge, that all may be taught to be wise and to have knowledge" (D&C 46:18)

"To another faith by the . . . Spirit" (1 Cor. 12:9)
"exceedingly great faith" (Moro. 10:11)
"to some it is given to have faith" (D&C 46:19)

"to another the gifts of healing by the . . . Spirit" (1 Cor. 12:9)
"the gifts of healing by the . . . Spirit" (Moro. 10:11)
"to others it is given . . . to heal" (D&C 46:20)

"To another the working of miracles" (1 Cor. 12:10)
"work mighty miracles" (Moro. 10:12)
"to some is given the working of miracles" (D&C 46:21)

"to another prophecy" (1 Cor. 12:10)
"prophesy concerning all things" (Moro. 10:13)

"to others it is given to prophesy" (D&C 46:22)

"to another discerning of spirits" (1 Cor. 12:10)
"the beholding of angels and ministering spirits" (Moro. 10:14)
"to others [is given] the discerning of spirits" (D&C 46:23)

"to another divers kinds of tongues" (1 Cor. 12:10)
"all kinds of tongues" (Moro. 10:15)
"it is given to some to speak with tongues" (D&C 46:24)

"to another the interpretation of tongues" (1 Cor. 12:10)
"the interpretation of languages and of divers kinds of tongues" (Moro. 10:16)
"to another is given the interpretation of tongues" (D&C 46:25)

SELECTED BIBLIOGRAPHY

Listed here are some of the sources that have been cited in this book. The reader may find this collection useful as a guide for further study. Here and throughout the notes, the archives of The Church of Jesus Christ of Latter-day Saints in Salt Lake City is abbreviated as LDS Church Archives. Also, the L. Tom Perry Special Collections, located in the Harold B. Lee Library at Brigham Young University, Provo, Utah, is referred to simply by the collection name (L. Tom Perry Special Collections).

BOOKS

Allen, James B., Ronald K. Esplin, and David J. Whittaker. *Men with a Mission: The Quorum of the Twelve Apostles in the British Isles.* Salt Lake City: Deseret Book, 1992.

Anderson, Dawn Hall, and Marie Cornwall, eds. *Women Steadfast in Christ: Talks Selected from the 1991 Women's Conference.* Salt Lake City: Deseret Book, 1992.

Asay, Carlos E. *In the Lord's Service: A Guide to Spiritual Development.* Salt Lake City: Deseret Book, 1990.

Ballard, M. Russell. *Our Search for Happiness: An Invitation to Understand The Church of Jesus Christ of Latter-day Saints.* Salt Lake City: Deseret Book, 1993.

———. *Counseling with Our Councils: Learning to Minister Together in the Church and in the Family.* Salt Lake City: Deseret Book, 1997.

Benson, Ezra T. *The Teachings of Ezra Taft Benson.* Salt Lake City: Bookcraft, 1988.

Brewster, Hoyt W., Jr. *Prophets, Priesthood Keys, and Succession.* Salt Lake City: Deseret Book, 1991.

Cannon, Donald Q., and Lyndon W. Cook, eds. *Far West Record: Minutes of The Church of Jesus Christ of Latter-day Saints, 1830–1844.* Salt Lake City: Deseret Book, 1983.

Clark, James R., comp. *Messages of the First Presidency of The Church of Jesus Christ of Latter-day Saints.* 6 vols. Salt Lake City: Bookcraft, 1965–1975.

Cowley, Matthias F. *Cowley's Talks on Doctrine.* Chattanooga, TN: Benjamin E. Rich, 1902.

———, comp. *Wilford Woodruff: History of His Life and Labors.* Salt Lake City: Bookcraft, 1964.

Durham, G. Homer, comp. *Gospel Standards: Selections from the Sermons and Writings of Heber J. Grant.* Salt Lake City: Improvement Era, 1981.

Ehat, Andrew F., and Lyndon W. Cook, eds. *The Words of Joseph Smith: The Contemporary Accounts of the Nauvoo Discourses of the Prophet Joseph.* Orem, UT: Grandin Books, 1991.

Garrett, H. Dean, ed. *Regional Studies in Latter-day Saint History: Illinois.* Provo, UT: Department of Church History and Doctrine, 1995.

Gates, Susa Young. *Lydia Knight's History.* Salt Lake City: Juvenile Instructor Office, 1883.

Gibbons, Francis M. *Dynamic Disciples, Prophets of God: Life Stories of the Presidents of The Church of Jesus Christ of Latter-day Saints.* Salt Lake City: Deseret Book, 1996.

Goates, Brent L. *Harold B. Lee: Prophet and Seer.* Salt Lake City: Bookcraft, 1985.

Hartley, William G. *My Best for the Kingdom: History and Autobiography of John Lowe Butler, A Mormon Frontiersman.* Salt Lake City: Aspen Books, 1993.

Hinckley, Gordon B. *Teachings of Gordon B. Hinckley.* Salt Lake City: Deseret Book, 1997.

Jenson, Andrew. *Latter-day Saint Biographical Encyclopedia.* 4 vols. Salt Lake City: The Andrew Jenson History Company, 1901–1936.

Jessee, Dean C., ed. *The Personal Writings of Joseph Smith.* Salt Lake City: Deseret Book, 1984.

Kenney, Scott G., ed. *Wilford Woodruff's Journal: 1833–1898.* Midvale, UT: Signature Books, 1985.

Kimball, Edward L., ed. *The Teachings of Spencer W. Kimball.* Salt Lake City: Bookcraft, 1982.

Kimball, Spencer W. *Faith Precedes the Miracle.* Salt Lake City: Deseret Book, 1972.

Lee, Harold B. *Stand Ye in Holy Places.* Salt Lake City: Deseret Book, 1974.

Ludlow, Daniel H., ed. *Encyclopedia of Mormonism.* 4 vols. New York: Macmillan, 1992.

Lundwall, Nels B. *Assorted Gems of Priceless Value.* Salt Lake City: Bookcraft, 1944.

———, comp. *Masterful Discourses and Writings of Orson Pratt.* Salt Lake City: N. B. Lundwall, 1946.

Madsen, Carol Cornwall, ed. *In Their Own Words: Women and the Story of Nauvoo.* Salt Lake City: Deseret Book, 1994.

McConkie, Bruce R. *Doctrinal New Testament Commentary.* 3 vols. Salt Lake City: Bookcraft, 1965–1973.

———. *Mormon Doctrine.* Salt Lake City: Bookcraft, 1966.

———. *A New Witness for the Articles of Faith.* Salt Lake City: Deseret Book, 1985.

Middlemiss, Clare, comp. *Cherished Experiences from the Writings of President David O. McKay.* Salt Lake City: Deseret Book, 1955.

Morgan, Nicholas G., Sr., ed. *Eliza R. Snow: An Immortal.* Salt Lake City: Nicholas G. Morgan Sr. Foundation, 1957.

Nelson, Russell M. *The Gateway We Call Death.* Salt Lake City: Deseret Book, 1995.

Newquist, Jerreld L., comp. *Gospel Truth: Discourses and Writings of President George Q. Cannon.* Salt Lake City: Deseret Book, 1987.

Nibley, Preston. *The Presidents of the Church.* 13th edition, revised and enlarged. Salt Lake City: Deseret Book, 1974.

Pace, Glen L. *Spiritual Plateaus.* Salt Lake City: Deseret Book, 1991.

Packer, Boyd K. *Teach Ye Diligently.* Salt Lake City: Deseret Book, 1975.

Peterson, Janet, and LaRene Gaunt. *Elect Ladies.* Salt Lake City: Deseret Book, 1990.

Pratt, Orson. *Orson Pratt's Works.* Salt Lake City: Deseret News Press, 1945.

Pratt, Parley P. *Key to the Science of Theology.* Salt Lake City: Deseret Book, 1965.

———. *Autobiography of Parley P. Pratt.* Salt Lake City: Deseret Book, 1985.

Richards, Stephen L. *Where Is Wisdom?* Salt Lake City: Deseret Book, 1955.

Roberts, Brigham H. *Defense of the Faith and the Saints.* Salt Lake City: Deseret News Press, 1907.

———. *Seventy's Course in Theology.* 5 vols. Salt Lake City: Deseret News Press, 1907–1912.

———. *A Comprehensive History of The Church of Jesus Christ of Latter-day Saints.* Salt Lake City: Deseret News Press, 1930.

———, ed. *History of the Church.* 7 vols. Salt Lake City: Deseret Book, 1948–1950.

Robison, Parker P., ed. *Orson Pratt's Works.* Salt Lake City: Deseret News Press, 1945.

Smith, George D., ed. *An Intimate Chronicle: The Journals of William Clayton.* Salt Lake City: Signature Books and Smith Research Associates, 1995.

Smith, Hyrum M., and Janne M. Sjodahl. *Doctrine and Covenants Commentary.* Revised edition. Salt Lake City: Deseret Book, 1960.

Smith, Joseph F. *Gospel Doctrine.* Salt Lake City: Deseret Book, 1949.

Smith, Joseph Fielding. *Church History and Modern Revelation.* 4 vols. Salt Lake City: The Church of Jesus Christ of Latter-day Saints, 1946–1949.

———. *Doctrines of Salvation.* 3 vols. Salt Lake City: Bookcraft, 1954–1956.

———. *Take Heed to Yourselves.* Salt Lake City: Deseret Book, 1966.

———. *Essentials in Church History.* Salt Lake City: Deseret Book, 1969.

Snow, Eliza R. *Biography and Family Record of Lorenzo Snow.* Salt Lake City: Deseret News Press, 1884.

Spencer, Orson. *Letters Exhibiting the Most Prominent Doctrines of The Church of Jesus Christ of Latter-day Saints.* Salt Lake City: George Q. Cannon and Sons, 1891.

Stuy, Brian H., ed. *Collected Discourses.* 5 vols. Burbank, CA, and Woodland Hills, UT: B.H.S. Publishing, 1987–1992.

Talmage, James E. *Jesus the Christ.* Salt Lake City: Deseret Book, 1983.

———. *The Articles of Faith.* Salt Lake City: Deseret News Press, 1901.

Tate, Lucile C. *Boyd K. Packer: A Watchman on the Tower.* Salt Lake City: Bookcraft, 1995.

Top, Brent L., Larry E. Dahl, and Walter D. Bowen. *Follow the Living Prophets.* Salt Lake City: Bookcraft, 1993.

Tullidge, Edward W. *The Women of Mormondom.* New York: Tullidge and Crandall, 1877.

Watson, Elden J., ed. *Manuscript History of Brigham Young: 1801–1844.* Salt Lake City: Smith Secretarial Service, 1968.

Watt, George D., ed. *Journal of Discourses.* 26 vols. Liverpool, England: Samuel W. Richards and Sons, 1852–1886.

Webster, Noah. *An American Dictionary of the English Language.* New York: S. Converse, 1828.

Wesley, John. *The Works of John Wesley.* Grand Rapids, MI: Zondervan, 1958.

West, Franklin L. *Life of Franklin D. Richards.* Salt Lake City: Deseret News Press, 1924.

Whitney, Helen Mar. *A Woman's View: Helen Mar Whitney's Reminiscences of Early Church History.* Provo, UT: BYU Religious Studies Center, 1999.

Whitney, Orson F. *Life of Heber C. Kimball.* Salt Lake City: Kimball Family, 1888.

———. *Elias: An Epic of the Ages.* New York: O. F. Whitney, 1914.

———. *Saturday Night Thoughts.* Salt Lake City: Deseret News Press, 1921.

———. *Through Memory's Halls: The Life Story of Orson F. Whitney.* Independence, MO: Zion's Printing and Publishing, 1930.

Widtsoe, John A. *Program of The Church of Jesus Christ of Latter-day Saints.* Salt Lake City: The Church of Jesus Christ of Latter-day Saints, 1937.

———. *Evidences and Reconciliations.* Salt Lake City: Bookcraft, 1987.

Williams, Clyde J., ed. *The Teachings of Harold B. Lee.* Salt Lake City: Bookcraft, 1996.

Woodruff, Wilford. *Leaves from My Journal.* Salt Lake City: Juvenile Instructor Office, 1881.

AUTOBIOGRAPHIES

Hamblin, Jacob. Autobiography. L. Tom Perry Special Collections Library, Brigham Young University, Provo, UT.

Hancock, Levi Ward. Autobiography. L. Tom Perry Special Collections Library, Brigham Young University, Provo, UT.

Hyde, William. Autobiography. L. Tom Perry Special Collections Library, Brigham Young University, Provo, UT.

Lightner, Mary. Autobiography. *Utah Genealogical and Historical Magazine,* Writings of Early Latter-day Saints.
Mace, Wandle. Autobiography. L. Tom Perry Special Collections Library, Brigham Young University, Provo, UT.
Pulsipher, John. Autobiography. L. Tom Perry Special Collections Library, Brigham Young University, Provo, UT.
Pulsipher, Zera. Autobiography. L. Tom Perry Special Collections Library, Brigham Young University, Provo, UT.
Rollins, James Henry. Autobiography. L. Tom Perry Special Collections Library, Brigham Young University, Provo, UT.
Skanchy, Anthon L. Autobiography. Translated and edited by John A. Widtsoe. *Improvement Era,* vol. 18, no. 2, December 1914.
Walker, William Holmes. Autobiography. L. Tom Perry Special Collections Library, Brigham Young University, Provo, UT.
Young, Alfred D. Autobiography. L. Tom Perry Special Collections Library, Brigham Young University, Provo, UT.
Young, Margrette W. Autobiography. LDS Church Archives, Salt Lake City, Utah.

FOR FURTHER READING

Arnold, Mervin B. "Seek Ye Earnestly the Best Gifts." *Ensign,* March 2005, 64–67.
Ashton, Marvin J. "There Are Many Gifts." *Ensign,* November 1987, 20–23.
Barrett, William E. "The Blessings of the Holy Spirit." Chapter in *The Restored Church,* 615–34. 7th edition. Salt Lake City: Deseret Book, 1953.
Cannon, Donald Q. "Miracles: Meridian and Modern." In Bruce A. Van Orden and Brent L. Top, eds., *The Lord of the Gospels,* 23–37. Salt Lake City: Deseret Book, 1991.
Clark, J. Reuben, Jr. "The Gift of Tongues at Pentecost." *Millennial Star,* vol. 91, 10 October 1929, 647, 649–53.
Cowley, Matthias F. "Gifts of the Gospel." *Improvement Era,* vol. 2, no. 6, April 1899, 447–51.
Cullimore, James A. "Gifts of the Spirit." *Ensign,* November 1974, 27–28.
Faust, James E. "Communion with the Holy Spirit." *Ensign,* March 2002, 3–7.
Freeman, Robert C. "Paul's Earnest Pursuit of Spiritual Gifts." In *The Apostle Paul, His Life and His Testimony: The Twenty-third Annual Sidney B. Sperry Symposium,* 34–46. Salt Lake City: Deseret Book, 1994.
Hales, Robert D. "Gifts of the Spirit." *Brigham Young University Fireside and Devotional Speeches, 1992–93,* 135–46. Provo, UT: BYU Publications, 1993. Also in *Ensign,* February 2002, 12–20.
Holzapfel, Richard Neitzel. "Salvation Cannot Come without Revelation." *In Doctrines for Exaltation: The 1989 Sperry Symposium on the Doctrine and Covenants,* 87–95. Salt Lake City: Deseret Book, 1989.

Johnson, Lane. "How to Receive Spiritual Gifts." *Ensign,* December 1975, 46–47.
Oaks, Dallin H. "Revelation." *Brigham Young University Fireside and Devotional Speeches, 1981–82,* 20–26. Provo, UT: University Publications, 1982.
———. "Spiritual Gifts." *Ensign,* September 1986, 68–72. Also in Mary E. Stovall and Carol Cornwall Madsen, eds., *A Heritage of Faith: Talks Selected from the BYU Women's Conferences,* 28–39. Salt Lake City: Deseret Book, 1988.
Packer, Boyd K. "Personal Revelation: The Gift, the Test, and the Promise." *Ensign,* November 1994, 59–62.
Perkins, Jerry. "God Tailors Revelation to the Individual." In Byron R. Merrill et al., comps., *The Heavens Are Open: The 1992 Sperry Symposium on the Doctrine and Covenants and Church History,* 257–75. Salt Lake City: Deseret Book, 1993.
Richards, Stephen L. "Gifts of the Gospel." *Improvement Era,* May 1950, 371, 419–21.
Romney, Marion G. "Gifts of the Spirit." *Improvement Era,* June 1956, 422–25.
Smith, Joseph Fielding. "Seek Ye Earnestly the Best Gifts." *Ensign,* June 1972, 2–3.
Woodger, Mary Jane. "Frontier Prophetesses: The Gift of Tongues as Manifested by Latter-day Saint Women in Southern Alberta, 1894–1930." In Dennis A. Wright et al., eds., *Regional Studies in Latter-day Saint Church History: Western Canada,* 123–38. Provo, UT: Department of Church History and Doctrine, 2000.

INDEX